"*Coaching Supervision* challenges us to reflect on the supervision and what's required to navigate the pathwa scape incorporates cultural sensitivities, research and a incorporates foundational footholds of ethics, model working. This book will both extend and embed vital ᴋɴᴏᴡɪᴇᴅɢᴇ.

– Tammy Turner, Founder, The Centre for Coaching
Development and Supervision, ICF Master Certified
Coach, MAICD, CSA and AAOS, Australia

"The contributor list of this book reads like a compendium of current thought-leadership in coaching supervision. I am delighted to see writers (and maybe more importantly practising coaches and supervisors) from different psychological fields and backgrounds joining a rich exploration and explanation of the range of purposes and strengths of supervisory work in the C21st."

– Jenny Bird, Executive Coach. Coaching Supervisor,
BA (Hons) Oxford, ICF Master Coach, UK

"It's good for a profession's world to be jostled at its outer edges from time to time. It challenges us to examine whether we have begun to hold a "flat world" view of what we do and how much we might have invested in who we have become, as opposed to who we might become. There will be at least one chapter in this book that will jostle pleasantly and at least one whose jostle might not be so welcome. Both reactions are grist for the mill for supervisors."

– Patricia (Pat) Marum, Certified Coach Supervisor, ICF Assessor,
ICF Mentor Coach, Southern Arizona ICF Past President, USA

"This book is a profound exploration of the growing field of coach supervision. Each chapter and contributor draws our attention to the nuances of the supervision experience; provoking the reader to consider fresh perspectives while broadening and deepening the landscape of this essential practice. A true contribution to the field and a must read for the serious coach practitioner and coach supervisor."

– Pam McLean, Ph.D., CEO Hudson Institute of Coaching,
Author, *Self as Coach, Self as Leader*, USA.

Coaching Supervision

Coaching and mentoring supervision is a rapidly expanding field. This book is a curated collection of contemporary thinking; presenting cutting-edge contributions from international writers, leaders in the professional field, academics and practitioners who offer a range of accessible applied research, practice examples, case studies, guidelines and reflective prompts to readers. As in art galleries, some pieces require reflection – and return visits may be necessary. The work is edgy and new, and yet totally grounded in the coaching and mentoring supervisor experience, bringing pragmatic solutions to current complex challenges.

Over the last decade coaching supervision has moved from a rare and privileged audience to being common place amongst 'best practice' coaches. This book harnesses the current surge in curiosity, knowledge and practice in coaching and mentoring supervision and provides a collective statement of our times. Each chapter, in its highly individual way, equips us to face the demands of the VUCA environment. In turn, the book resources coaching and mentoring supervisors to support their supervisees – coaches and mentors who work with leaders, grappling with global, community and personal challenges, in this uncertain, fast moving world. Supervision for mentors is developing alongside coaching supervision and at present there appears to be no obvious distinctions with little current research focussing on the mentoring supervision experience. However, its distinctive identity is still forming. We invite mentors, and mentor supervisors, as they read these works, to consider the emerging similarities and differences in addressing requirements for mentoring supervision.

The book brings together pioneering research and practice and as such will remain current for many years. This book will be popular with experienced professionals who want to stretch and deepen their practice, keep up-to-date with current studies, challenge and catalyse their own thinking, and embrace learning from real-world practitioner examples and applied research.

Jo Birch brings 20 years' experience providing supervision to coaches, psychotherapists and leaders. She is a passionate member of international professional, research and practice communities – previously Director, Coaching Supervision Academy, and Chair, BACP Coaching. She writes and presents on supervision, ethics and cross-cultural practice.

Peter Welch is a coach, coach supervisor, thinking partner and thought leader. As co-founder of the Association of Coaching Supervisors (AOCS) he is influential in the coaching field, by supporting individuals and by contributing to organisations and publications. He draws on a rich tapestry of current thinking in coaching, change, transition and leadership development.

Routledge-EMCC Masters in Coaching and Mentoring

Series Editors: David Clutterbuck and Irena Sobolewska.
Associate Series Editors: Julie Haddock Millar and Agnieszka Bajer

This series is published in collaboration with the European Mentoring and Coaching Council (EMCC).

Routledge-EMCC Masters in Coaching and Mentoring provides critical perspectives in coaching and mentoring. It aims to avoid the overcrowded basic coaching/mentoring textbook market and focus instead on providing a toolkit for topics outside of core theory but necessary to become a mature practitioner.

The series will appeal to those studying to obtain certificates, diplomas and masters in coaching and mentoring, alongside experienced practitioners who wish to round out their practice using selected essential reading as part of their continuous professional development.

Coaching and Mentoring in the Asia Pacific
Edited by Anna Blackman, Derrick Kon and David Clutterbuck

Coaching Supervision
Advancing Practice, Changing Landscapes
Edited by Jo Birch and Peter Welch

The Art of Listening in Coaching and Mentoring
Authored by Stephen Burt

Coaching Supervision

Advancing Practice,
Changing Landscapes

Edited by
Jo Birch and Peter Welch

Routledge
Taylor & Francis Group

LONDON AND NEW YORK

First published 2019
by Routledge
2 Park Square, Milton Park, Abingdon, Oxon OX14 4RN

and by Routledge
52 Vanderbilt Avenue, New York, NY 10017

Routledge is an imprint of the Taylor & Francis Group, an informa business

© 2019 selection and editorial matter, Jo Birch and Peter Welch; individual chapters, the contributors

British Library Cataloguing-in-Publication Data
A catalogue record for this book is available from the British Library

Library of Congress Cataloging-in-Publication Data
Names: Birch, Jo, 1957– editor. | Welch, Peter, 1950– editor.
Title: Coaching supervision : advancing practice and changing landscapes / edited by Jo Birch and Peter Welch.
Description: Abingdon, Oxon ; New York, NY : Routledge, 2019. | Series: Routledge EMCC Masters in Coaching and Mentoring | Includes bibliographical references and index.
Identifiers: LCCN 2019007113 (print) | LCCN 2019008445 (ebook) | ISBN 9780429282898 (eBook) | ISBN 9780367244989 (hardback : alk. paper) | ISBN 9780367255657 (pbk. : alk. paper)
Subjects: LCSH: Personal coaching.
Classification: LCC BF637.P36 (ebook) | LCC BF637.P36 C636 2019 (print) | DDC 158.3—dc23
LC record available at https://lccn.loc.gov/2019007113

ISBN: 978-0-367-24498-9 (hbk)
ISBN: 978-0-367-25565-7 (pbk)
ISBN: 978-0-429-28289-8 (ebk)

Typeset in Bembo
by Apex CoVantage, LLC

Contents

Contributors

Sabreena Andriesz (PhD MCC) is known for her integrative approach. She is passionate about partnering her clients towards the fulfilment of their desired performance targets and catalysing individuals, and their organisations, to live and work with cultural authenticity and courage. Sabreena has devoted the past 18 years to senior executive coaching and team development with over 4,500 hours of coaching experience in diverse industries focussed primarily on leadership development. Sabreena is a Master Certified Coach, with a PhD in Organizational Development and Change as well as double master's degrees in Social Science and Human Development. She is also accredited to administer various psychometric testing instruments. Sabreena is Past President of the International Federation Singapore Chapter from 2009 to 2011 and serves her professional community of practice through mentorship, supervision and facilitation of adult learning and development in small and large groups. www.theconsciouschoice.com

Jo Birch (MA) is an international executive coach, psychotherapist and accredited (CSA) and approved (EASC) supervisor. Jo has been practising for over 20 years. She is an active and respected member of the professional community: passionate about engaging in deep dialogue and partnering with colleagues across the world to enhance and extend coaching practice in service of clients. She writes and presents on supervision, ethics and cross-cultural practice, and was Series Editor of *Thinking Global in Coaching Today*. Previously Chair, BACP Coaching, Jo continues to be engaged in developing the field: exploring coaching supervision with Association for Coaching Special Interest Group; undertaking autoethnographic research into 'supervision of supervision'; and providing supervision to rising coaches in Ethiopia with Global Supervisors Network. Jo is committed to continuous personal and professional development. As Co-Founder of the International Centre for Reflective Practice, Jo has sourced a wide range of webinars, retreats, workshops and supervision groups for international coaches and supervisors. Previously Director of CSA, Jo continues to deliver training in coaching supervision in the UK, Asia Pacific and beyond.

Paul Brown is Professor of Organizational Behaviour, Monarch Business School Switzerland; External Advisor, the International Energy Research Centre, the Tyndall National Institute, University of Cork, Ireland; International Chairman of the Vietnam Consulting Group, Ho Chi Minh City; and International Director of SIRTailors, HCMC. He teaches as a Guest Lecturer at the Fulbright Economics Teaching Program in HCMC and taught annually at the UK's Royal College of Defence Studies for 25 years. He has a long-standing professional advisory interest in how family businesses are handed on to the next generation. A clinical and organisational psychologist and executive coach and supervisor, he has in recent time co-authored *Neuropsychology for Coaches: Understanding the Basics* (2012), McGraw-Hill/Open University Press; *River Dragon* (a novel, 2014); *Neuroscience for Leadership: Harnessing the Brain Gain Advantage* (2015), Palgrave Macmillan (which won a category Gold in the 2016 Chartered Management Institute's 'Management Book of the Year' awards); and *The Fear-Free Organization* (2015), Kogan Page. Dr Brown lives in Laos, consulting worldwide. He has created and teaches a world-first distance-learning master's programme in Applied Neuroscience in Organisations and a CPD programme, The Science of the Art of Coaching. In Germany, he is attached to Eicke Leadership Academy.

Henry Campion has worked as a doctor (including a psychiatric internship), a TV program maker, a senior BBC manager, an executive coach and now a coaching supervisor accredited by Oxford Brookes University. He also holds a postgraduate diploma in Psychosynthesis (transpersonal) counselling – all of which gives him a wealth of experience to draw on. Dr Campion is particularly interested in how insights from neuroscience can inform coaching and coach supervision. He has presented on the functioning of the right and left brain to the International Coaching Supervision Conference, and on attachment theory to the Global Supervisors' Network. His website is www.coachsupervisor.co

David Clutterbuck is EMCC Special Ambassador and Co-Founder. He is author of two books on coach supervision, and author or co-author of more than 60 others. He is a veteran presenter at diverse global conferences. Visiting professor at four UK universities, he holds a postgraduate certificate in coach and mentor supervision. He also wrote the first English language book on team coaching and is currently leading the editorial team creating the first handbook of team coaching.

Kees de Vries (drs) is an executive life coach and supervisor with 30 years of experience in and active commitment to the coaching profession. He is an ICF certified coach (PCC status) and was trained and certified by Hudson Institute of Coaching (California, USA). Kees holds a MSc in Work and Organisation Psychology, and is a Registered Psychologist NIP/W&O. Furthermore, he is qualified as an accredited coaching supervisor by the Coaching Supervision Academy in London. Kees brings his naturally appreciative and humane presence, open-mindedness and free spirit to his coaching and coaching supervision sessions. Exploring, discovering, learning and letting new truths emerge through dialogue is Kees' core approach. Relationship, trust and fidelity are his anchors. Kees has been honoured with the 2014 ICF President's Award in recognition of his work to promote coaching in a humanitarian capacity. For eight years Kees has been actively involved in ICF's Ethics Independent Review Board, three years as Chair. He has since been an international ambassador and thought leader on ethics. Ethics that he defines as 'giving the very best of yourself in the present in service of the relationship with the other and the wider system'. Kees is currently partnering in conversations and dialogues about ethics and ethical guidelines for the coaching supervision practice.

Kathryn M Downing, (JD, PCC) comes with a joyous commitment to lifelong learning and belief in the value and rewards of regular reflective practice. Her expertise and passion are in virtual supervision. She supervises small groups and individuals and relishes working with coaches who are committed to continuing to learn about themselves and their coaching practice. She is currently engaged in doctoral research on the subtle art of small group supervision towards a Professional Doctorate (DProf) in Coaching Supervision at Middlesex University, London. Her research is infusing her supervision with greater experimentation, customisation and playfulness. She is a member of the Leadership Team at Hudson Institute of Coaching and faculty for Coaching Supervision Academy – UK and Asia Pacific. Kathryn is a Professional Certified Coach by the International Coach Federation, is certified by the Hudson Institute of Coaching and has a Diploma in Coaching Supervision from the Coaching Supervision Academy in the UK. She is a Certified Daring Way™ Facilitator and Case Consultant, based on the research of Dr Brené Brown. Her educational background includes a JD from Stanford University School of Law. She lives with her husband and two beloved dogs in Santa Barbara, California.

Louie J N Gardiner, BA (hons), MBA, FRSA, PhD Researcher, Lead Presence in Action Practitioner and Learning Partner, Executive Coach-Confidante, Coaching Supervisor, Systemic Change Catalyst and Facilitator: Louie is a pioneer practitioner and writer, contributing creatively to both academic and practice-based journals e.g. *Human Arenas, Cybernetics and Human Knowing, e-O&P Journal, Coaching Today, Book: The Collaboratory* and *the3rdi* magazine. Irrespective of the diverse roles she has undertaken throughout her working life, Louie has consistently generated new ways of unleashing learning and catalysing personal and systemic transformation – enabling people within organisational and community contexts and across cultures and generations to navigate complexities in life, work and relationships with greater integrity, joy and artistry. Her life-long learning has found coherent synthesis in the P6 Constellation and the Presence in Action praxis that has come into being as more practitioners have come to learn with her. The emerging Community-in-Practice galvanising around this unique praxis is testament to the integrity, accessibility, applicability and generativity of the approach – a glimpse of which is offered within Chapter 7. louie.gardiner@potent6.co.uk www.potent6.co.uk

Saba Hasanie has spent two decades focussing on executive coaching and leadership development in North America and Asia. Since moving to Singapore in 2010, Saba has leveraged her extensive commercial experience and background in M&A towards her practice focussed on coaching, developing and facilitating leadership programmes and organisational development projects. Saba undertakes a neuroscience-based approach that connects scientific understanding of the brain with psychological theory of behavioural change. Saba works primarily with clients in Technology, FMCG, Financial Services, Energy and Professional Services. Saba writes and presents on many topics related to leadership development and neuroscience and resides in Singapore as a Permanent Resident.

Patrick Hobbs is a highly experienced executive coach and coaching supervisor accredited with the Association for Coaching, the Association of Coaching Supervisors, the European Mentoring and Coaching Council and the International Coach Federation. He has coached leaders, executives and entrepreneurs across more than 30 countries, and he has helped to train and develop coaches in the UK and internationally. He understands both coaching and the supervision of coaching as fundamentally creative processes rooted in hearing a human being and helping the person connect with and bring to life what is important to them in the context in which they find themselves. He seeks to encourage and enable coaches to interact with the realities of human life and work with wisdom, compassion and humility, seeing the person not in isolation but in a wider community of existence. Before coming to coaching Patrick studied History and Creative Writing and spent some 20 years struggling with and overcoming disabling viral illness. He has a love of music and wild places, and he has been, among other things, a furniture-maker, a photographer and a poet. He has published one collection of poems, and his work has been featured on BBC Radio.

Alison Hodge is an accredited Executive Coach at Master Practitioner level with EMCC and an accredited Executive Coaching Supervisor with APECS and EMCC. Working globally as a coaching supervisor with individuals and groups of both internal and external executive and team coaches, she co-creates working agreements to explore their practice, their client work and their ongoing professional wellbeing. As an Executive Director and a senior member of faculty at Coaching Supervision Academy (CSA), Alison facilitates global webinars and supervises supervisors-in-training where group and team coaching is increasingly on the agenda for reflection. She completed her DProf in Coaching Supervision at Middlesex University in 2014. She is particularly interested in the relational phenomena that arise in supervision and how these can inform the supervisee about their own process with their client relationships, particularly when 'the client' is a team that is often operating in a complex, demanding organisational system in which the work is being delivered. Team coaches really appreciate this safe space to explore and reflect on their work. She has facilitated international workshops on team coaching as well as developed and delivered a four-day team coaching supervision development programme for supervisors of team coaches.

Lise Lewis is an executive coach and coach supervisor. She founded Bluesky International in 2000 following a rewarding career in HR to work with people wanting to achieve personal and professional ambitions through coaching/mentoring. She proudly supports the quality standards of the EMCC as a designer, international provider and trainer of EMCC accredited programmes in coaching/mentoring and coach supervision skills. Lise is an EMCC accredited Master Coach and Coach Supervisor, has an MBA, is a Chartered Fellow of CIPD and completed a Professional Doctorate in Executive Coaching with Middlesex University. Her research topic grew from observing the importance of feedback and a wish to improve the experience of this activity. This research is now the foundation of a book due for completion in 2019. Lise was EMCC International President 2011–2017 and is currently EMCC International Special Ambassador. Her role is to promote the professionalisation of mentoring, coaching and supervision including supporting the creation of a body of knowledge through research that informs professional practice.

Katherine Long is a highly experienced coach, supervisor and OD practitioner. Katherine formerly led the Master's in Coaching at Warwick University for several years, held the Chair of Association of Coaching Supervisors and developed some of the earliest EMCC accredited supervision programmes aimed at supporting organisational coach-supervisors to grow internal coaching cultures. Her 'Diamond Model' (Long, 2011) was one of the first to support a systems model of the practitioner as the basis for applying different lenses to developing 'self-as-instrument' through coach-supervision. Whole-systems thinking and stakeholder-based design has always been an important strand to her work, and Katherine now focusses on developing practice and thought leadership to support eco-systems leadership and communities of practice actively engaged in achieving environmental and social outcomes at regional to global levels through a range of partnerships. Addressing the need for paradigms that support greater levels of consciousness and integration between self and system, Katherine has been developing an eco-spiritual approach to support holistic leadership and organisation development through the lenses of presence, love, meaning and oneness. www.evolutionod.com

Michel Moral spent most of his career in an international environment as a manager and executive. At that time his activities were covering Eastern Europe, Middle East and Africa, i.e. 124 countries. This helped him to become an intercultural specialist. In 2003 he created a coaching and supervision practice, and he coaches executives, executive teams and organisations. He also trains coaches on team coaching in several French universities, and supervises coaches and trains supervisors around Europe. His supervisor's training school holds the ESQA from EMCC. He also participates in a Post Master Collective Intelligence curriculum at the French University of Cergy-Pontoise. He is the European Supervision Individual Accreditation (ESIA) workgroup leader in EMCC and participates in many activities related to supervision and research on supervision. He holds a master's degree in Science and Technology and a PhD in Clinical Psychology. He has published ten books related to management, coaching and supervision.

Elaine Patterson is an award winning international Accredited Master Coach, Accredited Coach Supervisor and writer. She is also a member of Senior Faculty for the Coaching Supervision Academy and has been a senior leader in highly complex political organisations. Elaine's vision and passion is to bring the humanising, energising and creative powers of reflection and reflective supervision to an international audience of leaders and development practitioners for great work and inspired living in today's constantly changing world. Elaine's creative partnership with Karyn Prentice as PattersonPrenticeDesigns is receiving international acclaim. Together they craft and host warmhearted and soulful retreat spaces for deep reflection and profound learning. Elaine's work with Jackie Arnold on Executive Reflection is profiled in the 2019 *UK Parliamentary Review for Leadership and Education*. Elaine takes her inspiration from her love of the arts, history, mediation, writing, poetry and Nordic walking. Elaine has developed a new lens for coaching and coaching supervision called 'The 7Cs' designed to bring our shared humanity to work. Elaine's new book *Reflect to Create! The Dance of Reflection for Creative Leadership, Professional Practice and Supervision* has just been published. Elaine can be contacted at Elaine@ep-ec.com or via her website.

Katharine St John-Brooks is an executive coach and consultant specialising in the strategic use of internal coaches within organisations. She has spent 15 years as an external coach and is the author of *Internal Coaching: The Inside Story*, based on research with 123 internal coaches and interviews with a myriad of learning and development professionals, lead coaches, coach trainers, coach supervisors and coach sponsors (Karnac Books, 2014). Katharine holds an MSc in Organisational Behaviour, an MA in Professional Development (Coaching) and is a Fellow of the Institute of Consulting. She has coached over 400 people across the public, private and not-for-profit sectors and currently focusses exclusively on Board level and CEO clients in her coaching work. She is very active within the EMCC and chairs EMCC UK's Third Sector Coaching & Mentoring Forum, which meets quarterly. She is also President of Link Age Southwark – a charity providing friendly volunteer support for isolated, older people living in Southwark which received the Queen's Award for Voluntary Service in 2018.

Eve Turner has had three careers: musician, BBC editor and senior leader, and coach, supervisor and facilitator. She won the Coaching at Work 2018 Award for Contributions to Coaching Supervision and is the 2015 holder of the EMCC European Coach of the Year Award along with research awards from Coaching at Work, the BPS's Special Group in Coaching Psychology and the Association for Coaching. Eve has Master Executive Coach and Supervision accreditation, and her qualifications include an MBA and MSc. Her love of writing has come full circle from journalist to now contributing to literature on subjects from ethics and contracting to supervision and regularly presenting at conferences. Her first book, co-edited with Stephen Palmer, was published in 2019: *The Heart of Coaching Supervision – Working with Reflection and Self-Care*. Eve successfully set up the Global Supervisors' Network (GSN) for qualified and experienced supervisors to continue learning, and there are virtual sessions monthly at no cost to members, as well as original research being done. She is a Fellow at both the University of Southampton and Henley Business School in the UK and loves football (soccer!) and tolerates going to the gym regularly! Contact Eve via eve@eve-turner.com.

Peter Welch is an executive coach, team coach, coaching supervisor, thinking partner and thought leader. As Co-Founder of AOCS★ he is influential in the coaching field by supporting individuals and by contributing to organisations, networks and publications. In his work he draws on a rich tapestry of current thinking in the fields of coaching, change, transition, OD, leadership development and coaching supervision. Peter's key purpose is to bring about change in behaviour and performance in his coaching clients, achieved through a powerful and diverse combination of approaches that help clients achieve their goals. Peter has worked with multinationals, government departments, smaller enterprises and in the performing arts. His clients include CEOs, board directors and business owners; he also works with a range of independent coaches and teams by providing coach supervision, to support and strengthen them in their roles. Peter's accreditations include the Association for Coaching and the Coaching Supervision Academy. He also holds a Certificate in Team Coaching, backed up by an MA in Learning Organisations. He keeps current through a wide variety of CPD and ongoing learning. As a key player in AOCS★ he helps to promote supervision, to engage with and develop the association's international membership and partnerships, and to enable organic global growth. ★ www.associationofcoachingsupervisors.com

Sandra Wilson has a Professional Doctorate in Coaching Psychology and is a Teaching and Supervising Transactional Analyst specialising in the organisational application of TA. Sandra is a Master Certified Coach with the International Coach Federation. Sandra's professional background is in Human Resources and Organisation Development with a large multinational manufacturing company. Her career evolved naturally from the role of internal consultant to that of external consultant. Sandra has over 25 years' experience as a supervisor of coaches, organisation development consultants, human resource professionals and students of TA. She works nationally and internationally across organisational hierarchies with a particular focus on organisational change. Sandra works with the concept of change being an event and the response to change being a series of transitions which are individual and collective psychological experiences. Her work spans Organisation Development, Coaching Strategy; Coaching; Supervising; and Professional Consultancy. Sandra offers accredited training in both Coaching and Supervision. Her area of interest is in working with psychodynamic theory to support the development of individuals' and teams' understanding of the unique role the unconscious plays in how human beings interact, communicate, build relationships and build organisations.

Series editor foreword

Coaching Supervision: Advancing Practice, Changing Landscapes

When the European Mentoring and Coaching Council (EMCC) first decided it was time to create a book series with a leading international publisher, one of the key prompts was the sheer volume of research and writing from our members in Europe and further afield. This very much reflects the origins of the EMCC, in the bringing together at the beginning of the 1990s of researchers, practitioners and users of mentoring, then coaching. As the world of coaching has expanded, the shelves now groan with interesting, sometimes entertaining books that have little, if any, evidential underpinning – the result of extrapolation of personal experience into generalised 'truths.'

Coaching Supervision: Advancing Practice, Changing Landscapes brings together a team of practitioner-researcher-academics, each of them exploring aspects of supervision at the edge of what is known and what is surmised. Like all good coaching conversations, it focusses less on creating certainties than on generating new questions and challenging assumptions. This takes us into the messy marshlands at the edge of coaching and supervision, where paths are unclear and shifting, where compasses don't always work and where it takes a lot of effort to retrieve your wellington boots from where they are stuck. And as with the marshlands, it takes a special type of person to relish the experience of being in the supervision hinterland – people like the contributors to this book!

The chapters that follow provide invaluable insights for supervisors and their coach clients into the complex systems into which every supervision session is embedded. The challenges for coaches and supervisors occur so often not just within systems, but in the interaction between systems and, indeed, systems of systems. Various chapters explore the coach-supervisor system, the internal systems related to how our brains make sense of complex situations, cultural and ethical systems and the looming threat (or opportunity) of adding Artificial Intelligence to the supervisor-coach dynamic.

One of the core objectives of coaching is to expand the horizons and awareness of coachees. Supervision can be seen similarly as helping to raise the horizons and awareness of coaches. Books such as this ground-breaking volume are essential in enabling the same shifts in the thinking of supervisors. From the series editing team, our thanks to all the contributors for the challenges and provocations they offer us.

David Clutterbuck

Introduction

Jo Birch and Peter Welch

As the art and science of supervision for coaches and mentors evolves, we are witnessing practitioners and researchers following diverse areas of interest, which broadens and deepens the scope, understanding and capacity within the field.

This exciting time is reflected in this book, which takes you, the reader, on a journey through a changing landscape – moving from the evolution and context for supervision; through the essence; into a deep dive into exploring practice; and out into future avenues of inquiry for the profession.

Each chapter has a signature identity coherent with its author(s) and their theme. You may experience some discomfort when faced with radical ideas, re-configurations of earlier thinking and challenging propositions. This is our current world, and these contributions reflect the expansion in reach and range of coaching and mentoring supervision research and practice.

In the book we see practitioners engaging with academia in a new way, bringing alive the concept of praxis – the embodiment of theory and research. The energy in the field of supervision is vibrant and dynamic. It is stretching knowledge in a multitude of ways and is variously diverse and distinctive in its design.

We hear much of the volatile, uncertain, complex and ambiguous (VUCA) world in which our coaches and mentors, and our clients as global leaders, find themselves working. The chapters in this book offer islands of sanity[1] amidst the complexities of this VUCA world – places to pause for a moment and reflect before re-entering the flow again.

We hope that understanding more about the practice of supervision – its capacity to support coaches and mentors to hold space for reflection and learning; and contribute to a mature dialogue in professional standards and ethics – will support our supervisees to go out into the world and engage more robustly and assuredly with the complexity of their work.

We open the book, in Chapter 1, with Long's dialogic, reflective approach to exploring the interconnected activities of coaching and supervision, 'Supervision and the seventh eye.' Long considers the history, the 'old skin,' and the current challenges and risks to the developing professions and their ability to serve the leadership challenges of the current time and the future. She takes a systems perspective utilising Eye 7 (from the Seven Eyed Supervision model) and the necessary shift from Ego to Eco.

Birch and Gardiner draw on their understanding of the nature of emergence and self-organising dynamics in complex living systems and offer the essence of supervision through 'Seven simple rules: an alternative lens.' From an exploration involving over 20 coaching supervisors, they discern system-wide behaviours manifesting through supervisors and supervisees, when supervision is 'at its best.'

Brown, Hasanie and Campion take the reader into uncharted territory with 'Neuro-behavioural supervision: applied Neuroscience in the context of coaching supervision.' Brown et al. offer propositions that provide the underpinnings for supervision based on current brain knowledge; they introduce us to the HASIE model, the first brain-based coaching model, and extend it for the first time into supervision and discuss the relevance of attachment theory in coaching and supervision relationships.

In her chapter 'The power and influence of the unconscious mind,' Wilson's research participants, all trained and experienced coaches, use metaphoric landscapes and symbolic representation to explore unconscious processes present in coaching supervision. Wilson introduces the unconscious as a self-perpetuating pattern of organising self in relationships. We need more than solitary self-reflection for increased self-awareness – we need others in conversation.

We move from the unconscious into the realm of emotion with 'Working in the shadows: pain and suffering in coaching and supervision.' Hobbs invites us to consider the wholeness of the human experience. He raises important questions about the potential extension of the coaching relationship if we embrace pain, grief and loss alongside joy, success and future potential. Hobbs provokes our thinking and invites us to consider the dangers of a blinkered or superficial focus on the positive.

Downing invites us to consider 'A new dimension? Using observational data in supervision.' Her doctoral research was stimulated by reflections on self-identity, and how this informs the way we bring material into coaching supervision. Downing explores the potential for video and audio recordings to enhance learning and illustrates the chapter with case studies and reflective questions.

Drawing on a complexity-thinking paradigm and Natural Inclusion, in 'Attending, daring, becoming: making boundary-play conscious,' Gardiner offers a core case study, using her own process to illuminate challenges during a period of growth and change. A long-standing supervision group holds integrity and safety as they move into a new way of being together.

Andriesz explores the advancement of Asian leaders in Singapore in 'Extending ourselves as supervisors: stepping outside our cultural conditioning.' She discusses the potential impact of Western-centric models predominant in coaching and coaching supervision practice. The field of coaching orientates coaches towards the future and avoids delving into the past. This can be a conundrum for coaches when they encounter a person's cultural belief system.

In 'Moving from frozen code to live vibrant relationship – towards a philosophy of ethical coaching supervision' De Vries argues that journey-ethics rather than destination-ethics is more relevant to coaching supervision. He welcomes the reader into a dialogic journey building trust and deep connection in which both supervisor and supervisee are open to the emerging truth.

St John-Brooks builds on her original research in 'Supervision for internal coaches' and deploys contemporary study findings and new case studies to extend knowledge in this field. She explores the nature and function of supervision for internal coaches; the degree to which it is being delivered; alternatives; differences in respect of the supervisor role; and some challenges specific to internal coaches that may be brought to supervision.

In 'Guidelines for team coach supervision,' Hodge and Clutterbuck use research survey results and professional experience to identify some of the dimensions involved in the challenging and demanding work of a team coach. They draw conclusions about the need, nature and purpose of supervision in supporting coaches in this complex environment.

Patterson draws on her experience, practice and research to consider the wider application of supervision in the executive fields. She invites us to connect at the level of our shared humanity and to extend our thinking beyond the 'known.' She poses reflective questions that engage us in the exploration.

'Supervision of supervision' has become common practice; however, there is almost no literature or research on this practice to date. Moral and Turner examine the findings of their recent study, conducted through the Global Supervisors' Network, in 'Supervision of supervision' and consider the implications for supervisors and the field of supervision.

The book is drawn to a close by the chapter that really opens us to the future: Lewis and Clutterbuck's 'Co-evolution: exploring synergies between Artificial Intelligence (AI) and the supervisor.' They draw our attention to the changing world of technology and the growth of Artificial Intelligence in the coaching and coaching supervision field. In referring to broader research and the impact of AI in global business, Lewis and Clutterbuck join with us in wondering how we prepare for the future when the future is unknown.

This book is a gallery of pioneering work, curated to stimulate, challenge and inspire you as we journey through the changing landscape. There are cutting-edge contributions from some of the finest practitioners and researchers in the field. As in art galleries, some pieces invite reflection – and return visits may be necessary. The work is edgy and new, and yet totally grounded in the coaching and mentoring supervisor experience, bringing pragmatic solutions to current complex challenges.

Note

1 Wheatley, M. (2017). *Who Do We Choose to Be?* Oakland, CA: Berrett-Koehler.

1   Supervision and the seventh eye

Katherine Long

> We must be willing to get rid of the life we've planned, so as to have the life that is
> waiting for us. The old skin has to be shed before the new one can come.
>
> Joseph Campbell (Campbell, 1991)

Introduction

This chapter explores coaching and coach supervision through the 'seventh lens'
of the Seven Eyed Supervision model (Hawkins and Shohet, 2000), particularly
examining some of the core assumptions which have shaped coaching as we
know it today, as well as the relationship between the twin systems of coaching
and supervision, and how they stay relevant in a changing world.

Given this seventh lens invites our awareness of the macro systems and trends
which encompass the work of coaches (or coach-mentors) and supervisors, the
focus of this piece is intentionally broad-ranging, attempting to bring both an
'emic' (as seen from within a professional or social community) as well as an
'etic' view (as seen from the outside).

This chapter also attempts to weave in some of the themes which have surfaced when practitioners gather to explore their work from a meta-perspective,
and what may be crystallising from those inquiries. The research data for this
chapter is therefore emergent and dialogic in nature, and includes conversations
which I have hosted across different groups of coaches and supervisors including: live research with coaches (Long, 2014); the 'Squaring the Circle' session at
the International Conference on Coach Supervision (2014) exploring the role
of supervision in the transfer of learning from individual interventions to the
wider organisation; workshops exploring so-called macro 'Ego to Eco' shifts
with alumni of OCM, Ashridge and the International Centre for Reflective
Practice, as well as with the Critical Coaching Research Group; conversations at
the 'Across Boundaries' international supervision Open Space event co-hosted
by the Association of Coaching Supervisors (AOCS) and OCM in 2016; the
West Midlands Organisation Development Network Europe (ODNE) community and AOCS joint event ('Systems of Change – Joining the Dots' Theory-U
based inquiry) in 2017; and conversations with several cohorts of students in
the Master's in Coaching programme at Warwick University. These discussions

have focussed on a central question exploring how both practitioners and the professional bodies constantly evolve to remain relevant and 'fit for practice.'

To avoid confusion, it's important from the outset to clarify the terms 'coaching' and 'supervision' as they are used in this chapter, as depending on your viewpoint, you might interpret them in one or more of the following ways:

- As practice, i.e. the actual activity of coaches (or coach-mentors) and coach supervisors (or coach-mentor supervisors if you prefer) as it occurs in real life, in all its hybrid forms, including virtual and AI coaching platforms, such as MIT's Coach Otto, or the Pocket Confidant self-coaching app;
- As a set of widely recognised definitions, ethical standards and competences created by professional bodies to which practitioners are expected to adhere;
- As the global community of all practitioners (irrespective of professional membership), operating within diverse niches, markets and cultures around the world;
- As coaching and supervision are understood and experienced from outside the profession by individual or organisational clients, by adjacent professions (counselling, organisation development, training and teaching, etc.) or by society at large;
- As referring to the formalised practice of a timeless skills set and dialogic approach to human development which will continue to exist whether coaching, mentoring and supervision as we currently know them remain as distinct professional activities or not; or
- As a meta-perspective of the conjoined fields of coaching and supervision as a whole, which includes but does not purely consist of professional bodies and academia, and the way in which this dual system engages with its neighbours and stakeholders.

Reflection

- Notice your responses to the previous list of possible meanings. Which feel familiar or strange? Which do you resonate with? Do you have any strong reactions to any? Was there anything else you would have changed or added?
- What does this tell you about the way your supervision practice is focussed, as well as what you may be privileging, and what may be in your blind spot?
- What might be the response(s) of the professional bodies or communities of practice which you may be aligned to or be a member of, and what does this tell you about their way of seeing the world?

In this chapter, we will be considering coaching and supervision from the final description in this list, i.e. a meta-perspective on a dual system, which can be seen as a composite of each of the other previous interpretations. In this way, coaching and supervision are not seen as just one 'thing,' or even as two separate things, but as a dynamic exchange between multiple players which creates a macro entity. This description may feel unfamiliar to those whose habit or preference is to clearly delineate these activities, as opposed to viewing them as interacting and changing elements within a wider whole.

Here you are invited to adopt a more environmental, systemic perspective, which sees coaching and supervision as interconnected activities occurring within a broader and highly diverse ecology. To use an analogy from nature, whilst it is possible to analyse a woodland by categorising its separate species, it provides little understanding of how a woodland actually functions. In a dynamic and more holistic understanding of a woodland, we pay attention to how pioneer species create soil through the help of enabling micro-organisms to colonise and make way for an increasing diversity of life-forms inhabiting complex and mutually sustaining niches. Similarly, held in the matrix of overlapping socio-economic, political and environmental systems, coach-mentoring and supervision can be seen as a twin system which has evolved through time and which includes individual practitioners, academia, course providers and professional bodies.

Indeed, when it is seen in this way, one could argue that supervision, given its competences and parameters are currently determined by the coaching bodies themselves, depends upon a very close relationship with the professional bodies for its own survival; supervision therefore can be seen as both a product and a partner of the coaching profession, and unlike the relationship between some other professions and their regulatory bodies, there is very little 'arm's-length' relationship. Furthermore, supervisors may also be coaches and providers of coach education, and therefore have an interest in meeting standards set out by professional bodies, and indeed may be embedded within them as active members. This is not an attempt to argue for separation, but an invitation to acknowledge that there is a symbiotic relationship between supervision and coaching, and this will be important to consider in relation to the arguments explored throughout this chapter.

As is hopefully becoming clear, the intention for this thought piece is to provide a springboard for reflection and dialogue, to consider practice and professionalism from a more ecological frame, and from time to time you will be invited to pause and simply notice your own relationship to the content, and what it suggests to you regarding further inquiry or possible next steps, including ideas for exploration in group supervision. Assuming you are either a coaching or supervision practitioner (and quite possibly both), you have a stake in their combined futures and are therefore not a passive reader, but one who has a role to play in what each becomes.

A brief timeline of coaching

> I think calling it climate change is rather limiting. I would rather call it the *everything change*. Everything is changing in ways which we cannot yet fully understand or predict.
>
> Margaret Atwood (Finn, 2015)

Before we attempt to look forward to how coaching and supervision lean in to the challenges and opportunities of the future, it may be helpful to take a retrospective look at how they evolved into their current forms, and to remind ourselves of world events happening at the time. Coaching as we know it today does not have a precise start date, but according to Brock (2014), one of the leading researchers of the history of coaching, the earliest coaching programmes or companies emerged within the UK and the US in the early 1980s, following publications such as Gallwey's *Inner Game of Tennis* in 1974, the year Nixon resigned, followed by Fournies' *Coaching for Improved Performance* in 1978, the year the first IVF baby was born, and Megginson's *A Manager's Guide to Coaching* in 1979, the year Britain elected Margaret Thatcher.

Whilst coaching has a mixed provenance, whose roots extend back much further in time, drawing as it does on a number of philosophical traditions, we can see that the 1980s and 90s were a significant period for coaching, which was marked by the successive founding of many professional bodies: the European Mentoring and Coaching Council in 1992, not long after the collapse of the Berlin Wall in 1989 and Mandela's release in 1990, then the European Association for Supervision and Coaching in 1994, International Coach Federation in 1995, Société Francaise de Coaching in 1996, Worldwide Association of Business Coaches and Association for National Organisations for Supervision in Europe in 1997 and Association of Coaching in 2002, the year following the destruction of the World Trade Center. A later clustering of organisations such as Coaches and Mentors of South Africa and Asia Pacific Alliances of Coaches established themselves in 2007, signalling the spread of coaching globally, the year the first iPhone came out. Although a number of these organisations have advocated for supervision right from the start, the widespread acceptance of supervision as a key element of professional practice has taken much longer to be adopted, with ICF only formally recognising supervision (in contrast to mentor coaching) much later.

To put this timeline into a wider socio-economic context, the launch of many professional coaching and supervision bodies pre-dates the advent of the major social media platforms which shape today's global communication (LinkedIn was founded in 2002, Skype in 2003, Facebook in 2004, YouTube in 2005, Twitter in 2006). Indeed, e-mail was still a relatively new phenomenon when EMCC was founded. As well as preceding social media, the founding of most of these coaching and supervision bodies pre-dates the collapse of Lehman Brothers in 2008 and the subsequent worldwide financial crisis from which economies are still recovering today. Both the rise of social media and the global banking crisis are just two of many mega-trends and events occurring since the foundations of coaching as a profession were laid, and it is worth considering how even just these two, and their combined ripple effects, have had a significant impact on the wider contexts in which coaching and supervision take place.

For example, in response to the ongoing legacy of austerity which the banking crisis created, we see many organisations, and especially the public sector, under constant pressure to do more with less, and consequently needing to explore partnerships with a wide range of organisations operating across their geographic footprints to deliver shared services (Cullen, Willurn, Chrobot-Mason and Palus, 2014; Senge, Hamilton and Kania, 2015). This has forced a different perspective on leadership, with early adopters of living systems thinking such as Bateson, Capra, Maturana and Varela increasingly influencing more mainstream approaches to change, a radical shift from purely transactional and even transformational paradigms regarding leadership.

We also see the rise of a new generation of platform-based enterprises disrupting traditional organisations, which must either re-invent themselves or be left by the wayside. According to Matt Kingdon, co-founder of ?WhatIf!, almost three-quarters of the UK's largest companies in their 2014 survey admitted to reliance on fading revenue streams, and more than a quarter feared that their current business model would no longer work by 2017. "Despite recognising the acute need for innovation, most corporate leaders are struggling to create the conditions for new ideas to thrive. With a few notable exceptions, our research shows efficiency-focussed leadership, disconnected structures and laborious processes are stunting hopes of an innovation-led UK recovery. Swift action is needed to generate sustainable economic recovery" (Groom, 2014).

Broadening the historical and environmental context yet further, there is a significant debate within scientific communities (Crutzen and Stoermer, 2000) to rename the geological era we are now living in, proposing that the Holocene, a relatively stable inter-glacial period which started approximately 11,650 years ago, has already ended, and that humanity has now entered the Anthropocene, where human activity is the dominant influence on the climate and environment. In ways which are unprecedented and far-reaching, human beings now have the single greatest impact on the planet, and we are already starting to witness what is being termed as the sixth mass extinction of species. When we deeply engage with this reality, it invites us to profoundly examine our moral purpose, and hopefully to be brave enough to question our actions and our paradigms. In Einstein's words, "We cannot solve our problems with the same level of thinking that created them.", and it is above all a crisis of perception that the planet is facing.

As coaching and therefore supervision are primarily engaged in human development and activity, it is critical to consider how supervision partners with coaching to develop post-conventional thinking and ethics (Puka and Kohlberg, 1994; Rooke and Torbert, 2005; Scharmer and Kaufer, 2014) in relation to these existential challenges. And in the words of Joseph Campbell at the start of this chapter, we may need to shed an old skin before the new one can come.

Reflection

- What is your own timeline in relation to being a practitioner?
- What macro changes have been significant during that time? In what ways have they impacted on your clients, and on the environment?
- In what ways have you adapted your practice in response?
- What, if anything, are you letting go of in your practice and in your thinking to better serve the needs of the world today and tomorrow?

Group supervision idea

- Invite members of the group to stand in the timeline of when they first started coaching. There may be several timelines – formal coaching, informal coaching, etc.
- From 'oldest' to 'newest' invite each to reflect and share the wider organisational and/or socio-economic context when they began their practice.
- Open up a group or pair/trio discussion as to how the context shaped their approaches at the outset, and notice what has since changed both in the external environment and correspondingly in their practice.
- Take some time to ground yourselves in the present moment (e.g. body scan, mindfulness or focussing practice), and to collectively invite a sense into what might be wanting to emerge.
- Give time for individual sharing without interruption or discussion, and after each has spoken, invite some meta-reflection on what the group is noticing, and what that might mean for their practice.

Challenges and risks for coaching and supervision

> The greatest danger in times of turbulence, is not the turbulence itself, but to act with yesterday's logic.
>
> Peter Drucker (Drucker, 2009)

Given the scale of these changes, it would be naïve to pretend that these macro trends and events might not challenge some of the dominant narratives and assumptions which shaped coaching and supervision in its inception. To build our understanding of the wider context accompanying coaching's timeline, we now turn to discourse analysis and stage development theories to help us to discern crucial patterns.

In Western's typology of leadership discourses (Western, 2013) the so-called Messianic leadership discourse peaked in the 1980s and 90s (and as we have established, this was the period that most of the professional coaching bodies arose).

The distinctives of the Messiah discourse were in creating entrepreneurial and dynamic yet highly conformist cultures. Longer-term impacts of this discourse risked creating totalising and fundamentalist mindsets, with organisational cultures that resisted critical reflection and diversity.

Western's Messiah discourse echoes Rooke and Torbert's 'Achievist' leadership stage (Rooke and Torbert, 2005), and in *Spiral Dynamics* (Beck and Cowan, 1996) this is largely consistent with aspects of the fifth level, sometimes referred to as 'strive-drive' and characterised by materialist, strategic, ambitious and individualistic values.

Yet, new paradigms for organisations and leadership have been emerging since the early 2000s. Western labels the subsequent wave of leadership discourse as 'Eco,' characterised by connectivity, distributed leadership, ethics, sustainability and leading adaptive networked organisations. Described elsewhere as collective leadership and systems leadership, it relates to much wider societal shifts described by futurists Otto Scharmer and Gerd Leonhard as 'Ego to Eco' changes, with 'Ego' denoting mindsets and structures which are based on an ultimately individualistic approach to leaders and organisations, often hierarchical, narrowly defined and with a tendency to linear thinking. For example, Leonhard's background in the music industry led him to observe how that sector transformed under the new pressures created by digital downloading and then streaming, moving from an 'Ego' state characterised by pyramidic organisations with high levels of centralisation, hyper-competition, monolithic and proprietary – a 'one to many' models – to a more fluid 'Eco' state characterised by more distributed power expressed through networks of hubs, using interoperable systems – a 'many to many' model.

Regarding the shift towards 'Eco,' spiral dynamics and other stage development theories posit that stages of evolution will always oscillate between an individual and a collective focus, embodying a higher level of complexity at each stage. These stages are accelerated via changing environmental circumstances, and shifts in consciousness are adaptive responses to new levels of complexity spanning multiple levels of system, and not purely because of an individual or organisational desire to become more 'evolved.' Indeed, such shifts are always accompanied by new challenges as we are currently witnessing via the egoic needs of social media giants to control and use private data.

It is worth considering the extent to which the majority of coaching at its outset was focussed on 'Ego' needs, insofar as it served leaders at the top of their hierarchies, who were often closely mirrored in terms of status and background by the coaches who worked with them, and with coaching treated as a largely stand-alone intervention. The 'Eco' domain suggests possibilities for coaching to become much more embedded and normalised within all levels of organisation and society as an integral part of many types of development activities throughout education and beyond, with greater mutuality of learning in 'many to many' exchanges.

Indeed Western (2012) highlights the relationship between macro socio-economic trends and their potential impact on micro-practices in coaching, with the suggestion that rather than coaching being monolithic in its approaches and standards, it should naturally evolve and flex in accordance with changes in the wider environment. There are therefore significant implications for practitioners, not least how they negotiate scrutiny by the professional bodies, whilst staying adaptive to meet the changing needs of the world.

Reflection

- What aspects of the 'Messiah' or 'Ego' discourses do you recognise as having impacted the twin systems of coaching and supervision in relation to the professional bodies, to training providers and to practitioners?

- To what extent are your clients or the context you are coaching in operating within this paradigm? In what ways might they be seeking to change?
- What tensions, if any, can you identify in relation to how coaching and supervision adapt and evolve not only in relation to content, but also in the ways in which they are applied?

Group supervision idea

- Introduce, in whatever way seems appropriate (pre-reading, YouTube clip, etc.), the idea of 'Ego' and 'Eco' discourses to create a shared understanding.
- Designate one end of the room as 'Ego,' and the other as 'Eco,' and invite participants to find a space in the spectrum (or cycle if you prefer) which resonates with their current lived experience (whether in life in general, or in their coaching practice – decide what feels right). Allow each person to speak briefly about where they have placed themselves and why.
- Invite participants to then find the place which represents where their clients are positioned, and which direction they are facing. Give space for each person to express what their clients may be experiencing in relation to this polarity.
- Now invite participants to find the place which represents a range of key players in the coaching-supervision system (e.g. professional bodies, academia, internal coaching, independent coaches and supervisors, training organisations, etc.). Again, allow space for each representative to speak from their place on the spectrum.
- Open a discussion about the key themes emerging, paying attention to the distribution of different elements along the spectrum, and what implications there may be for the coach-supervision system, as well as for practitioners with their clients.

Given some of the significant shifts within organisational and leadership discourses as highlighted earlier, there is a corresponding need to regularly examine assumptions and practices. Here we will focus on three key risks of defaulting to the 'Ego' discourse as it relates to coaching and supervision:

1 *Risk of creating standardisation and loss of critical analysis*

Being in the business of change and transformation presents an interesting paradox; whilst coaches support clients to navigate, adapt and improvise in the face of increasingly complex and chaotic change environments, coaching bodies have over the last years invested heavily in creating and promoting standardisation with regard to practice, ethics and accreditation.

As might be expected, we see some interesting anomalies amongst the largest professional bodies, which subsequently can impact on how supervision is framed. ICF's certification system excludes mentoring from its standards, whilst at the same time requires coaches to work with mentors as part of the credentialing process. The EMCC on the other hand embraces both mentoring and coaching without specifically differentiating between coaching and mentoring competences, and yet to date, does not formally recognise team coaching, whilst the ICF does. Furthermore, EMCC and AC have co-created a 'Global Code of Ethics' which aligns with but does not include ICF, which has its own code. Regarding supervision, we have further distinctions; AC has created a range of categories of supervisor which specifically includes non-coaching supervisors (i.e. from counselling and related backgrounds, and not necessarily with experience of coaching).

Whilst such differences are inevitable, one of the risks which the gravitational pull of these professional bodies exerts on its membership is the narrowing of critical and open questioning of core assumptions. If I am a member of ICF I am likely to end up having an ICF shaped conversation, or if a member of EMCC, then an EMCC shaped one, neither of which is entirely enabling of fully open inquiry. It is telling that at the 'Across Boundaries' Open Space conference (Welch and Long, 2015), in an environment attended but not hosted by any of the standard-setting bodies, amongst a seasoned group of supervisors and providers of supervision qualifications, the most well-attended session focussed on addressing a simple question 'What Is Supervision?', generating a rich discussion drawing on diverse perspectives from representatives working across a number of continents regarding the need for a more culturally aware and nuanced understanding of supervision

2   *Risk of diminished diversity and inclusion of practitioners and practice*

Another risk to coaching and supervision's ongoing relevance relates to barriers to entry and participation, which the profession may unwittingly collude with by creating processes for accreditation which have the potential to marginalise would-be practitioners. In unconsciously mirroring client systems and their core paradigms, there is a risk that all the way from the selection and training of coaches and supervisors (both internal and external), from the make-up of training providers themselves, through to commissioning, matching and sponsorship the cumulative effect of small but significant levels of unconscious bias filters out practitioners and potential coachees, not only on the basis of protected characteristics (e.g. age, disability, gender reassignment, marriage or civil partnership, pregnancy and maternity, race, religion or belief, sex and sexual orientation), but also relating to professional and socio-economic background and level of education. When this occurs, not only does it make coaching and supervision appear anachronistic and biased, it also weakens its capacity to address client issues of equality, diversity and inclusion with integrity. Where diversity coaching *is* offered, it has often been in conjunction with leadership programmes targeting minority groups, rather than directed at addressing systemic conscious and unconscious bias and inclusion more widely. It is perhaps timely that we reframe coaching not as just an individual or even a team intervention, but as an inherently systemic intervention (i.e. intervening within a wider system) whether that is the intention or not, and that as such, coaching has the power to reinforce or challenge tacit assumptions regarding power and privilege.

Reflection

- How well does the coaching body you align to represent minority groups?
- Reflecting back on the coaching assignments you have engaged in over the last 12 months, how diverse is the make-up of the coaches (or supervisees) when compared to the national population?
- If you work with or are part of an internal pool of coaches, how well does your membership reflect the make-up of the organisation as a whole?

Group supervision idea

- Invite each participant to share what they feel they have in common with the other members of the group.
- Then invite each participant to share what they believe makes them different from other members of the group.
- What does this data around similarity and difference tell you about the strengths and weaknesses of the group to bring diverse perspectives to bear when exploring practice together?
- How will you include missing or underrepresented perspectives on practice?

The risk of homogeneity extends also to practice. HBR's 'Wild West of Coaching' (Sherman and Freas, 2004) highlighted many pertinent issues of coaching at the time, not least the challenge of building a shared understanding of what constituted effective practice. This threw down the gauntlet to the coaching community to ramp up efforts to build credibility and to 'tame' the wildness. Yet one questions whether 'taming' and delivering quality always equate to the same thing (Garvey, 2014). When I first started coaching as Director of Studies in a language school, I'd read just half of John Whitmore's *Coaching for Performance*, exploring alternatives to a pure training approach to staff development. I intuited that the best way I could offer coaching was to coach pairs of teachers at similar stages of practice to explore shared developmental issues, as it happened, with relative success. No-one ever 'told' me that this was not the right way to coach, and yet when I began formal coach training, I unlearnt this approach swiftly in favour of 121 coaching, as no other method was role-modelled. In ways which we can hardly be aware of, coach development programmes funnel practice to favour conformity rather than experimentation, and unwittingly exclude creative approaches which may serve us in being more agile and responsive to changing client needs.

3   Risk of privileging linear and individualistic viewpoints at the expense of working with complex contextual issues

Another legacy of the 'Ego' and 'Messiah' discourses is the emphasis on individually framed and individualistic goals. Whilst organisational coaching increasingly supports multi-stakeholder contracting as good practice, and there is evidence that team and group coaching is on the increase (Mann, 2016; Coachsource.com, 2018), the primary emphasis has been on facilitating unitary change, even when desired changes may be co-dependent on many other factors involving numerous feedback loops across the system. In the example of diversity coaching, such initiatives can only backfire if the organisation is not engaged in supporting diversity and inclusion more widely, and may be undergoing simultaneous 'de-layering,' taking away the very roles which recipients of diversity coaching might have applied for.

Clearly coaches cannot be held solely accountable for the context in which they work. The way coaching is commissioned is often disconnected to wider strategic and organisational change initiatives. Despite the fact they have so much in common, the fields of organisation development and coaching have developed largely independently to each other. On Roffey Park's 'Map of OD' (Roffey Park, 2016) coaching is little more than a footnote, and many coaches are equally unaware of OD, yet a closer partnership between coaching and OD might yield more effective interventions on both sides, exploring the 'who?' the 'what?' and the 'why?' of organisation change in more co-ordinated ways.

Coupled with the risks of largely individual focussed interventions is the risk of coaching colluding with a linear set of approaches regarding goal setting and evaluation, regardless of rapid changes in the external environment. Snowden's Cynefin model (Snowden and Boone, 2007) predicts that when applying standard processes to problem-solving in complex change conditions (where the relationship between cause and effect can only be understood in hindsight) organisations will suddenly find themselves in chaos. A client recently shared with me how in her public sector organisation, in spite of 'doing all the right things,' they are feeling as though the 'walls of the box have just started crashing down, and we are all looking at each other like, what just happened?' When coaching assumes a simple, linear approach to change and performance, it may be at the expense of the wider system.

Opportunities for evolving profession and practice

> The growth of our challenges and the growth of our capacities are growing faster than we are yet able to comprehend.
>
> Andrew Zolli (Zolli, 2012)

With new challenges arise new possibilities, and in this final section we will explore what opportunities arise when leaning into some of the risks and tensions highlighted earlier. We will be applying two sets of lenses, environmental and appreciative, and considering how supervision can enhance a positive core of characteristics which are advantageous in evolutionary terms. These include the inter-dependent qualities of *adaptive action*, the capacity of coaching to respond effectively to wider environmental changes and needs, *integration*, the capacity to embrace and synthesise new practices, and *hybridism* and *polymorphism*, the ability to develop new and diverse forms.

1   *Adaptive action*

Capacity to adapt to changes in the external environment is a critical enabler for long-term survival, which coaching and supervision must be able to demonstrate in order to retain their relevance in the wider environment. Adaptive action can be highly beneficial for others also; taking an example from naturopathy, adaptogenic plants are valued for their remarkable ability to help the body to deal with a wide range of stressors and to support homeostasis, with the same plant being able to treat a wide range of symptoms.

Evidence of adaptive action in coaching, in relation to wider 'Ego' to 'Eco' shifts in organisations and in society, is seen by the way in which coaching has already begun to adopt a broader systems approach, as demonstrated through the mushrooming interest in systemic constellations, team coaching and organisational coaching. This systems focus is crystallising in more formal ways via new awards such as EMCC's International Standards for Mentoring and Coaching Programmes (ISMCP), and CIPD's award category for Best Coaching and Mentoring Initiative, which recognises strategic integration of coaching within organisational settings, as opposed to coaching as a standalone intervention.

For coaching to stay adaptogenic to client systems, it needs the freedom to intuit what is needed for those systems to find balance. Supervision can have a role to play by supporting practitioners to identify and stay true to high-level principles to serve client needs as opposed to conforming to detailed norms.

One example is in relation to ethical practice. As coaches must balance multiple stakeholder needs whilst working within the parameters of their own skills and integrity, the need to develop ethical maturity becomes more pronounced. A key question for coaches in the current context is whether they choose to simply maintain a single role, or whether the context is better served by their being adaptive in offering a range of roles supporting individual and collective change. The same question needs to be asked of supervisors, for example, what role they might play in offering a feedback loop by harvesting organisational and wider professional learning to inform and support development and adaptive action.

2   Integration

Another example of an evolutionary strategy is integration. In evolutionary biology, phenotypic integration is the capacity for a species to hold multiple traits within its DNA. In coaching, we see this exemplified in the generous holding of multiple strands of theoretical and philosophical 'DNA,' more recently welcoming in mindfulness (Silsbee, 2010; Hall, 2013), neuroscience (Brown and Brown, 2012; Rock and Page, 2013) and systems approaches (Whittington, 2012), which both confirm and confront previous paradigms.

This integration resists the creation of a single, dominant framework for coaching, and instead supports diverse expressions of practice. New approaches are communicated across the multiple relationships and channels criss-crossing the coaching-supervision system, enervated through conferences, research, publications, social media and networking events. Collective intelligence within the coaching-supervision system enables cross-pollination across different fields, and whilst professional bodies may be more singular in focus, real-life practitioners represent a wide and vibrant range of interests across different professional identities, suggesting potential for the coaching-OD and other divides to be straddled by practitioners, if not by professional bodies.

3   Hybridism and polymorphism

Hybridism is the capacity to create new subspecies in order to take advantage of different niches, such as Darwin's finches, adapting to different habitats across the Galapagos. Polymorphism, on the other hand, is an individual species' capacity to take on a range of forms, colours and sizes, for example, jaguars and black panthers, or within colonies of ants which share the same DNA but express that through a range of sizes and roles.

Hopefully it is not too difficult to see parallels across coaching and supervision. Several sub-types have existed for years but are often outside the focus of professional bodies, including lean management, sports, sales and call centre coaching. New hybrids include 'Personal Consulting,' (Popovic and Jinks, 2013) as a practice which bridges coaching and counselling, and it might be argued that team coaching is a hybrid of coaching, team development and OD. Health, wealth and sex coaching necessarily integrate diverse knowledge bases which fall beyond the scope of 'pure' coaching. In relation to polymorphism there are a widening range of niches: coaching in prisons, coaching in education, supporting soldiers back into civilian life, back to work schemes, not to mention applied coaching skills for managers and leaders, as well as Islamic (Allaho and Van Nieuwerburgh, 2017) and Christian (Collins, 2010) coaching. Whilst they may share some common characteristics, each will demonstrate distinctive features with regards to ethics, awareness of and ability to work with mental health issues, length and focus of coaching conversations.

Given the proliferation of varied coaching forms and contexts, it makes the possibility of clear differentiation to adjacent practices (mentoring, facilitation, team development, organisation development, counselling, leadership development) all the more challenging, and potentially counter-productive. Increasingly coaches need to act as professional shape shifters, constantly evolving themselves and their practice to adapt or specialise according to different client and contextual needs.

There are clear implications for supervision, indicating a need to broaden its taxonomy and widen its own approaches in equal measure. As coaching increasingly adapts to different niches, there may be scope for supervision to learn from a range of adjacent practices such as shadow consulting or clinical nurse supervision.

Reflection

- To what extent does your supervision practice act as a 'gate-keeping' function to encourage or discourage different forms of coaching practice? If so/if not what guides your action?
- What new or innovative approaches have you encountered via the coaches whom you supervise? What has been your response?
- How does adaptive action, integration and hybridism/polymorphism manifest in your own development and practice?

Group supervision idea

- Set up the following activity as an exercise to help coaches reflect on ways they are exploring adaptive action in relation to client needs and contexts.
- Invite coaches to create a composite 'island' or archipelago representing the shared contexts they operate within – this could be on flip-paper or represented spatially within the room. Encourage creative flair, and use topological features (cliffs, sandy beaches, dense woodland, etc.) as metaphors for the different 'habitats.'
- Introduce the metaphor of Darwin's finches as an expression of adaptive changes within a species and support a shared inquiry into all the different ways in which coaches are discovering new micro-practices or strategies which suggest evolving practices and approaches.
- Conclude with some time for meta-reflection and application work.

Final thoughts

> We are all time travellers, journeying together into the future. But let us make that future a place we want to visit.
>
> Stephen Hawking (Hawking, 2018)

Coaching and supervision are, like any approach to human development, products of the contexts and times in which they developed. This chapter has provided a highly condensed version of events, but which hopefully highlights some of the key wider environmental shifts and their significance for how supervision and coaching evolve to stay relevant. In relation to the current times, Scharmer talks about "the simultaneous existence of one world that is dying and another one that is being born," (Scharmer and Kaufer, 2014, p153) and coaching and supervision find themselves at the transition point between serving systems facing obsolescence, and new ones trying to find their way forward. An evolutionary approach suggests ways in which supervision can support ongoing relevance across paradigm shifts, yet it remains to be seen what an optimal relationship(s) between coaching and supervision could be, which can only be determined through ongoing inquiry across the wider community. I suggest that the primary role which supervision should play in the shared system of coaching and supervision is, in fact, to support sustainability, and to recognise that this is a shared role across multiple stakeholders.

> Sustainability is not an individual property but a property of an entire web of relationships. It always involves a whole community. This is the profound lesson we need to learn from nature.
>
> (Capra and Luisi, 2014, p. 355)

This re-framing of supervision transcends traditional functional roles of supervision, i.e. formative, normative, restorative (Inskipp and Proctor, 1995), and instead emphasises the promotion of the health, connectedness and ongoing relevance of coaching in all its variant forms so that we can continue to serve the needs of today and tomorrow.

References

Allaho, R. and Van Nieuwerburgh, C. (2017). *Coaching in Islamic Culture*. London: Karnac Books.
Beck, D. and Cowan, C. (1996). *Spiral Dynamics*. 1st ed. Oxford: Blackwell.
Brock, V. (2014). *Sourcebook of Coaching History*. 1st ed. CreateSpace Independent Publishing Platform.
Brown, P. and Brown, V. (2012). *Neuropsychology for Coaches*. Maidenhead: Open University Press.
Campbell, J. (1991). *Reflections on the Art of Living: A Joseph Campbell Companion*. Selected and edited by Diane K. Osbon, Quote Page 8 and 18. New York: HarperCollins.
Capra, F. and Luisi, P. (2014). *The Systems View of Life*. 1st ed. New York: Cambridge University Press, p. 355.

Coachsource.com. (2018). EC4R Full Report 2018. *CoachSource CONNECT* [online]. Available at http://coachsource.com/EC4RFULL2018 (Accessed 24 January 2018).

Collins, G. (2010). *Christian Coaching.* 2nd ed. Colorado Springs: NavPress.

Crutzen, P. and Stoermer, E. (2000). The 'Anthropocene'. *The International Geosphere – Biosphere Programme Newsletter May No. 41,* 20(41), 17–18.

Cullen, K., Willurn, P., Chrobot-Mason, D. and Palus, C. (2014). Networks: How Collective Leadership Really Works. *Ccl.org* [online]. Available at www.ccl.org/wp-content/uploads/2015/04/networksHowCollective.pdf (Accessed 24 January 2018).

Drucker, P. (2009). *Quoted in Neharika Vohra and Kumar Mukul, 'Relevance of Peter Drucker's Work: Celebrating Drucker's 100th Birthday', Vikalpa, 34(4), p. 7.*

Finn, E. (2015). An Interview with Margaret Atwood. *Slate.* Available at https://slate.com/technology/2015/02/margaret-atwood-interview-the-author-speaks-on-hope-science-and-the-future.html (Accessed 20 December 2018).

Fournies, F. (1978). *Coaching for Improved Work Performance.* 1st ed. New York: Van Nostrand Reinhold Co.

Gallwey, W. (1974). *The Inner Game of Tennis.* Random House.

Garvey, R. (2014). The Wild West of Coaching. *Coaching at Work,* 9(3), 57.

Groom, B. (2014). UK Big Business Lagging on Innovation Uptake. *Financial Times,* April 28.

Hall, L. (2013). *Mindful Coaching.* London: Kogan Page.

Hawking, S. and Livni, E. (2018). Please Allow Stephen Hawking to Explain Time, History, and God. *Quartz.* Available at https://qz.com/1464626/please-allow-stephen-hawking-to-explain-time-history-and-god/ (Accessed 16 November 2018).

Hawkins, P. and Shohet, R. (2000). *Supervision in the Helping Professions.* Philadelphia, PA: Open University.

Inskipp, F. and Proctor, B. (1995). *The Art, Craft & Tasks of Counselling Supervision, Part 2.* 1st ed. Twickenham: CASCADE.

Leonhard, G. (2014). Egosystem–Ecosystem. *Futuristgerd.com* [online]. Available at www.futuristgerd.com/share/2014/02/ego-system-ecosystem-gerd-leonhard-futurist-speaker.png (Accessed 24 January 2018).

Long, K. (2014). Mind the Gap: Is Coaching Always a Good Thing? *The OCM Coach and Mentor Journal,* 2–5.

Mann, C. (2016). *6th Ridler Report, Strategic Trends in the Use of Coaching* [online]. Available at www.ridlerandco.com/ridler-report/ (Accessed 24 January 2018).

Megginson, D. and Boydell, T. (1979). *A Manager's Guide to Coaching.* 1st ed. London: British Association for Commercial and Industrial Education.

Popovic, N. and Jinks, D. (2013). *Personal Consultancy: A Model for Integrating Coaching and Counselling.* 1st ed. London: Routledge.

Puka, B. and Kohlberg, L. (1994). *Kohlberg's Original Study of Moral Development.* New York: Garland.

Rock, D. and Page, L. (2013). *Coaching With the Brain in Mind.* Hoboken, NJ: Wiley.

Roffey Park. (2016). *Mapping the Field of OD With Roffey Park* [online]. Available at https://vimeo.com/165552818 (Accessed 24 January 2018).

Rooke, D. and Torbert, W. (2005). Seven Transformations of Leadership. *Harvard Business Review,* 83(4), 66–76.

Scharmer, O. and Kaufer, K. (2014). *Leading From the Emerging Future.* Kbh.: Nota.

Senge, P., Hamilton, H. and Kania, J. (2015). The Dawn of System Leadership. *Stanford Social Innovation Review,* Winter.

Sherman, S. and Freas, A. (2004). The Wild West of Executive Coaching. *Harvard Business Review,* 82(11), 82–90.

Silsbee, D. (2010). *The Mindful Coach*. Hoboken: Jossey-Bass [Imprint].

Snowden, D. and Boone, M. (2007). A Leader's Framework for Decision Making. *Harvard Business Review*, November.

Welch, P. and Long, K. (2015). Across Boundaries. *Aocs.pagelizard.com* [online]. Available at http://aocs.pagelizard.com/acrossboundaries/#acrossboundaries2015/across_boundaries_2015_e_magazine (Accessed 24 June 2018).

Western, S. (2012). *Coaching and Mentoring*. London: Sage Publications.

Western, S. (2013). *Leadership*. London: Sage Publications.

Whittington, J. (2012). *Systemic Coaching and Constellations*. London: Kogan Page.

Zolli, A. (2012, July). *Resilience: Why Things Bounce Back by Andrew Zolli and Ann Marie Healy*. New York: Simon & Schuster/Free Press. ISBN13: 9781451683844.

2 Seven simple rules

An alternative lens

Jo Birch and Louie J N Gardiner

A changing world, changing us

The focus of this book leans us towards the future of coaching supervision.[1] What is happening now that offers insights into what might become? Throughout this book, we are invited into little-explored avenues. Here, we found ourselves inspired to examine the generative nature of coaching supervision as it is emerging and manifesting in these, its embryonic years. Why? Because of a bigger question: how can we (collectively as agents in the system with myriad roles) understand, and more importantly, influence developments in a way that upholds and enhances ourselves, our practice and our field, and those engaged and impacted, locally and globally – now and in the future?

We experience and recognise the world as volatile, unpredictable, complex and ambiguous (VUCA).[2] We are not alone. Increasingly, more and more people are bumping up against this reality. Our clients find themselves facing tension-filled dilemmas: desperately wanting certainty, consistency, predictability and proof of impact; yet finding increasingly that their usual ways of thinking (simplistic cause-effect, quick fixes, change on demand) do not deliver. Our beliefs drive what we do and how we do it. This means that if our approaches are to change to better fit our complex, emerging future, we also need to think differently – we need a shift in paradigm (worldview) to open us up to those unimagined, unimaginable possibilities. Herein lies the rub. We cannot make paradigm shifts happen just because we want them. However, we can establish conditions that might facilitate a turn.

As coaching supervision professionals, what is our part in all this? What do we need to be able to know, do and be, to support those we serve to survive, lead and thrive in the world as it is?

To explore these questions, we adopted an iterative, emergent inquiry involving ourselves and others. Our methodology is consistent with a complexity-thinking paradigm[3] and informed by contemporary studies of human systems. The outcomes of our exploration comprise a radically simple contribution to the practice of coaching supervisors and to our emerging field. We do not have the space here to explore the wider ramifications of this statement. Instead we simply offer our thinking (thus far) as a spark, a catalyst to your own thinking.

We invite you to walk into the shallows with us, and if it resonates, please play with the ideas, open dialogues with friends and colleagues, and see where the swim takes you!

Setting the scene

We draw on our understanding of the nature of emergence and self-organising dynamics in complex living (adaptive) systems. We set the scene by first introducing you to the Stacey/Landscape[4] diagram and the concept of complex adaptive systems (CAS). This situates coaching and coaching supervision in a wider systemic context. Using the theory of 'simple rules,' we then direct our attention to the behavioural dynamics and patterns we and others recognise in and across our coaching supervision system. We propose that by bringing system-wide behaviours into view, we may be able to amplify those that (re)generate and support our practice, the field and those in the wider world we serve.

Surveying the landscape

Ralph Stacey first developed a heuristic to aid people in his organisation to appreciate and understand that not all was simple, certain and controllable. Later he rejected his own model, considering it too simplistic to be of value. Nevertheless, it remains in use because it serves as a useful bridge for understanding when traditional scientific thinking and approaches (objective, mechanistic, reductionist, linear) may be fit-for-purpose, and when alternative complexity lenses, with related approaches, may be more helpful. For example, Gardiner[5] uses the Stacey/ Landscape diagram to illustrate and leverage the similarities and distinctions between person-centred and goal-directed approaches to coaching, counselling and self-reflective practice. However, (Figure 2.1) we deploy it to situate coaching and coaching supervision in relation to their stages of emergence.

By way of example the arrows shifting from top right to bottom left depict indicative trajectories for both coaching and supervision. Both will have arisen from the unorganised realm, entering the Pattern-Forming realm with the arrival of training programmes and the formation of member organisations, then into the organised zone as those bodies morphed into accredited/accrediting entities. There is further convergence between some coaching accreditation bodies around professional ethics which suggests they are 'close to agreement' (vertical axis) about the nature of certain challenges, and that they are 'close to certainty' (horizontal axis), believing their course of action will address those challenges. Whilst there is divergence amongst many professional coaching bodies across the world, there is a similar propensity to establish competencies and accreditation procedures. Some are pursuing Royal Charter Status. This would, in all likelihood, drive the coaching profession in the UK towards increasing constraint (further into the Organised space), bringing with it tighter controls e.g. procedural compliance, quality assurance protocols and externalised assessment. Such moves may be fit-for-purpose in disciplines that require expert skills for known complicated tasks e.g. aircraft crew emergency procedures, some HR functions; repetitive functions where high levels of variability in the organising system can be eliminated as in IT, accounting or some manufacturing processes. Competency frameworks lose efficacy in the face of 'never-experienced-before' situations typical of the VUCA world in which many coaches, mentors, supervisors and their clients are operating.

As of 2018, coaching supervision as a field of practice is relatively young with few practitioners across the world. Its emergent, self-organising nature is illustrated by the creation of the Global Supervisors' Network in 2016 as a response to the dearth of continuing professional development (CPD) opportunities for experienced, senior practitioners. Initiated by Eve Turner, the group quickly established itself and continues to expand as a self-sourcing, mutually resourcing advanced learning network. It is simple in form and process and has few constraints. This facilitates the presence of diversity, invites reciprocity and generates learning exchanges within. Being in it, noticing the nature of what is in play and being able to consciously influence such systems distinguish complexity-attuned from conventional practitioners.

Arguably, as coaching supervisors, we are all called to attend to such complexity: to see, understand and act differently; to engage with not-knowing; and to notice patterns and take conscious action without being attached to predetermined outcomes. As professionals in service, we enable our clients to weave across the landscape of complexity (infinity symbol in Figure 2.1),

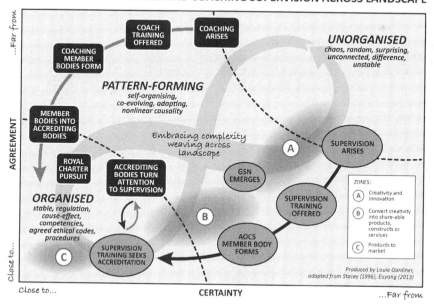

TRAJECTORY OF COACHING AND COACHING SUPERVISION ACROSS LANDSCAPE

Figure 2.1 Emergent trajectory of coaching and coaching supervision fields

attending to what is present and calling for attention: e.g. sensing when a shift towards embracing difference and creativity is called for, or when decisions and time-bounded plans need to be enacted (Figure 2.1).

To better understand the aforementioned framing, we need to appreciate that coaching and coaching supervision are interdependently linked and that those of us working within them act as complex adaptive systems (CAS) (Figure 2.2). What do we mean by this? A CAS comprises similar and diverse agents (individuals) who interact, generating patterns (behavioural, organisational, cultural, etc.) that come to exemplify the CAS. These patterns then, in iterative fashion, influence and shape the interactions and behaviours of the agents.

Referring to Figure 2.1, CAS tend to shift from unorganised (top right) to organised states (bottom left). If their pattern-forming abilities become overly constrained, they will die, disintegrate or erupt! What can we do to keep alive the adaptive pattern-forming propensities in coaching and coaching supervision so needed in today's reality?

According to CAS scientists[6] and researcher-practitioners,[7] system patterns evolve in relation to certain conditions: the *systems/containers* in which we find ourselves, the *differences/distinctions* between us and the nature of our *exchanges/ relationships*. When it comes to humans, our perspectives also come into play. When one of these conditions changes, the others are influenced in a nonlinear fashion. In other words, we cannot predict how all other conditions will shift, nor how this will affect the overall pattern. We only know that something will change . . . eventually. To influence a CAS we need only act on one variable, knowing that the others will be affected anyway.

Complex adaptive system (CAS) representation

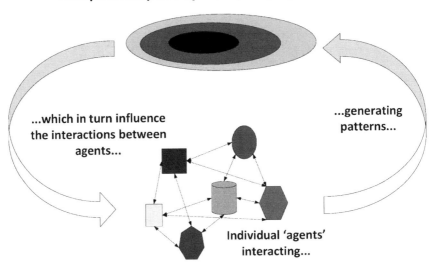

Figure 2.2 Complex adaptive system (CAS) representation (re-presented from Eoyang, G. and Holladay, R. (2013))

The theory of 'simple rules'[8] illuminates the self-organising behavioural dynamics in complex adaptive/living systems like ants, schools of fish, flocks of birds and human beings. Craig Reynolds (1987), a computer scientist, found how to create computer simulations of flocking birds, which he called *Boids*! He discovered that by coding a very few 'simple rules,' drawn from the observable behaviour in the flock, his computer Boids would produce complex swarm patterns similar to those we see in nature.

We, as human beings, also co-evolve behavioural rules in the groups of which we are a part – usually non-consciously. We embrace and adopt those behaviours as part of being in that group – not because we are told to do so. When several of us embody the same behaviours, we find ourselves generating patterns that epitomise us as a group, system, organisation, community, school, culture, etc. Becoming aware of ourselves and this process can help us leverage our self-organising propensities. By naming and consciously embracing behaviours that show us at our best, we can amplify desirable group patterns. When as individuals we take on these behaviours as our own – as in starling murmurations – we in effect self-organise through our peer-to-peer interactions, and in the process, our group patterns become more internally coherent *without the need* for externalised control mechanisms. We again draw an example from the Global Supervisors' Network. CPD webinars are delivered voluntarily and are free to attend, and we consistently see very high attendance ratings – almost always 100%. In our experience 'free' events frequently experience high drop-out rates. We suggest there are 'simple rules' playing out in the GSN system that are generative and appreciated by group members that guide 'following through' on commitments to attend webinars.

This leads us into our inquiry. What 'simple rules' already exist in coaching supervision that support and uphold its emergence as a coherent, generative professional field and as a practice? By amplifying our generative, pattern-forming, adaptive behaviours and capacities we hope to better resource individuals and the wider system to deal with a complex, unpredictable world.

Engaging with voices in the system

In order to find the 'simple rules' at play in our system we began a reflective process. We started scoping 'what we knew' and used our own experiences as supervisors and as supervisees. We intended to bring into awareness our sense of the 'DNA' of coaching supervision, the essence. What is this activity, this 'way of being'? How would we know it when we came across it?

Starting with ourselves

We chose Eoyang's[9] complexity tool *Radical Inquiry* to extrapolate similarities and differences between coaching supervision and counselling supervision as a starting point. Simply, this process involved an exploration of 'Doing, Knowing and Being.'[10] We noticed (amongst other things) a crucial difference related to the context of the overall activity. Coaching explicitly operates within a complex stakeholder environment, open to multiple systemic influences at any point in the coaching contract, process and field. This complexity must inevitably be present within coaching supervision.

Through this initial scoping we were able to distil our first tentative list of simple rules. We put these aside and set out to explore with a wider cohort of colleagues.

We could have taken our distillation to colleagues asking them to confirm, deny or amend. Bringing forward concrete statements to be judged as right or wrong would have taken our inquiry into the bottom left hand corner of the Landscape diagram. We believed a more generative approach was required.

We engaged three further primary sources of data. Two 'in-depth' interviews with recognised professionals in the coaching supervision field, and one group dialogue with 20 coaches (18 of whom are experienced coaching supervisors) within a Special Interest Group[11] focussing on coaching supervision in a professional body.

Broad, open questions inspired dialogue with our peers that was unconstrained by our first reflections. As their data and perspectives accumulated, fresh connections and resonances appeared, enabling us to adapt and hone our original distillation into the following seven 'simple rules.' This represents our shift into the bottom left of the Landscape diagram.

In-depth interviews

We conducted semi-structured, recorded dialogues exploring the nature of coaching supervision drawn from personal experience.

Group dialogue

We adopted a similar semi-structured, reflective group conversation guided by a series of small prompts.

- As supervisor or supervisee, tune into a coaching supervision experience that for you was 'supervision at its best.'
- What did you feel and/or think?
- What did you notice?
- If this is supervision 'at its best,' what is happening on other occasions?

Simple rules? Not simple, not rules!

Simple rules[12] are neither simple, nor rules – the two words constitute a linguistic term that describes a set of behaviours already present in a system. These are not abstract ideals to be enforced; rather they are descriptors of current practitioner behaviour which we have drawn out from the study with colleagues.

In the following text we offer our distillation of simple rules already present in coaching supervision, generative behaviours that enhance practice.

We offer a brief commentary for each and use the voices of participants as illustrations.

1   Attune to self
2   Engage with love
3   Serve the intention
4   Hold the space, work with the edges
5   Illuminate and explore what is calling for attention
6   Dare to call it out
7   Attend to the relationships, individuals and situational contexts

This set of simple rules equips us with a framework to apply in our own practice. It enables us to notice the patterns that arise from the interplay between these behaviours within supervision sessions, enacted by both supervisor and supervisee, and within the wider field when practitioners live their practice.

1   Attune to self

We noticed a focus on 'arriving' that suggested more than practical preparation. Colleagues spoke of an intentionality guiding the 'way' in which they came to the supervision space: a focus on self-awareness as an essential building block to arriving centred and available to 'self' and 'other.' This included putting aside worries, thoughts and feelings about the past, and concerns for the future, and freeing from formal knowing and certainties – not discarding, or discounting, merely laying these to one side to be fully present in relation to the other.

> How well can we as supervisors help our supervisees prepare and know what to bring and how to do it? It takes time to build a relationship.

> . . . I had to overcome my anxiousness, my nervousness, my feeling 'you may not be so good', 'you may need to do some more training . . . You may need to!' But I said to myself 'keep on working,' this whole light in myself. To say nothing more, nothing less. My commitment was all.

> That depends on all the 'head' stuff I have at my disposal, the years of learning and training and reading and practice . . . and then you can fly. You learn the models and then you throw them away.

2   Engage with love

We noticed our attraction to, and our struggle with, the word 'love.' We wondered if it would be acceptable within our field, and yet the way our colleagues spoke encouraged us to stay with what we believe is true of supervision in coaching and mentoring. In this practice, we believe there is a strong thread of 'love,' a deep valuing of the person, and of humanity. This was described in many ways:

> I have a person in front of me, I have a soul (here).

> We did some deep work . . . resourcing her . . . what was really important to me, and what I think made the work possible was a heart-to-heart connection.

I think the 'Hero's Journey' comes to mind . . . a lot of what we are doing is helping each other to translate language, our language, the language of the soul.

(Coaching supervision is) . . . for me, in the truest sense of the word, spiritual. I'm not meaning religious.

. . . the humanity of the work . . . where the relational piece becomes so fluid and true and honest that we get into that space where we are all one, we are all actually interconnected.

And part of deepening the curiosity and the inquiry is that people start being able to self-observe, but with kindness, crucial, crucial kindness.

3   Serve the intention

We chose the verb 'serve' as used by Robert Greenleaf[13] (referring to 'servant leadership'). It offers a radical shift in framing from the old conventions about leadership and followership. In serving the intention we include identifying and clarifying the purpose of our work together, what we, in each relationship, mean by coaching supervision, and following through with coherent actions and ways of being.

Through 'serving the intention' we also illuminate a commitment to 'we,' to the relationship and to the mutuality of learning within and from each other in the supervision relationship, to both parties being open to being changed, yet not expecting or driving for change.

We see profound and distinct patterns emerging for coaching supervision:

When I am coaching, I often get a sense I am holding up a mirror to the coachee, and when I am supervising it's like there are two mirrors reflecting back and you are seeing the infinite.

. . . felt very intimate . . . being very much together, a sense of a sort of midwife to something that was being born in her.

Lightness characterises a lot of the real learning, there's a kind of humour when people get enough reflective space that they can actually see themselves.

Something about translating . . . whether I am translating inside myself, what I am trying to say . . . the other person too. The ups and downs and translating a meaning of language, feelings, emotions, what's right and wrong . . . and the self-limiting part. One of the things I have benefitted so much from is trusting in another. Either way, as a supervisor or as a supervisee.

Crucial to our capacity to serve the intention is to see ourselves in the other and to help them see themselves through us:

I can also get a very strong sense . . . of being in a hall of mirrors, but a living hall of mirrors, as the field gathers and the information gathers, and the movement of thinking and sharing and conversing happens, you start to get all these echoes, relational echoes . . . and you realise it is in the room with you . . . As the space gets bigger and bigger and yet full of these halls of mirrors, moving mirrors suddenly insight comes, emergent learning. Often, it's not me that gets it. That's not important. They get it. There's a calm at the end of it. There's a calm.

One colleague describes holding his purpose as supervisor, despite the tension it sometimes generates in him. He talks about being committed to providing a space for the supervisee to find her own answer.

> It reminded me of a very recent experience with one of my supervisees. It takes a lot of time to start feeling (and) expressing yourself . . . it took 50 minutes, I wanted to scream, the solution was in front of her . . . it wasn't for me to guide her. It was really difficult for me. She was stuck, she was stuck . . . and at the very end found this very simple question . . . she understood, she was transformed with light. Very intense. Very distinctive this supervision, and for me as well, this is the commitment that comes to my soul.

Here we see the interdependency of the simple rules. In this beautifully vivid account the supervisor also engages with love; and attunes to self.

4 Hold the space, work with the edges

We create and maintain the container for the 'work' of coaching supervision. In this distinct space, bearing witness to another in their 'being,' we also attend to intrapersonal processing and interpersonal dynamics in the context of our contracted relationship.

The space – the coaching supervision session or series of sessions – is held not only by process and quality but by explicit and implicit contractual, psychological and ethical boundaries. These 'edges' further define the space at any moment in time and are far from absolute. They are perceptual, contextual and – in this complex world we are embracing – forever shifting, requiring continuing mutual vigilance.

Often the 'edges' come more acutely into view as we approach them, sometimes in an ethical dialogue, a change in contract, a disturbance in the here-and-now. Bringing the edges under scrutiny enables exploration, testing and adapting, helping us keep steady yet moving. To work with the edges requires awareness of the roles of structure and fluidity in establishing and deepening safety and trust – each of us, ourselves, as well as in our relationship.

> . . . it's rather like building a house, you've got the fabric, you've got the bricks and then you put in the windows and you let the light in.

> . . . and it's only when you live in it that you make it a home.

The trust and holding . . . the space . . . because otherwise the (my) resistance would just have been resistance but instead it moved swiftly on to curiosity . . . and that enabled me to go deep.

There was a 'relationship, rapport and ritual' that was very much there and that underlined . . . working together for a while . . . the way in which we explicitly and implicitly contracted to work together.

. . . for me, those insights, that shift is what I am here to do, a real sense of having met the need. Curiosity, openness, development of the relationship, trust, deep trust, mutual respect. The openness enables these insights to emerge.

5   *Illuminate and explore what is calling for attention*

Colleagues described a process of attuning to what was spoken and unspoken, and to what was happening within the supervision relationship. With an attitude of acceptance, the exploration proves liberating and enabling.

. . . it was very clean . . . the supervision . . . going with where I was going and where my energy was, what my focus was, paying attention to where my attention was . . . sometimes opening out, going just beyond, or just to the side . . . but not taking their own (the supervisor's) direction.

. . . conscious that I was processing it as we were talking.

. . . and yes, it includes competencies . . . in the business world they know this phrase, it can be a little anchor for some people.

We mustn't go looking for the dramatic all the time.

Normalising . . . do this balance between knowing and not knowing. It really helps me to think 'actually, I'm doing okay here.'

Sometimes it is the nuance, not a big ethical issue, not a big dramatic issue but sometimes just unhooking stuff or liberating things.

The deepest attention to every subtle 'note' of the conversation, mine and theirs, to the direction of it, the feeling tone of it, something I might notice in somebody's face, something I notice in my own body. What's that telling me? . . . I am paying enormous detail, forensic attention, to every aspect of that conversation as it unfolds . . . I register all my own body stuff, I register the body in front of me . . . I can feel the conversation, the kind of rhythm of it, what it is doing, the content of course, is part of all this, but I think the real magic is in what the content sparks off in both of us and in the dialogue we are generating together. That's exciting and that's what seems to drive us both towards learning, illumination and change. Resolution has come. We sit. It is very spacious and satisfying. My work is done here today. We've got it.

In our inquiry with colleagues, they made no explicit mention of 'working with difference' – an element we included in our original distillation. In their comments, we see an acceptance of what is present; however, we remain curious as to whether this is sufficient in addressing some of the divisions and unconscious biases that play out in society which may be reflected in our practice as coaching supervisors.

6   *Dare to call it out*

Coaching supervision is not always a comfortable conversation. Our colleagues described a willingness to be disturbed as a crucial and valued part of the exchange.

> I really loved . . . that I felt challenged, you know that bit of churning.

> I don't think the depth of relationship happens instantaneously . . . we may feel a rapport and a trust but it's only when I experience that being tested does the depth come. The true connection, not only to be serious but to laugh at the human condition – and easy with the difficulty and all of the paradoxes that are there.

Each simple rule is supported by all the others. In 'dare to call it out' we need to be attuning, illuminating, attending, holding, working and serving with deep, broad awareness to help us move beyond our own judgments and conclusions of the other, ourselves, the situation and context. Our 'calling it out' first brings the lens of curiosity to ourselves and, in doing so, liberates us to recognise what we might usefully reflect.

This 'daring' might be conveyed by staying connected to painful and challenging explorations such as the unravelling of complex ethical questions. In this example, we again see an interplay between engaging with love, serving the intention, working with the edges (in this case ethics), and illuminating and exploring what is calling for attention:

> (I felt) nervous at the start . . . relieved, as I told the story and felt supported, not judged. Supported but challenged. The supervisor didn't make me feel that she was in any way judging (me). In fact, I don't think there was a lot said, but the body language was normalising. This gave me permission to think this *was* a pretty tricky situation (and she) challenged me not to move away from the problem . . . to have some thoughts about what possible conversations I could have with my coachee. I was conscious I was processing it as we were talking. We didn't even come up with a solution! Because it *was* a very difficult ethical issue . . . and it was how to hold the ethics *and* support the coachee.

7   *Attend to the individuals, relationships and situational contexts*

In adopting the lens of complex adaptive systems, we need to consider the 'part, the whole and the greater whole.' This complexity notion enables us to see patterns across the system, displayed and experienced as fractals[14] i.e.

using the here-and-now pattern to illuminate a part greater or smaller than the current moment. We might see patterns in the supervision dyad that reflect those at play elsewhere; and we might also create and influence patterns in the system.

> . . . my experience was the pleasure of making a felt connection after a process of following . . . and trying to get a sense of what this is about, and then the shift for them into an awareness about how they have played into the situation – they have understood something about themselves which they can take back into their coaching in the future with different clients. So, it's about how *they* as individuals affect the system, as opposed to what the client is bringing.

> . . . the way this is all being described amongst professionals . . . the sort of texture that you are getting in the conversation today . . . how you can project that (supervision) is not just a compliance issue but as something that really benefits them (coaches). I think this is tremendous.

> Coaches also in their own style were used to thinking fast, being solution focussed, yet you were trying to introduce a practice where the process was the thing, and the relationship was the thing, in other words the relationship became the conduit for learning.

Final comments

Drawing on our reflections and experiences, and those of 22 other practitioners, we have distilled an elegantly concise articulation of seven[15] simple rules of coaching supervision. We do not claim this to be a comprehensive nor final list, yet we are confident in and excited by the rules. Why? Because we recognise them in play when we, in our supervision relationships (as supervisors and supervisees), are at our best; and we bear witness to them in others.

We also believe that if enough of us proactively and consciously adopt them, we will co-evolve a new way to bring coherence to our emerging personal and professional practice. To this end, we encourage you to share them with others, inviting observations and reflections in our mutual learning places and spaces.

Acknowledgements

We are grateful to the following practitioners for their wholehearted engagement and contribution to this chapter:

> Association for Coaching (AC) Coaching Supervision Special Interest Group (SIG), March 2018: Jeannette Marshall (AC Director of Accreditation); Anne Calleja (Chair, AC SIG); Margaret Barr (Administrator, AC SIG); AC Director of People and Organisations; and members Angela Dunbar;

Benita Treanor; Carol Whitaker; Catherine Mulcaster; Eve Turner; George Karathanos; Henry Campion; Jane; Jenny Maddox; Lorenza Clifford; Lynne Cooper; Marie Faire; Peter Welch; Sarah Gilbert; Umut Ahmet Tarakcı.

Coaching Supervision Academy: Edna Murdoch and Miriam Orriss (Co-founders) for in-depth interviews, January 2018.

Notes

1 Coaching supervision: at present there is not a distinct identity for mentoring supervision, and therefore coaching supervision is applied in both contexts.
2 (Whiteman, 1998; Bennett and Lemoine, 2014; CIPD, 2014).
3 (Gardiner, PhD pending publication).
4 (Stacey, 1996; Olson and Eoyang, 2001b; Zimmerman, 2001; Holladay, 2012).
5 (Gardiner, 2013).
6 (Prigogine and Nicolis, 1971; Prigogine, 1980; Prigogine and Stengers, 1984; Holland, 1992).
7 (Eoyang, 2001; Olson and Eoyang, 2001a, 2001b; Cabrera, 2008; Cabrera and Colosi, 2008; Eoyang and Holladay, 2013).
8 (Holladay, 2005; Patterson, Holladay and Eoyang, 2013).
9 (Eoyang, 2010; Eoyang and Holladay, 2013).
10 In this chapter, space prohibits deeper discussion of this stage of our initial inquiry
11 Association for Coaching (AC) Coaching Supervisor Special Interest Group (SIG): comprised of AC members who are interested in supervision. The group is voluntary and has no formal standing or accountability. However, it is a vehicle through which the AC leadership team engages regularly with members.
12 Chapter 7 herein offers a case in which simple rules are used in a Community-in-Practice (Gardiner, 2019).
13 (Greenleaf, 1998).
14 Repeating patterns that emerge across scales in a system/context.
15 In this method, ideally there should be no less than three and no more than seven simple rules. Each should start with a verb and be expressed in the positive. They should be general enough to apply to anyone in the system in which they manifest and specific enough for each individual to recognise how they apply to them in their unique role.

References

Bennett, N. and Lemoine, G. J. (2014). What a Difference a Word Makes: Understanding Threats to Performance in a VUCA World. *Business Horizons*, 57(3), 311–317.

Cabrera, D. (2008). *Distinctions, Systems, Relationships, Perspectives: The Simple Rules of Complex Conceptual Systems* [Lecture]. Citeseer, unpublished.

Cabrera, D. and Colosi, L. (2008). Distinctions, Systems, Relationships, and Perspectives (DSRP): A Theory of Thinking and of Things. *Evaluation and Program Planning*, 31(3), 311–317.

CIPD. (2014). *Leadership: Easier Said Than Done*. London: CIPD.

Eoyang, G. (2001). *Conditions for Self-Organizing in Human Systems*. Doctor of Philosophy Thesis. The Union Institute and University.

Eoyang, G. (2010). *Radical Inquiry*. Circle Pines: HSD Institute.

Eoyang, G. and Holladay, R. (2013). *Adaptive Action: Leveraging Uncertainty in Your Organization*. Stanford: Stanford University Press.

Gardiner, L. J. N. (2013). Adaptive Capacity: Looking at Human Systems Dynamics. *Coaching Today*, 6, 19–24.

Gardiner, L. J. N. (2019). Our Emerging Community-in-practice – Making Boundary-play Conscious. In Birch, J. and Welch, P. (eds), *Coaching Supervision: Advancing Practice, Changing Landscapes*. Abingdon, UK: Routledge.

Greenleaf, R. K. (1998). *The Power of Servant-Leadership: Essays*. San Francisco, CA: Berrett-Koehler Publishers.

Holladay, R. (2005). Simple Rules: Organizational DNA. *OD Practitioner*, 37(4).

Holladay, R. (2012). *Adaptive Action: Landscape Diagram*. HSD Institute. http://wiki.hsdinstitute.org/landscape_diagram

Holland, J. H. (1992). Complex Adaptive Systems. *Daedalus*, 17–30.

Olson, E. E. and Eoyang, G. (2001a). Using Complexity Science to Facilitate Self-Organizing Processes in Teams. *OD Practitioner*, 33(3), 37–44.

Olson, E. E. and Eoyang, G. (2001b). *Facilitating Organization Change: Lessons From Complexity Science*. San Francisco, CA: Jossey-Bass/Pfeiffer.

Patterson, L., Holladay, R. and Eoyang, G. (2013). *Radical Rules for Schools: Adaptive Action for Complex Change*. Charlestown SA, USA: HSD Institute.

Prigogine, I. (1980). *From Being to Becoming: Time and Complexity in the Physical Sciences*. San Francisco: W. H. Freeman.

Prigogine, I. and Nicolis, G., 1971. Biological order, structure and instabilities. Quarterly Reviews of Biophysics, 4(2-3), 107–148.

Prigogine, I. and Stengers, I. (1984). *Order Out of Chaos: Man's New Dialogue With Nature*. Toronto: Bantam Books.

Stacey, R. (1996). *Complexity and Creativity in Organizations*. Oakland, CA: Berrett-Koehler Publishers.

Whiteman, W. E. (1998). *Training and Educating Army Officers for the 21st Century: Implications for the United States Military Academy*. Army War College, Carlisle Barracks, PA.

Zimmerman, B. (2001). *Ralph Stacey's Agreement & Certainty Matrix*. Available at www.plexusinstitute.org/edgeware/archive/think/main_aides3.html (Accessed 19 December 2018).

3 Neuro-behavioural supervision

Applied neuroscience in the context of coaching supervision

*Dr Paul Brown, Saba Hasanie and
Dr Henry Campion*

Introduction

The twenty-first century has seen two remarkable developments in the slow process of understanding human behaviour. The first is that a variety of modern imaging technologies make it possible to see the brain functioning in (almost) real time. This marks a major scientific shift towards the prospect of understanding cause and effect relationships in human behaviour.

The second is the gradual development of an understanding that human beings are not, essentially, psychological systems but, like the rest of the physical world, *energy* systems, and that the mechanisms of directing energy within the individual are emotional, not cognitive. Descartes' dictum that *I think, therefore I am* is being superseded by a reformulation that proposes *I feel, therefore I can think I am.*

Both of these developments have significant implications for the practice of both executive coaching and coaching supervision.

Background

Coming as it does from psychotherapies rooted in differing (and often competing) schools of psychology, executive coaching has surprisingly insecure foundations. The purpose of this chapter to offer a sense of an underpinning structure for coaching supervision that is grounded in replicable science and that supports a systematic approach to supervision in coaching.

First, the insecurity of the existing foundations is briefly described. It should be noted in passing, though, that the notion of grounding supervision – and coaching as a whole – in replicable applied neuroscience will not be to everyone's taste. Existing approaches have depended on a range of self-sustaining metaphors such as the analogy of the rider and elephant to illustrate the role of the conscious mind in relation to the whole organism (Bachkirova, 2011), as a sufficient means of understanding how coaching works without reference to an underpinning neurobiology.

The Oxford English Dictionary defines psychology as:

> the scientific study of the human mind and its functions, especially those affecting behaviour in a given context.

Unfortunately, the discipline of twentieth century psychology failed to come to any fundamental, shared or even operational conclusions about what 'the mind' might be; so its primary purpose – *the scientific study of the human mind* – gained little traction. Instead there was a proliferation of theory and supposition, in the applied field particularly. Wikipedia[1] lists 51 different schools of psychology appearing in the twentieth century. They generated between them a wide variety of therapies, variously classified,[2] with 161 differentiated types of psychotherapy listed.[3]

So it could well be argued that the body of knowledge called human psychology developed more as a set of theologies, or belief/assertion systems, than as a replicable scientific body of knowledge. One serious consequence is that its applied practitioners fail to share a common body of knowledge that, through practice, continuously seeks both to be tested and to contribute to emerging knowledge. The recent convincing evidence adduced by Crews (2017) of the largely fraudulent bases of Freud's classic case studies – accounts of what *ought* to have been happening in therapy, not what was *actually* happening – adds credence to the observation that much of what was taken for fact in twentieth century psychology regarding human behaviour proves to have been, in the absence of replicable evidence, *description* not *explanation*. Dawes (1994) was an earlier protagonist of the fallacies underlying psychotherapeutic 'truths.'

For the practice of executive coaching this raises the question: *where does our understanding of the coachee come from?* And, by extension, as a supervisor: *where in supervision does an understanding of the coach's understanding of the coachee come from? What is our shared professional frame of reference? Do we indeed have one?*

For example, bearing in mind that we all carry around with us our cultural assumptions, attitudes and 'explanations' about human behaviour, it is not uncommon to hear a coach observe during supervision that a coachee 'is resistant' to something or other. While readily used as if it were explanatory rather than descriptive, and as if it were telling us something about the inner state of the coachee upon which behaviour was predicated, 'resistance' is in fact a phenomenon of the coach's experience, not the coachee's.

The neuroscientific assumption is that the coachee's brain, being the organ of adaptation, always seeks to adapt its behaviour to its current circumstances in the best way possible based on its meaning-making processes, i.e. how it makes sense of life events, relationships and the self. So the aim of supervision in coaching is to help the coach to find ways of understanding the bases of the coachee's adaptation, and the particular personal goals being served, rather than trying to 'explain' the 'resistance', and then to work out how to change the coachee's meaning-making to effect an adaptive shift in pursuit of the coaching goals.

The same is also true for the supervision of team coaching and, in a wider context, for organisational change programmes. The brain could not possibly be the organ of resistance at the same time as being the organ of adaptation. What it always seeks is the best adaptation *in context*, both externally and internally, and consequent upon that individual's (or team's, or organisation's) accumulated prior experience.

This reformulation of elements of human behaviour from a neurobiological point of view is summarised in the propositions about the brain and its workings in the following text. By and large, neuroscientists in laboratories are less interested in human behaviour than in the brain and the workings of the nervous system as a whole – the way the brain and the heart and the gut are connected and reciprocally influence each other. It is the field of *applied neuroscience* that sets out to take laboratory findings and extract from them the value that they have in organisational settings.

Main propositions about the brain that a supervisor needs to know

It was only in 1980 that the first clinically useful brain images (MRI scans) were created. Before then it was not possible to see the normal everyday brain working. Electrical patterns tracked through electro-encephalography (EEG) recordings, first recognised in 1938 as a means of understanding some aspects of the workings of the brain, gave indirect measures of brain activity and, with increasing technical sophistication, the capacity now to track specific reactions at millisecond intervals. But it is only in the twenty-first century that developments in imaging technology have led to extraordinarily detailed pictures of the brain and its cellular workings.

New sciences have arisen in consequence, notably connectomics (Seung, 2012), which extends thinking about the structure and function of the brain into working out how 86 billion brain cells having highly differentiated functions all work together to make an integrated whole, and epigenetics (Lipton, 2005; Dispenza, 2014), to which more detailed reference will be made later.

In the propositions that follow, it should be borne in mind that (as is always the case in evolving sciences) not all of the statements made are based on cast-iron scientific agreements. They are working assumptions that provide the underpinnings for supervision based on the present state of knowledge about the brain.

1   *The brain has evolved as a three-part system – the so-called triune brain.* Put very simply, the brain stem on the underside of the brain, at the top of the spinal cord, is the 'reptilian brain,' and manages all the bodily functions that keep us alive and which we are completely unaware of until they go wrong. It is the first part of the brain to develop *in embryo*. In the centre of the brain is the limbic system or 'mammalian brain,' which manages emotions and memory. It develops second embryonically. Covering both these systems is the cognitive cortex, looking much like a large walnut, though much softer and more squidgy in texture. The essential discovery of the twenty-first century is that the brain works from the bottom up, not top down. That is to say, it is driven by the central emotional system not, as has generally been thought, by the higher cognitive system. Hyphenate the word *emotion* into *e-motion*, and it becomes apparent that embedded in the concept of the emotions is energy and action. Rita Carter's *The Brain Book* (2014) has excellent 3-D illustrations of the brain.

2   *The brain manages its own energy and, in complex relationship with the heart and gut, manages the energy of the whole body.* It is the energy management system for everything. Watkins (2014) has recently proposed that the heart is the central management system for energy in the body and that the rhythms of the heart regulate the brain, not that the brain establishes the rhythms of the heart. It is a debate in progress. What is certain is that the heart, brain and gut are completely interlinked.

   The brain is also much more directly affected by the gut than has previously been understood. The millions of microbes in the gut − the microbiota − are in a continuous signalling relationship with the brain. This has considerable implications for the way diet affects behaviour.

3   *The brain has decided what is to happen next before an individual has conscious awareness of that decision.* The brain can react to sensory input and prepare the necessary subsequent actions within 85 milliseconds. It takes 250 milliseconds for that decision to get into conscious awareness. This raises the uncomfortable but undeniable possibility that we are not nearly as much in charge of ourselves as we would like to think we are. The function of our cognitive brain is to make sense of what the brain has already decided to do. While it may have the power of veto, it does not initiate the brain's actions. The philosophical questions of free will and 'free won't' have become hot topics again as a result of this knowledge.

4   *The brain is the organ of relationship* − a proposition first proposed by Dan Siegel as part of his formulation of the neurobiology of relationships. (see Siegel (2012) for his developing views). 'Mind,' for Siegel, is an expression of the way that the brain organises itself and its outputs around the continuous dynamic of managing information, energy and relationship.

5   *Male and female brains function differently.* Not surprisingly there is a great deal of controversy over this subject, but work at the University of Pennsylvania suggests conclusively that the differences are readily observable.[4] This has significant implications for the role women and their contributions play within organisations that are *different* to men's. It also has considerable implications for the almost-unexplored topic of the impacts of sex differences in coaching and supervision.

6   *We each act in the way that we do because of the way we each have learned to see the world around us.* There is no need for complex metaphors like Id, Ego and Superego to 'explain' human behaviour. We are essentially pattern-recognition systems, and whatever our life-patterning has been will create the responses that are unique to each of us.

   This is an amazingly simple yet complex re-statement of why each of us is the person that we are with the reactions that each of us have, and needs a little elaboration.

   Watson and Crick's 1953 discovery of the double helix as the structure of DNA led to wide-ranging suppositions in the Western world that genes were the essential controllers of behaviour. However, as genetic inquiry expanded throughout the second half of the twentieth century, it became apparent that genes could express themselves in a wide variety of ways. The question then arose: what is it that instructs the gene how to express itself? Twenty-five years ago, cell biologists began to understand that it is the way we see things (perception) that triggers the neurochemistry that instructs the gene how to express itself. This is the field of epigenetics.

Think of the gene as a most extraordinary store cupboard. Within the cupboard are the ingredients for creating any recipe imaginable. The question at any moment in time is: what recipe is called for right now? It is the function of the neurochemistry of perception to instruct the gene (DNA) how to express itself, and the gene in turn instructs the RNA how to create the mix of proteins that will produce the appropriate and adaptive behaviour. There is no behaviour without an underlying neurochemistry.

Imagine a situation in which you are arriving at your normal place of work and you suddenly see an old friend who you have not met for three or four years. The instant delight and recognition of each other that you both express happen without any conscious control of expression. It would have come from the way you 'see' each other. If a colleague is with you arriving at your office, they will not have the same reaction to that person. It is not within their prior patterning. There may be pleasure at your pleasure but not the same reaction to someone who is otherwise a stranger.

This is true for every reaction of every moment of the conscious day. It is what makes each of us unique. The question for supervision, as for coaching, is, firstly, how to get into an understanding of this uniqueness; and secondly, how to manage that understanding in the coachee's interest.

7   *As a consequence of proposition 6, we each have a unique Self.* Although the neurobiology of the Self is not yet well understood, it is useful to think of it as the central integrator, maintaining from within the storehouse of encoded memory a continuous representation of its Self that both we and others observing us recognise as having consistency and familiarity. Nothing can be part of the Self that has not been previously stored: but not everything that has been stored may be in regular use by the Self. The practical question, then, is how to get into an understanding of the individual's Self such that the Self is itself the main agent of achieving the goals of supervision or of coaching. A key aspect of understanding the Self is recognising those stored memories, both conscious and non-conscious, which is why an understanding of the coachee's emotions and observable neurochemistry can provide useful access data. For instance, a coachee may not have conscious awareness of shame but may be flooded with cortisol that stems from a non-conscious reaction to a current scenario.

8   Finally, modern brain science makes it clear that we humans are *self-regulating complex adaptive systems*. The persistent and continuously fascinating dilemma for understanding another person is having an explicit frame of reference. In supervision, it is about understanding what one person (the supervisor) understands about another's understanding (the coach's) of

another person (the coachee) and then being able to set that understanding within a common frame of reference that is shared by the rest of the profession.

In summary, then, the brain is an emotionally driven system that controls everything we do; sets up an action before we are conscious of it; and lets us think that thinking is what controls us. While coaching requires an understanding of the uniqueness of the coachee, coaching supervision requires an understanding of both the coach and the coachee. The supervisor also requires some deep working knowledge of them-Self within the same framework coaches are using to understand the coachees they bring to supervision. Put together, these factors make for a triadic interplay that characterises the circumstances of supervision.

It follows that the contribution that applied neuroscience might make to supervision could be part of a wider contribution to the practice of the coaching profession as a whole. In both supervision and the practice of coaching there is, from an applied neuroscience perspective, a need to understand the individual within the framework of what is currently known about the brain and its relationship to behaviour. It is by looking at how we do that that the underpinning structure of a brain-based approach to supervision will become apparent.

The underpinnings

While coaching as a profession has reached some agreement as to technique – listening skills and the like – it has not yet agreed upon the common shared professional knowledge base that all coaches should have. Should all coaches have a common armamentarium of psychometric skills, for instance, such as Torbert's *Leadership Development Framework* (Rooke and Torbert, 2005)? Should all coaches understand and/or be able to monitor heart-rate variability as an accurate record of stress reduction?[5]

Perhaps even more fundamental is the question of whether all coaches – and by extension all supervisors – should be required to have a practical grasp of meaning-making and the adaptive shift referred to earlier. Without it, it is difficult to see how the coach or supervisor might, on a skilled professional basis, evoke sustained behavioural change. Both must have a common frame of reference for understanding the coachee's 'why' to be able to help with the 'what' and the 'how' (Figure 3.1).

This question is important because it moves supervision out of the entirely private domain – what happens between a supervisor and a coach – into a shared public domain – what *should* happen between a supervisor and a coach.

The aim of this section is to provide a working approach to agreeing working practices within the public and professional domain. It proposes the coach supervisor needs to share a common frame of reference with the supervisee that is not just a frame of reference contained within a specialised descriptive framework – be it Gestalt, Integrationist, Solution-Focussed or any other such

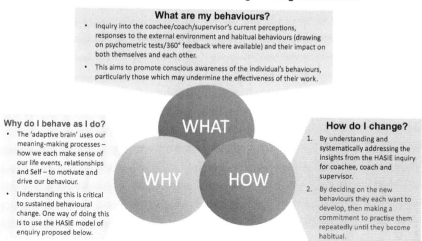

Core Elements of a Shared Meaning-Making Framework

What are my behaviours?

- Inquiry into the coachee/coach/supervisor's current perceptions, responses to the external environment and habitual behaviours (drawing on psychometric tests/360° feedback where available) and their impact on both themselves and each other.
- This aims to promote conscious awareness of the individual's behaviours, particularly those which may undermine the effectiveness of their work.

Why do I behave as I do?

- The 'adaptive brain' uses our meaning-making processes – how we each make sense of our life events, relationships and Self – to motivate and drive our behaviour.
- Understanding this is critical to sustained behavioural change. One way of doing this is to use the HASIE model of enquiry proposed below.

WHAT

WHY   **HOW**

How do I change?

1. By understanding and systematically addressing the insights from the HASIE inquiry for coachee, coach and supervisor.
2. By deciding on the new behaviours they each want to develop, then making a commitment to practise them repeatedly until they become habitual.

Figure 3.1 Establishing a shared understanding of meaning-making as between coach and coachee and between supervisor and coach

frame of reference – but one that is common to all coaches and that is *explanatory*, not just *descriptive*.

The first requirement is to have a framework of inquiry into the uniqueness of the individual. For such purposes Brown and Brown (2013) developed for their *Science of the Art of Coaching* teaching programme a model based upon a synthesis of developmental psychology and attachment theory that links straight into organisational behaviour and that is consistent with modern neuroscience. Called the HASIE model, it is named after its dimensions of Hierarchy, Attachment, Siblings and other peer groups, Identity and Emotional tapestry.

Its use proposes and presupposes that a coach needs to understand, through systematic inquiry, the biographical bases of a coachee's meaning-making that ultimately influence behaviour. It provides an evidential framework for the supervisor to understand what the coach understands of the coachee. Beyond this, it is also a framework for the supervisor to understand how coach and supervisor make meaning of what is happening both between coach and coachee, and between coach and supervisor, within the supervisory relationship.

The coachee is, at any moment in time, their presenting past, as is the coach in supervision. They can bring nothing else but the past to a coaching or supervision session; but in bringing the presenting past they bring the whole of themSelf. A supervisor needs to understand the coach as much as the coach needs to understand the coachee. For the presenting past is the key to the epigenetics of producing the appropriate and adaptive behaviour needed to achieve supervisory and coaching goals.

Table 3.1 Key dimensions of the HASIE model

Dimension	Description	Significance in an organisational setting
Hierarchy	Hierarchy examines the authority-based relationships in a coachee's life, beginning with parents.	These create an understanding of the templates of leadership the coachee is most likely to exhibit.
Attachment	Attachment theory explains how adults create, sustain and manage relationships.	Examining this area creates a better understanding of how a coachee approaches the creation and maintenance of relationships
Siblings	Examining the role that peer groups (including siblings) have played in a coachee's life gives insight into how the coachee approaches, and the importance they give to, teamwork in an organisational setting.	Understanding the role that the coachee tends to prefer taking within the team-based environment is a critical aspect of this dimension
Identity	Organisational identity is formed through a complex interaction between self, social identity and environmental context.	By examining the evolution of core aspects of the coachee's sense of self and group over time, we understand some of the non-conscious biases that may influence the coachee's interpretation and subsequent behavioural choices.
Emotional tapestry	Understanding the neuroscientific basis of how coachees acknowledge and process emotions is critical to an awareness of the relationship between behaviours and meaning.	This helps us understand the non-conscious patterning of behaviours that takes place in an organisational setting.

The HASIE model has been elaborated by Hasanie for use in her doctoral work around the neuroscience perspective of meaning-making for coachees in coaching. Each dimension has been expanded for classification purposes (Table 3.1).

When examining meaning-making in the context of the HASIE model, it is important to explore this at both conscious and non-conscious levels of awareness. At a conscious level, this can be explored using:

- Narration and autobiographical inquiry – the process of having the coachee narrate the story/stories of their life to better understand how they have interpreted and made meaning of their experiences and how this impacts the way they live today; and
- Exploration of the dimensions of the HASIE model to gain insights into why they value certain leadership styles and approaches and avoid others; how they create and form relationships; how they look at teamwork and the role they play within teams; and their own sense of self and the difference between their inherited identity and the one they have constructed for themselves.

Before examining the non-conscious level, it is important to first define 'non-conscious.' Unlike the Freudian model of the unconscious mind where mental processes exist at the conscious, preconscious and unconscious levels, with the latter often being associated with negative or escape-based emotions, our definition is more inclusive.

Firstly, even mental processes at a conscious level are influenced by the non-conscious; one cannot be assessed without the other. Secondly, we have learned through the applied neurosciences that the brain is an emotional energy management system, using emotions based on both attachment and escape emotions. A definitive model of the emotions – the London Protocol – has been delineated in Brown and Dendrowskyj (2018), linking emotions to the nervous system and behaviour. The experiences which shape a coachee's emotional tapestry are ones which have become ingrained in how their brain operates. So the non-conscious describes the activity of all those mental processes which may be influencing the coachee's behaviour but of which they are unaware.

At the non-conscious level, this includes consideration of:

- Emotions and experiences and their link to conscious memory (which must include a review of both attachment and escape emotions);
- Memory formation and recall and its relationship to behavioural patterning; and
- Neurochemistry: both attachment and escape emotions involve the release of neuroactive chemicals which can have a profound impact on brain functioning and resulting behaviours.

The use of the HASIE model in supervision can yield valuable insights for coaches (Table 3.2).

Table 3.2 Using the HASIE model in supervision

Dimension	Insight
Hierarchy	How the coachee's relationship to authority is evoking assumptions/judgments in the coach
Attachment	• Projection of coach's attachment relationship needs onto the coachee • Judgments on quality and quantity of attachment relationships based on coach's sense of meaning-making
Siblings	Insight into the coaching relationship dynamics via the coachee's experiences of other peer-based relationships
Identity	Exploring identity as object in order to serve both the coaching and supervision relationship
Emotional tapestry	Access to non-conscious meaning-making and ensuing behavioural patterns

Hasanie has identified the following steps in applying the HASIE model in her work:

1   To link conscious awareness of life events to the emotional patterning and meaning-making that has emerged from those events;
2   Through the emotional patterning insights, to link non-conscious expression to non-conscious and conscious behavioural patterns;
3   To use the insights generated in Steps 1 and 2 to identify and create sustained behavioural change; and
4   To link the adaptive changes required to neuro-behavioural modelling techniques that evoke an emotive expression of curiosity (and the resulting neurochemical reward of dopamine release).

So it is proposed that supervision in coaching should, as part of the larger development of executive coaching as a profession, similarly rely on an agreed model derived from reputable sources supported, as for example in Western medicine, by a systematic method of inquiry. Both the model and the means of inquiry will themselves then be subject to systematic progressive development and revision as well as benefiting from pragmatic confirmation in use, which is part of the proper processes of any knowledge-based profession.

One dimension of the HASIE model that draws on material that has already been extensively researched is attachment, which plays a key role in how we relate to one another. The 'attachment pattern' which develops in infancy becomes internalised as a working model for relationship throughout life. Since relationship is core to the work of both coaches and coaching supervisors, it makes sense for them to be familiar with attachment theory.

The initial role of the attachment system is to ensure the survival of the infant. When it feels threatened or distressed in any way, it strives to find a safe haven with food, warmth and protection in the arms of its mother (or primary care giver). Table 3.3 shows how the infant's attachment pattern depends on how the mother habitually reacts to its distress. A positive response is likely to lead to a secure attachment pattern and a negative response to one of three insecure patterns.

Mikulincer and Shaver (2016) describe how the attachment pattern which emerges from these primary care experiences becomes embedded in the neural connections of the infant's brain as a 'prototype' internal working model. This then underpins a more dynamic current working model which evolves in response to later relational experiences and which serves to modify the prototype attachment behaviours (Figure 3.2).

The majority of adults are variably securely attached: they are variably self-confident and variably ready to trust in others. Those with manifest insecure attachment have greater difficulty relating to others; they tend to either avoid intimacy or social interaction (avoidant) or become anxious, or both. These behaviours emerge most strongly under stress (Table 3.4).

Table 3.3 Development of attachment patterns

Attachment pattern	SECURE	INSECURE		
		SELF-RELIANT	ANXIOUS	FEARFUL
Mother/ primary care giver's response to attachment behaviour	Emotionally available, attentive and responsive, providing a 'safe haven' and a 'secure base'	Remote, unresponsive; can't handle intensity of infant's demands; love conditional on good behaviour	Uncertain, inconsistent, unpredictable; little correlation between infant attachment behaviours and care giver availability	Highly stressed by infant's demands; may react with abuse – denial, violence or both – towards the infant

Note: The majority of infants develop the same attachment pattern as their mother/primary care giver (Fonagy, P., Steele, H. & Steele, M. (1991)).

Evolution of the Internal Working Model

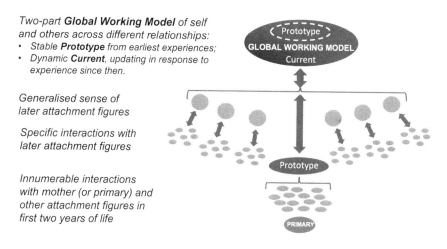

Two-part **Global Working Model** of self and others across different relationships:
• Stable **Prototype** from earliest experiences;
• Dynamic **Current**, updating in response to experience since then.

Generalised sense of later attachment figures

Specific interactions with later attachment figures

Innumerable interactions with mother (or primary) and other attachment figures in first two years of life

Figure 3.2 Generating the inner working landscape

It is easy to see how the attachment pattern of the coach can have a profound impact on their work with coachees. For example, while a secure coach will be open to whatever the coachee might bring, an apparently self-reliant (or 'avoidant') coach is likely to have difficulty in responding to the coachee's emotions, causing them to steer the coachee towards a more cognitive stance. This may be exacerbated in that self-reliance, though a product of insecure attachment, may

Table 3.4 Characteristics of adult attachment patterns

Pattern	SECURE	SELF-RELIANT	ANXIOUS	FEARFUL
Characterised by:	Low anxiety/ low avoidance	Low anxiety/ high avoidance	High anxiety/low avoidance	High anxiety/ high avoidance
Experienced as:	Likely to be trusting and confident.	May seem rather remote. Can be defensive.	May seem rather needy.	May struggle to relate; may behave unpredictably.
Self-worth	Positive view of self, attachments and relationships. Optimistic about outcomes.	Positive view of self, less so of attachments and relationships.	Lack of self-worth, blaming themselves for attachment figure's lack of responsiveness.	Lack of self-worth, with unconscious, negative views about self *and* attachments.
Intimacy & in/dependence	Comfortable both with being emotionally close to and depending on or being depended on by others, and with being alone or not accepted by others. Tend to be more satisfied and adjusted in their relationships than other patterns.	Independent, seeking lower levels of intimacy. Tend to see themselves as self-sufficient without the need for close relationships, wanting neither to depend on nor to be depended on by others.	Want relationships with high levels of intimacy, approval and responsiveness from others, often more than those others would like. May experience anxiety only alleviated by contact with the attachment figure. May value intimacy so much that they become overly dependent.	Uncomfortable with high levels of intimacy, wanting relationship yet feeling undeserving and at the same time unable to trust or depend on others for fear of getting hurt.
Emotional regulation	Balanced for both positive and negative emotions.	Emotionally over-regulated, hiding or suppressing feelings, seeming defensive or emotionally vacant.	Emotionally under-regulated, with high levels of expressiveness, worry and impulsiveness in relationship.	Emotionally over-regulated, suppressing and denying feelings and uncomfortable expressing affection.

Note: "Most adults are securely attached": in a three-way analysis of secure, dismissive and anxious/preoccupied in non-clinical individuals, 58% were secure (quoted by Cozolino, L. (2014), p 150).

lead to a coaching style that relies on the coach's profound sense of their own rightness, one of 'knowing the answer.' (For an interesting example of this see Kets de Vries, 2018.) In contrast, an anxiously attached coach may come across as over-emotional and approval-seeking, distorting the coaching relationship and causing the coachee to distance themselves from the coach. It is not difficult to generalise these patterns to organisational settings.

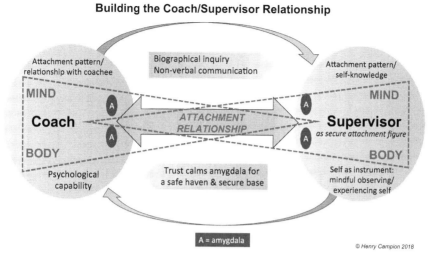

Figure 3.3 The working relationship between coach and supervisor

Figure 3.3 describes in attachment terms the working relationship between supervisor and coach. In the process of any supervision it may be that an especially strong relationship develops between supervisor and coach, just as it can between coach and coachee. Although some coaching models and rules of practice strongly disavow the development of any kind of (mutual) dependency, this flies in the face of neuropsychological reality: it is in the nature of effective relationships to be interdependent.

A key element in the relationship is trust. Trust calms the amygdala – those parts of the right and left hemispheres dedicated to first line scrutiny of stimuli for their emotional loading, and especially danger – and in so doing opens up the brain to the possibility of creating new pathways or enlarging old ones. As the primary task of the brain is to secure the well-being of its owner, to rely on the known is much safer than relying on something new. So adaptive change can only take place when the emotional conditions are right. The amygdala are the guardians of that process.

This process can be important, for example, in the sense of rightness associated with the self-reliance pattern mentioned earlier. Though self-reliance may be a valuable attribute in many circumstances, the forming of effective relationships where growth is of the essence, as in coaching and supervision, is not one of them.

A concept many coaches and supervisors will be familiar with is the 'internal supervisor' which enables the coach to grow professionally within the supervisory relationship. Figure 3.4 suggests how this might happen.

In therapy, the treatment of attachment disorders depends first and foremost on creating a secure attachment relationship. While supervisors are not

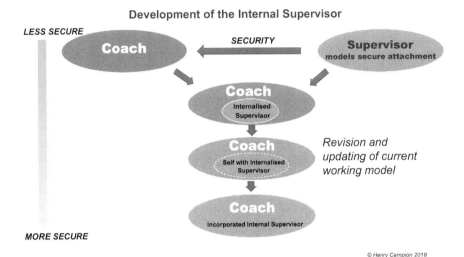

Figure 3.4 The gradual development of security within the supervision dyad

therapists, they can still model the qualities of a secure attachment figure. A suitably experienced supervisor can, within contractual and ethical boundaries, also help the coach to address attachment issues for the benefit of both their coachees and themselves (while recognising there may be situations where, just like their coachees, the coach needs to consider therapy). Such issues might include understanding more about their own and their coachees' respective attachment patterns and how they might interact; and for an insecurely attached coach, making a shift towards the 'earned security' of becoming more securely attached (Figure 3.5).

The foregoing has been distilled into a first set of principles of neuro-behavioural supervision.

Principles of neuro-behavioural supervision

1   The aim of the neuro-behavioural supervisor is to deepen the expertise, resilience and professionalism of the coach. Given the crucial importance of the coaching relationship to the success of coaching, a key part of the work is to raise the coach's awareness of their own and their coachees' unique, largely non-conscious patterns of relating, and then work with the coach to refine them in line with the supervision agreement. The coach learns how to become more fully present with the coachee, to deepen their understanding and compassion for the coachee and how they see the world and to be more aware of and manage the impact of their own issues on their coaching.

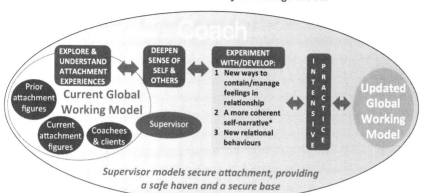

Figure 3.5 Working with attachment in coach supervision

2   The neuro-behavioural supervisor's approach is rooted in an understanding of the neurobiology of the human brain, the 'organ of relationship.' As it grows, a baby's brain is shaped by the interaction between its genes and the environment, particularly through the baby's relationship with its mother from before birth into early childhood (and subsequently with other close care givers). The patterns of relationship or attachment which become embedded during that time form that person's basic working model for relationships for the rest of their life.

3   Over time, the different demands on the individual mean the original working model needs updating and refining. The brain's neuroplasticity, the remarkable and life-long ability of its existing neurons to grow and connect in new ways and even for new neurons to appear, allows people to learn new and more integrated patterns of relationship.

4   The neuro-behavioural supervisor works with the whole person of the coach by modelling a relationship of openness, honesty and trust led by curiosity and appreciation. Through biographical inquiry and narration they explore the coach's early experience of relationship using the HASIE model and help the coach reflect on how that might impact on their work with coachees.

5   The neuro-behavioural supervisor becomes familiar with the unique patterns of behaviour that characterise each coach's ways of relating to themselves and others, including their coachees, and the narratives they use to make sense of them. The supervisor is a close observer of both verbal and non-verbal communication, challenging the coach at both a

cognitive and emotional level when there is a mismatch. They also know themselves well enough to distinguish their own somatic and emotional experience from the coach's.

6   Equally the coach must, like the proverbial light bulb, want to change. The desires and motivation which drive human behaviour come from the energy of emotions which originate within the limbic system of the brain. This permeates the body through extensive connections with the central and extended nervous system, including those of the heart and gut, as well as the hormonal and immune systems. In supervision as in coaching, it is the energy mobilised by the experience of relationship with the coach or supervisor that powers change.

If this sounds similar to psychotherapy, that is because psychotherapy, coaching and supervision, in their multitude of forms, all have the same basic aim, which is brought into sharp focus by taking a neurobiological perspective: to change the neural connections in a person's brain with a view to helping them function and relate in more rewarding ways. Distinctions between past and future orientation are beside the point. The true differences lie in the purpose of the different types of intervention and the nature of their objectives.

In conclusion

It is arguable that the twenty-first century will create a body of neuroscientific knowledge that re-defines our understanding of human behaviour. Newton and his seventeenth century contemporaries taught themselves to practise the experimental philosophy that became physics. They showed that there were lawful relationships, not just a God, that governed the complexity of the world. It may not be too much to claim that the insights of modern neuroscience into the way energy, enabled by the emotions, flows within the human system will revolutionise our working models of human behaviour. At this stage of knowledge it certainly looks as if there is the real prospect that explanatory rather than just descriptive models will emerge.

Human beings are fundamentally habit-based adaptive creatures. This is a proposition that holds true even when a person appears to be in some kind of apparent self-destruct mode. At any point in time we are each making the best adaptation that our own particular system permits. And we are doing it without conscious control, though with varying degrees of success in trying to make sense of it consciously.

This first statement of the use of applied neuroscience within supervision has proposed that a structure for supervision, based on a systematic understanding of the data that biographical inquiry yields about the individual, would be applicable both to the coach-coachee relationship and the supervisor-coach relationship. This would give a common basis of making meaning based on the best understanding available of the way the brain works in creating the specifics of human behaviour. It is as important for the supervisor to have a working model of the coach as it is for the coach to have a working model of the coachee, both grounded in an energy/emotions model of adult functioning.

In this context the HASIE model provides a neuroscientific basis combined with developmental psychology for a coach to understand meaning-making in the coachee. Through the process of biographical inquiry and narration, HASIE allows the coach to see the world through the coachee's eyes. This foundational understanding of the coachee provides an excellent construct between the supervisor and coach to examine through a joint perspective how the coachee may be invoking reaction, and in consequence perception, in the coach.

HASIE also reveals the emotional and ensuing behavioural patterning on both a conscious and non-conscious level for the coachee. The non-conscious patterning within the coach and coachee relationship also exists within the supervisor and coach relationship. In essence, the supervisory relationship is dealing with the non-conscious patterning of three key stakeholders: supervisor, coach and coachee. What this chapter has not set out to do is describe in detail how to do it. That comes from workshop teaching and coachee-facing experience, not book learning. Rather, it asks nothing less than that supervisors engage with the development of a practice based on a common core of knowledge to the benefit not only of the practice of supervision but also of the long-term development of the profession itself.

Notes

1 https://en.wikipedia.org/wiki/List_of_psychological_schools
2 https://images.search.yahoo.com/yhs/search;_ylt=AwrgEZFNN7JakU0AP3oPxQt.;_ylu= X3oDMTByNWU4cGh1BGNvbG8DZ3ExBHBvcwMxBHZ0aWQDBHNlYwNzYw--?p= Forms+of+psychotherapy&fr=yhs-Lkry-SF01&hspart=Lkry&hsimp=yhs-SF01
3 https://en.wikipedia.org/wiki/List_of_psychotherapies
4 https://images.search.yahoo.com/yhs/search;_ylt=AwrgEZPFO7Na_HEA17QPxQt.;_ylu= X3oDMTByNWU4cGh1BGNvbG8DZ3ExBHBvcwMxBHZ0aWQDBHNlYw NzYw--?p=University+of+Pennsylvania+mens+and+womens+brains&fr=yhs-Lkry-SF01& hspart=Lkry&hsimp=yhs-SF01
5 www.heartmath.com/

References

Bachkirova, T. (2011). *Developmental Coaching: Working With the Self.* Maidenhead, Berkshire: Open University Press/McGraw-Hill Education.

Brown, P. T. and Brown, V. (2013). *The Science of the Art of Coaching.* A CPD programme developed at the request of the Association for Coaching, still actively delivered. For information contact ptbpsychol@gmail.com

Brown, P. T. and Dendrowskyj, T. (2018). Sorting Out an Emotional Muddle. *Developing Leaders,* Spring 2018 Issue, pp. 26–31. Available at https://iedp.cld.bz/Developing-Leaders-issue-29-Spring-20181/30/

Carter, R. (2014). *The Brain Book: An Illustrated Guide to Its Structure, Function and Disorders.* 2nd ed. London: Dorling Kindersley.

Cozolino, L. (2014). *The Neuroscience of Human Relationships: Attachment and the Developing Social Brain.* NY & London: W.W.Norton & Company.

Crews, F. (2017). *Freud: The Making of an Illusion.* London: Profile Books.

Dawes, R. M. (1994). *House of Cards: Psychology and Psychotherapy Built on Myth.* New York: Free Press.

Dispenza, J. (2014). *You Are the Placebo: Making Your Mind Matter.* London: Hay House, Inc.

Drake, D. B. (2009). Using attachment theory in coaching leaders: The search for a coherent narrative. *International Coaching Psychology Review*, 4(1), 49–58. (Available at groups. psychology.org.au/Assets/Files/ICPR%204_2.pdf)

Fonagy, P., Steele, H. & Steele, M. (1991). Maternal Representations of Attachment during Pregnancy Predict the Organization of Infant-Mother Attachment at One Year of Age. *Child Development*, 62(5), 891–905.

Kets de Vries, M. F. R. (2018). *Riding the Leadership Rollercoaster: An Observer's Guide.* London: Palgrave Macmillan.

Lipton, B. H. (2005). *The Biology of Belief: Unleashing the Power of Consciousness, Matter and Miracles.* London: Hay House, Inc.

Mikulincer, M. and Shaver, P. (2016). *Attachment in Adulthood (2nd Edition): Structure, Dynamics and Change.* New York: Guilford Press.

Rooke, D. and Torbert, W. R. (2005). Seven Transformations of Leadership. *Harvard Business Review*, April 1.

Seung, S. (2012). *Connectome: How the Brain's Wiring Makes us Who We Are.* London and New York: Allen Lane/Penguin Books.

Siegel, D. (2012). *A Pocket Guide to Interpersonal Neurobiology.* New York and London: W.W. Norton & Company.

Watkins, A. (2014). *Coherence: The Secret Science of Brilliant Leadership.* London: Kogan Page.

Watson, J. D. & Crick, F. H. C. (1953). Molecular Structure of Nucleic Acids: A Structure for Deoxyribose Nucleic Acid. *Nature*, 171, 737–738.

4 The power and influence of the unconscious mind

Dr Sandra Wilson

Introduction

The inspiration for this chapter comes from my research which set out to explore the influence of the coach's unconscious mind on the coaching process. This research was based on the psychodynamic concept that the unconscious mind is omnipresent and a strong influence on thoughts, feelings and behaviours, and sought to ascertain the extent to which the coach's unconscious mind is at work in the coaching process. Brunning (2006) suggests that the term 'psycho-dynamic' links *psycho (from the Greek psyche meaning soul or mind)* and *dynamic (from the Greek dynamis, meaning strength or power)*. Thus, psychodynamic work is based on ways of understanding how the mental forces operating intrapersonally and interpersonally in and between individuals and groups affect their thinking and behaviour.

The participants are professionally trained and accredited coaches, working as either internal or external coaches. The research invited participants to explore their lived experience in relation to the intrapersonal process, the interpersonal process, relationships with parties to the coaching contract and the coaching process. The data collection followed three distinct yet inter-related stages, engaging participants in semi-structured interviews using metaphor, symbolic representation[1] and creation of metaphoric landscapes,[2] culminating in indirect observation of the coach at work.

The narrative was a journey of discovery for both myself as researcher and the participants, with data emerging that identified the coach's relationship not only with the external parties but also with the different parts of self. In the three stages of this journey, the participants travelled from mental activity, reflecting on lived experience, perceptions and events, to the exploration of mental processes and constructs which were inferred, discovered and translated into conscious awareness throughout the research interviews.

The significance of this research is the consideration of where the need for psychological awareness sits within the context of professional coach education and accreditation, which moves the coach beyond technique to psychological understanding, self-awareness and self-regulation. In the context of coach supervision, it begs the question, 'How can we as supervisors support continuing coach education through helping surface the coach's unconscious mind to explore how it may be clouding or illuminating their work?'

I invite the reader to consider as they read to consider, 'What does this mean for me and my supervision practice?'

The psychodynamic approach

I don't intend to cover in detail the theoretical base which was the foundation on which I sought to make sense of the emergent data. For those readers not familiar with the psychodynamic approach the following narrative gives an overview of approach and a brief description of the key concepts which were used in the data analysis. References are given should the reader be interested in gaining a deeper understanding.

'Psychodynamic' is an umbrella term that refers to models of the mind that are primarily concerned with unconscious processes. All psychodynamic models can be traced back to Freud and psychoanalysis. Many theorists developed Freud's ideas in different directions and founded their own schools of psychodynamic thinking. Transactional Analysis, Adlerian, Jungian, Reikian and Gestalt are all psychodynamic models.

The underlying principle shared by these approaches is that we all have an inner world that has a powerful influence on how we think, feel and behave. This inner world comprises feelings, memories, beliefs and fantasies. It is partly conscious, in that we know about it and have access to it; but it is largely unconscious, meaning that we are unaware of it and therefore are unable to access it. Freud believed that behaviour could be understood if only we looked closely enough. Central to Freud's viewpoint is that we rarely deal directly with external reality, rather we interact with the world based on internal representations, so we see the world in terms of internal concerns. In the psychodynamic view, behaviour is the result of the interplay of conflicting internal forces.

The core models which were used in the data analysis were:

- Defence mechanisms – an internal process used to distort or deny reality and avoid exposure to hurt or harm. (See Freud, 1951; Berne, 1966; Mellor and Schiff, 1980; Peltier, 2009.)
- Adaptation – taking on an identity to please the authority figures on whom we depend for survival. (See Kets de Vries, 1991; Levinson, 1996; Berne, 1966.)
- Fantasy – the idealised notion of whom and what we are in the world of work; referred to as the ego ideal. (See Czander, 1993; Peltier, 2009.)
- Social defences – a primary cohesive element which binds individuals in institutional environments. The theory suggests that we take up both conscious and unconscious roles. The social system allows for beliefs and behaviours manifesting to become defence mechanisms which allow us to manage threat and anxiety. (See Jacques, 1953; Diamond, 1993.)

- The organisation-in-the-mind – an internal model unique to the individual and part of their inner world creating a perception of how the person perceives how activities and relationships are organised, structured and connected internally. The theory suggests that it is with the organisation-in-the-mind that the individual interacts. (See Armstrong, 2005.)
- Transference and counter-transference – those aspects of relationships that are shaped by preconceptions and transferred on to the actual relationship with a real person or group, thus limiting, confining and sometimes distorting the reality of the relationship.

Psychodynamic models and coaching

The literature review carried out for the research showed the authors who write about the psychodynamic models do so with authority and give a good account of how coaches can work with these models in service of their clients. The coaching literature focusses on the development of skills and use of models in support of the client. In much of the work there is an implicit assumption that the coach has taken responsibility for understanding their intrapersonal process and used psychodynamic theory for self-understanding before they use it with clients. I have found this not to be the case in my work as a coach mentor and coach supervisor, and I challenged the thinking of these authors as part of the research.

Coaching is a relational process, and coaches need a high level of self-awareness to serve their clients well. In reading coaching literature, there is a lack of commentary on the coach's self-awareness or an assumption that the coach is self-aware. I could find no definition of self-awareness anywhere in coaching literature, and where it is mentioned in the context of the coach, it is generally assumed that this is achieved through self-reflection and introspection. The psychodynamic models say that people provide explanations for their behaviour. Based on my understanding of these models, I would argue that these explanations are rationalisations, and when people do not understand their behaviour, they invent justifications. If the psychodynamic models are valid, then people are largely unaware of the influence of the unconscious mind. Looking at self-awareness through the psychodynamic lens, I suggest that self-awareness cannot be achieved through self-reflection and introspection. However, this is one of those perceived truths that everyone believes. The coaching literature reviewed does not specify this truth per se, but I think there is a distinct possibility that as a profession we are deluding ourselves. There may be a further assumption that successful coaching is independent of the capacity for introspection and self-analysis. Bachkirova (2011) addresses some of my concerns in her writing on the concept of self as an instrument. She argues eloquently that the traditional focus for coach training is on the development of skills and knowledge and that the next step in coach development should focus on the self and the reflexivity of the coach. I agree with her, and my experience of assessing and supervising coaches suggests that six years after Bachkirova's writing, there is a still a lack of reflexivity on the part of the coach. And this is where supervision can add value.

The research outcomes

To help the reader understand the outcomes of the research Figure 4.1 gives an overview of the stages of the research process. The interviews were all conducted face-to-face.

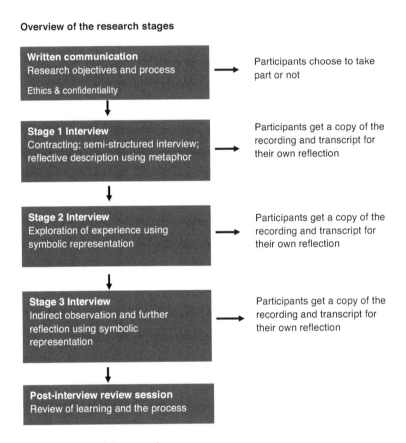

Figure 4.1 Overview of the research stages

The three aspects of self

An outcome of the research was the concept of the three aspects of self which I described as:

- *The idealised self* – this emerged as I considered the data collected from the stage 1 interviews. The early part of the interview focusses on how the participants both perceive and experience themselves using a simple narrative. The latter part of the interview invites deeper reflection using metaphor. This generated information on how they both perceive and experience themselves in relation to other parties to the contract and consideration of how this influences the process of their work.

- *The authentic self* – this emerged as I considered the data collected from the stage 2 interviews. The second stage interview sought deeper reflection and exploration about how they experience the parties to the relationship and how they make meaning of that experience. What the participants reported was a deeper understanding of their unconscious process and how this might be impacting on their work.
- *The unconscious self* – this emerged as I considered the data from the stage 3 interviews, which included indirect observation of the participants coaching. The data emerging from this stage in the process showed that the participants' perceptions and experiences of the parties to the contract influenced how they work. The name was chosen to conceptualise the idea of the unconscious mind and its influence on how humans connect and work.

Although the descriptors emerged as I considered the data from each stage in the research, the themes had relevance at each stage and captured the participants' awareness and insight.

These three aspects of self were derived from and supported by data which emerged from the questions addressed at each stage in the interview process. The interviews focussed on three areas which connected to the three aspects of self and sought to draw out deeper reflection and consideration of the unconscious mind:

- *Focus on self* – this theme explored the participants' beliefs and experiences of their way of being as a coach. It communicates an expanding awareness as the research process unfolds, taking the participant from discursive narrative to deeper meaning and reflection on their sense of self.
- *Focus on relationships* – this theme explored participants' experiences of their relationship with the parties to the contract. They reflect more deeply on whom they are as a coach in the relationship. The use of symbolic representation invites deeper reflection and consideration of how the coach's perception may influence their work. At this stage, participants are exploring their experience and feelings about the parties to the contract and the coaching process.
- *Focus on the unconscious process* – this theme captured the emerging understanding of the unconscious mind and its influence on the coaching process.

Throughout the three stages of the research, there is an expanding awareness of the power of the unconscious mind and its influence on the coaching process, but the greatest awareness came from stage 3.

The focus of the interviews at each stage in the process allowed the data to be grouped and analysed as shown in Figures 4.2, 4.3 and 4.4.

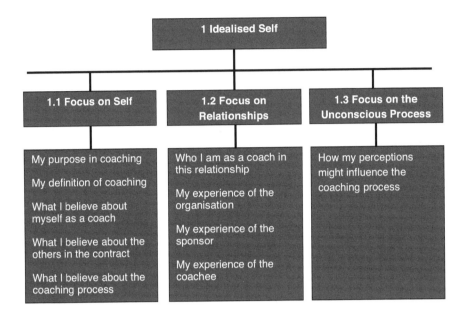

Figure 4.2 Idealised self (1)

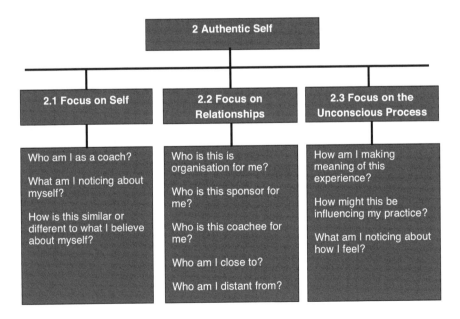

Figure 4.3 Authentic self (2)

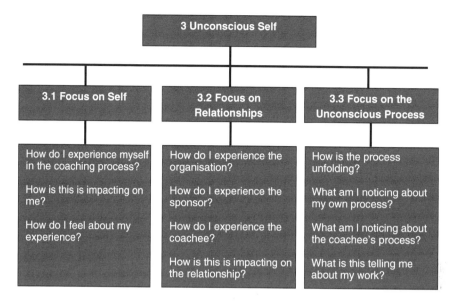

Figure 4.4 Unconscious self (3)

Source: Schiff, J. et al. (1975) *Transactional Analysis – Treatment of Psychosis.* San Francisco: Harper & Row.

The idealised self

In the first interview the coaches answered the questions with ease, and the information seemed readily accessible to them. It appeared this was the sort of 'script' they use with potential coachees to explain the purpose of coaching, the coaching process, how they work as a coach and what the organisation gains from coaching. I experienced this as a presentation of how they think they should be, the idealised self, and, consequently, who they believe they are.

When participants were invited to reflect using metaphor they stepped into a more reflective space and took longer to answer the questions. They described themselves in a positive way, and the organisation, the coachee and the sponsor in a more negative way. I had a sense of hopefulness about themselves as coaches and the coaching process, whilst the other parties to the relationship were presented as 'hopeless.' They seemed to see the coaching process and themselves as a source for good in what they perceived as challenging times in the organisation.

My interpretation is that their unconscious mind held them in a position above the other parties, and I was left thinking there was an element of discounting and grandiosity.[3] The voice tone, tempo and body language caused me to sense the participants believe their actions and words empower others and create a significant catalyst for change in the world in which they operate. On the one hand, the coach needs to believe they can be a positive force for change and feel confident and competent in their work. On the other hand, if this belief is not surfaced and dealt with in awareness, they may unconsciously co-create an authority relationship with the coachee based on power and powerlessness. Participants seemed resistant to the concept that their experiences as defined by metaphor would have any impact on the work they did. The metaphors were starting to draw out the mental constructs that were informing their perceptions, and it is difficult to see how these would not inform behaviour and, thus, their interventions in the coaching process.

My curiosity was raised by their resistance, and I thought they were protecting something personal to them. This is understandable – they have chosen to train for and work in a particular role. The responses at this stage led me to consider what had emerged was an enactment of a role, with the unconscious mind reflecting 'this is how I must be seen.' I did not believe they were 'hiding' anything but rather explaining their perception, ergo their reality, ergo their experience. Six of the eight participants could not conceive they were anything other than fully present with their coachees, moment by moment, without any intrapersonal process dynamics or intra-psychic experiences influencing them. They reported being fully aware and conscious in the moment, which I believed to be their truth. If we look at the coaching competence of 'presence,' it means more than being fully aware and conscious in the moment; it means deep listening and going beyond one's preconceptions and historical ways of making sense of the world. This means being aware of these things and being able to self-regulate to achieve 'presence.'

The authentic self

This second stage interview process encouraged the participants to look deeper at themselves, their relationships with the parties to the contract and the potential impact on their work. Their choice of symbols gave a sense of what might be held in their unconscious minds. The process allowed them to see that in their choice of symbols, they were telling their story in a different way and, I believe, a more authentic way. The symbols they chose gave strong clues about what they regarded as having value, goodness and use in its own right or, indeed, the opposite. Their articulation of how they experienced the symbols as empowering, mystical, protective, magical, dangerous, threatening and so on indicated the role and function of that symbol for them. All the symbols served a purpose in both the relationship and the process. The placing of the symbols allowed participants to reflect on the perceived distance between the parties to the relationship. It emerged that undoubtedly the coach-coachee relationship is a close one, with the other relationships being more distant.

This part of the process confirmed we all have an unconscious mind which has the potential to influence what we say and do. The material generated identified the participants having a psychological level to the relationship with the parties and the coaching contract. The symbolic representation surfaced how the participants were seeing and experiencing the other parties to the contract, the unconscious and, therefore, the unspoken beliefs they held. The establishment of the coaching contract creates a 'coaching world'; the data emerging at this point reinforces how the coach has an inner world within the coaching world. If the coach has this inner world, then I believe it is safe to assume the other parties to the contract do also. The question that remains is the extent to which this creates an unconscious dynamic which influences the work being done.

The unconscious self

In this part of the process, participants were asked to review an event after it had happened and to reflect on what they were noticing in the review they had not noticed in the moment. In this context, they were engaged in retrospective detection or reflection-on-action. All the participants changed their metaphoric landscape; then they considered the attributes and location of the symbols. In each of the sessions, I noted that participants changed:

- The relationship between two symbols;
- A change in the configuration of the symbols;
- A change caused by the unfolding process; and
- A change in the pattern of the relationships.

Each of these changes seemed to have its own logic of change, and a change at one level influenced a change at other levels. In other words, the interaction between the coach and coachee caused changes in the metaphoric landscape; thus, when something changed in the relationship between them, it caused a change in the relationship with the sponsor and/or the organisation. This move-ment of symbols and exploration of what was happening in the relationship allowed the participants to discover new information.

My analysis is that there is always a voice of judgment in the intrapersonal and interpersonal processes. The participants initially believed they had the capacity to suspend judgment, the imposition of their pre-established frame of reference and mental models. The creation of a metaphoric landscape using symbolic representation challenged that belief and uncovered data that hitherto had not been accessible.

Deeper levels of exploration seemed to create deeper levels of awareness both of themselves and of the larger whole. By the end of this process the participants had shown a capacity for deeper seeing and noticing the effects this awareness had on their understanding, their sense of self and others. The final session showed a depth of understanding about the unconscious process and its capacity to impact the work they do that I did not believe possible at the end of the first sessions. At the outset, the participants reported they were fully present and in the moment in the coaching process, and yet by the end of the process realised this was not so and were able to own their preconceptions and historical ways of making sense of the coaching encounter.

Research data and psychodynamic theory

I did not consciously fall in line with the psychodynamic concept of the different parts of self. The descriptions I chose were an attempt to make sense of the phenomena emerging from analysis of the data. What emerged was data supporting the notion of there being more than one self within the coach and a sense there is a place in the mind to which unacceptable feelings or fantasies are banished. The three aspects of self are depicted as internal objects and analysed in the context of internal and external relationships without consideration of how these aspects may be connected to the internal aspects of the psyche that are developed in childhood and present in all relationships.

By the end of the second stage interviews, I had a sense that the participants were developing a new understanding of how they made meaning of themselves, the relationship and the deeper, below-the-surface reasons for human behaviour. At this stage the participants had started to:

- Acknowledge the existence of a multi-layered collage of images in the human unconscious; and
- Develop an understanding that these unconscious images are linked to the way they work; although at this stage, they seemed unsure how these images were affecting their work.

The data from the stage two interviews correlates with the notion of the unconscious mind and unconscious psychological process. This connects with the concept of the psychological level of the contract (Berne, 1966). Berne suggests that there is always a psychological level to a contract, and he described it as the unconscious and, therefore, unspoken aspects of the relationship which influence the way the parties engage and communicate with each other. The psychological level of the contract started to emerge in the stage 2 interviews through the deeper exploration of how the participants were experiencing all the parties to the contract, themselves included. If they hold unconscious and unspoken beliefs, then it would logically follow that this will impact on the work because they are not accessing information that may be a hindrance.

There are two perceivers of the metaphoric landscape, the participant who detected the symbolically significant patterns across their experience and me as the researcher who noticed the patterns of their verbal and non-verbal expressions and then made the interpretation connecting their emerging story to existing theory. I am confident in saying there is an unconscious process at work and it influences the coaching process.

At the third stage in the process, using indirect observation, the participants identified when they had noticed something change in the coaching process and, therefore, in their work. They connected with the characteristics of the symbols they had chosen and identified thoughts, feelings and behaviours that had hitherto been inaccessible. Alongside this their perception shifted; they seemed to let go of the 'idealised' self and accept the human side of the self.

Interestingly, although they seemed to have let go of the idealised self, there were flashes of it from time to time, suggesting unconscious processes were still at work. What emerged, however, was an acceptance and understanding of how the unconscious mind was influencing them moment by moment in the coaching process. Despite the emerging awareness, they were focussed on what they were doing rather than their way of being, which suggests they were thinking about their performance as a coach rather than exploring the unconscious process and what prompted it to emerge in the way it did. The fact they chose to avoid the expression of authentic feelings suggests that they were still not fully in touch with, or accepting of, their unconscious self. They seemed restricted by their inner world, which was dynamic and changing and, thus, created inner turbulence. The pressure came from both internal and external sources and created the turbulence. As the new information emerged, so did their discomfort about the changing relationship they had with themselves. The external source, the research process, was the event that created the turbulence.

The data suggests they were getting a strong sense of their inner world and noticing through reflecting on their video recording how powerful this influence can be on how they think, feel and behave. Wilson (2010) explains the concept of gradations of consciousness, so that some parts of our unconscious mind are more readily accessible than others. She uses the metaphor of an iceberg to reflect on how we see and experience ourselves and others. What is on the surface is readily visible and generally acceptable but is only one-third of who we really are. Two-thirds of the iceberg is below the surface, feeding and informing thoughts, feelings and corresponding patterns of behaviour. At this stage, the participants were submerged and considering aspects of themselves that had hitherto been beneath the surface.

The organisation in the mind emerged strongly in the third stage interviews. The fact that the participants stayed with the same symbol to represent the organisation seemed significant (although some of them rearranged the placement at different times in the session). The participants held a fixed belief about the organisation, which did not change throughout the two sessions when they worked with symbols. By moving the symbols in response to something they noticed in the recording, they were having an emotional response to the organisation which impacted their experience and, therefore, their work in the moment. The organisation in the mind refers not only to the conscious and unconscious mental constructs and the assumptions the individual makes, it also refers to the emotional resonances which register and are present in the mind of the participant (Hirschhorn, 1990). When the participants were asked to reflect on their experience of the organisation, they were looking into the inner world of the organisation and to the world within a world, that is, their inner world. There seemed to be both a connection and a disconnection between the inner world of the organisation and the inner world of the participant, and this was reflected in their responses on how they were experiencing the organisation. I noticed at this stage the tension shifted around the relationships, sometimes being between the coach and coachee, the coach and sponsor, and the coach and the organisation.

The choice and placement of the symbol in the developing metaphorical landscape and the descriptions given by the participants relating to the characteristics of the symbols yielded information on the potential transference and counter-transference in the relationships. I believe the participants started their involvement in the research process in transferential relationships with other parties to the contract. The relationships seemed to be shaped by preconceptions that were transferred onto the actual relationships and which had the potential to confine, limit and distort the reality of the relationships. They reflected the persona of the sponsor through the characteristics of the symbol, and they chose to stay with the same symbol throughout sessions 2 and 3. This suggests although they moved the symbol around the landscape to create a different imago, they did not change their perception of the sponsor. This further suggests that their choice of symbol may not have wholly represented their experience of the sponsor but may also have included other experiences outside of this relationship. The lack of interaction with the sponsor may not have allowed the participants to experience and, therefore, collect data which challenged the preconceptions they held. Thus, the chance to explore a confronting reality was limited.

Staying with this theoretical concept, I considered something similar to be at work in their relationship with the coachee. Most of the participants kept the same symbol to represent the coachee throughout the process, with only two changing the symbol. Working with Obholzer's (2006) suggestion that it is never irrelevant to question the presence of transference and counter-transference in a relationship, I believe that although the transferential relationship may not be present always in the coaching process, it is most likely to be there some of the time. Given the individual potential for co-creating transferential relationships and the transferences generated by the organisational structure, which has levels of authority and status differentials, as well as complex systems of roles and relationships, it is difficult to conceive that the coaching relationship can be completely free from transference. People bring their psyche and personal history to every relationship; therefore, the participants will behave towards the parties to the contract in the same way that they behave towards other significant people. The reflection on their own process in the relationship with the coachee gave a strong indication of moments of transference. There was a deepening awareness of what was happening under the surface of the relationships. The strongest data comes from the relationship between the participant and the coachee, where the participant noticed their actions and reactions to what was happening in the relational process. They noticed the cause and effect of the interactions they were having with the coachee, the moving towards or moving away from each other. In essence, they were surfacing new information on the dynamics of the relationship.

The research process challenged the participants' beliefs about themselves, the parties to the relationship and the coaching process. In the early stages, they were living a core set of beliefs they had about themselves as coaches and the coaching process. Through engaging in reflection and creating the story, these beliefs were put under the microscope and challenged more by themselves than by me. Reflecting on how participants transformed their understanding of themselves, the parties to the relationship and the process connect to social defence mechanisms (Jacques, 1953). In the beginning, participants were using defence mechanisms to distort or deny reality so that they were not exposed to fear or anxiety. Their unconscious was working in the research process in much the same way as it was in the coaching process. Initially we had a parallel process[4] running. In the first interview I experienced the participants as protecting themselves, their professional identity and their competence. Fear or anxiety was most probably present for them because they had engaged in a process which put their professional practice under the microscope. This resulted in the use of defence mechanisms to keep threatening feelings and painful thoughts outside of their awareness. This suggests they were distorting reality to protect their sense of self.

As the interviews progressed and they stepped into their inner world, they employed defence mechanisms less overtly. Their attachment to the symbols they chose suggests, however, they were still employing defence mechanisms. The discomfort they experienced moment by moment in the coaching process raised anxiety which moved them away from the experience, the ability to sit with the anxiety and to be curious. Thus, the unconscious mind was motivating their behaviour as a defence against anxiety, which, in turn, moved them away from dealing with what they experienced in the moment. My role as a researcher was to elicit their mental constructs and interpret their experiences in the light of the emerging data. I am compelled to say that I did notice an emerging awareness of the unconscious mind and how this was impacting on the relationships and the process. Most awareness came from the stage 3 interviews. They became aware of something new when they could 'observe' themselves at work. The data points to evidence that the unconscious is at work in all aspects of relationships to a lesser or greater degree. Nin (1903–1977) said: "We do not see things as they are; we see things as we are" (cited in Blenkiron, 2005, p. 49), and this seeing of what we expect to be there can make the discovery of something new virtually impossible.

Six of the eight participants reported in the post-research review session that they continued to use symbolic modelling post-research involvement. These six participants said they had both gained insight and created strategies for noticing their perceptions of the coachee, the sponsor and the organisation to change their response in real-time interactions. Three of the eight said they were keeping a reflective journal, accounting for what happened in a session and processing what they noticed, what their thoughts were and how they felt. The other three said they were using metaphoric landscapes prior to starting work with new coachees to surface perceptions they were holding that might impact on the work they would engage in. All eight said they had richer material for supervision because of their involvement in the research. I was left with a strong sense of the participants being dedicated to their own learning.

Implications for supervision

I am interested in continuing in coach education beyond professional accreditation and the role of supervision in this developmental arena. How we define supervision and its functions will determine how we contract and work with our supervisees. The following narrative offers further reflection from me on what emerged from the research together with reflective questions for the reader to consider. The core questions I invite the reader to consider are:

> *How can I support my supervisees to explore their inner world to bring the unconscious into conscious awareness?*
> *How can I explore my inner world and notice what might be influencing my work as a supervisor?*

Supervision and the growing edge

The research suggests that some of the time coaches were operating in a restricted zone, within their own frame of reference, protecting their reality (see figure below). To be more effective in their work they must be prepared to use supervision to expand the boundaries and move beyond that restricted zone. The boundaries between

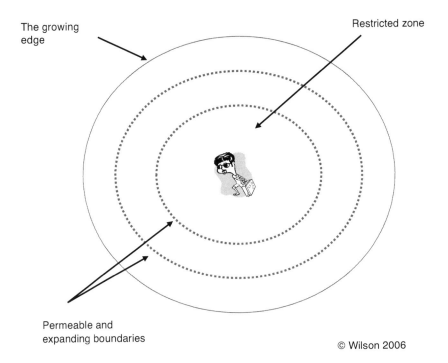

© Wilson 2006

Figure 4.5 The journey to the growing edge

the restricted zone and the growing edge become permeable and expanding. I see the role of the supervisor as to encourage, support and challenge the coach to move towards the growing edge. This move towards is the expanding awareness of the unconscious and how it influences our thoughts, feelings and consequently actions. This expanding awareness creates a more autonomous coach who can work more authentically with their clients.

Suspending our beliefs

As coaches and supervisors, we are required to suspend our beliefs, that is, to see freshly by stopping habitual ways of thinking and perceiving. Senge, Scharmer, Jaworski and Flowers (2007) suggest that there are risks involved in suspending beliefs, and to do so, individuals in the organisational helping professions are required to do personal work. They suggest this personal work is developing the capacity to be more aware of thoughts and feelings and how these impact inter-actions. To support the creation of awareness in others, coaches are required to be self-aware to ensure that, as far as is humanly possible, their unconscious process does not interfere with the work of coachees. I extrapolate this and suggest that as supervisors we need to ensure, as far as is humanly possible, our unconscious process does not interfere with the work of the supervisee.

Questions

> How can you work with supervisees to bring into awareness beliefs, thoughts and feelings that impact on their interactions in the coaching process?
> How can you become more aware of your own beliefs, thoughts and feelings that may be impacting your work?

Deepening reflective practice

I want to challenge coaches to deepen their reflective practice. There is work that coaches can do through self-reflection and considered thinking on what they take to the supervision process.

The research shows that the level of accreditation achieved by the coach is not a reliable predictor of the understanding they have of their own process, nor their level of self-awareness. In each of the three research encounters, all par-ticipants had insights into their unconscious process through reflective practice. Thus, I would suggest the supervision process should involve assessment of, and reflection on, recorded sessions. This allows supervisees to engage in reflexivity with the supervisor on what they perceived to be happening in the coaching encounter.

Questions

> What considered thinking do you want your supervisees to do before their supervi-sion session?

What is your reaction to the idea of listening to excerpts of your supervisee's work to create awareness and generate insights?

How might recording your supervision sessions invite deeper reflection of your practice?

Challenging professional assumptions

The study shows participants becoming much more reflective in their practice as the research unfolded. As a community, we should not assume that coaches can automatically reflect on their work, and my encouragement to supervisors is to consider how they might describe and demonstrate engagement in reflective practice in their work.

Questions

How do you measure your supervisee's capacity to engage in reflective practice?
How do you engage in reflection on your own practice?

Psychological awareness

Coaches, like psychotherapists and counsellors, help bring about important changes for individuals, groups and organisations. Consequently, their clients may be in a life situation which renders them vulnerable and possibly dependent. It is these occupational conditions that demand from the coach not only a high degree of professional competence and ethical awareness, but also a level of psychological understanding, a high degree of self-awareness and the capacity to self-regulate. The work of coaches can not only deeply influence their immediate client but impact other people and relationships. Thus, it is the individual coach's professional competence, self-awareness and self-regulation that are critical to the protection of the clients in their care.

The conclusion I draw from this research is that continuing professional development for coaches must place less emphasis on developing new skills and more on increasing psychological awareness, both in general and in the moment of the coaching conversation. Coaching and supervision are both reflective practices, aimed at enhancing understanding, making meaning, creating awareness and generating insights. De Haan and Graduates (2016) suggest that the coach should work on their own inquiry question in reflective conversation with others to prepare for working with the inquiry question of coachees. It is impossible not to be touched by the coaching relationship. The research validates this assertion, and it is a natural next step to train coaches to deal with their experience as it happens, what we call in coaching 'dancing in the moment.'

Questions

How do you encourage your supervisees to work on their own inquiry question?
What is your inquiry question that might be worthy of exploration?

Identity and the unconscious self

This research shows the coaches' attachment to their identity, and there is a possibility that protection of the idealised self is to do with protection of their reputation. In other words, *who they think they are is confused with who others think they should be.* Thus, they take on the identity of *who others think they should be as a coach; reputation and identity become intertwined.* As the research unfolded, the coaches faced confronting reality, and became more self-aware and able to contact the deeper aspects of the self to better understand who they are. As professionals we have an obligation to our clients to increase our self-awareness, to understand and acknowledge the meaning of what we do and the reasons behind our thoughts, feelings and actions. Freud (1951) stated that increasing self-awareness means discovering the unconscious origins of our everyday behaviour. The journey of self-discovery does not come about solely through self-reflection or introspection, yet it has become a perceived truth that we achieve self-awareness in this way.

Questions

> *How can you start to notice the supervisee might be protecting their identity and work with them to contact deeper aspects of self?*
> *What reflections do you have on your own identity and reputation?*

Deeper understanding

I encourage supervisors to consider how they support the development of the coaches they work with through developing competence in, and working with, psychodynamic models. Supervisors can challenge coaches who use psychological models to ensure that they are not only using them correctly and in a safe way, but using them to understand themselves better. We have a moral and professional duty to test theories and models on ourselves as practitioners before we use them with clients.

One of the things that struck me about the research was the significance of subjectivity and the different ways we emphasise relationships. In this I mean the relationship with the self, others and what we co-create in the coaching encounter. The research shows that being challenged to reflect on these relationships increases self-awareness and shifts mental constructs. It further shows that profound change in understanding happens through experience. Experiencing the use of metaphor and symbolism invites deeper reflection and understanding of the coaching encounter.

Questions

> *How might you use metaphor and symbolism to invite deeper understanding in your supervisees?*
> *How might the use of metaphor and symbolism create deeper understanding of the supervision encounter?*

Reflexive practice

At the heart of my research is the concept of the reflexive practitioner, and I believe achieving real reflexivity is crucial, whatever role we have in the coaching community. The research shows that central to the work we do in coaching is the relationship. It is crucial that as coaches and supervisors we pay attention to patterns in play between the parties to the relationship and that we can pay attention to these as they emerge.

Questions

> *How can you support your supervisees to surface and work on the patterns at play in the coaching relationship?*
> *How can you pay attention to the patterns at play in the supervision relationship?*

Surfacing the unconscious

As mentioned earlier in this text, even when the participants became more aware of how their unconscious mind was influencing them in the moment, they focussed on how this was impacting their performance rather than seeking to understand the impact on their way of being. Understanding our own unconscious process helps us as coaches and supervisors to find new and more authentic ways of relating. The research shows the importance of curiosity, critical reflection and creativity. There is an opportunity for all of us in the profession to allow ourselves the freedom to learn, to be curious and to explore the experience in the moment. The research shows the significance of the unconscious. The unconscious is not a place nor a thing but rather a self-perpetuating pattern of organising self in relationships that remains largely outside of awareness.

Question

> *What reflections or curiosity do you have as you reach the end of this chapter?*

And finally

Coaching and supervision are both relational processes. The research showed that coaching is not a one-person intervention; rather, it is a multi-party psychology. All the parties to relationship are in the coaching room in both the conscious and unconscious mind of the coach. If this is the case for the coach, it is likely to be the case for all parties to the relationship. It follows that, although ostensibly supervision is a one-person intervention, it is an extension of the multi-party psychology that is coaching.

Notes

1 Symbolic representation is the use of something familiar in daily life that possesses specific connotations in addition to its obvious meaning. It reveals something hidden from us.

2 Metaphoric landscapes are pictures that emerge through the exploration of situations, relationships and issues using symbols.
3 Discounting (Schiff et al., 1975) – blanking out of some aspects of the situation. Grandiosity (Schiff et al., 1975) – exaggeration of some feature of reality.
4 Parallel process: what is happening in one set of relationships is being played out in another set of relationships (Stewart and Joines, 2000).

Bibliography

Armstrong, D. (2005). *Organisation in the Mind*. London: Karnac.

Bachkirova, T. (2011). *Developmental Coaching: Working With* Self. Maidenhead: McGraw Hill.

Berne, E. (1966). *Principles of Group Treatment*. New York: Oxford University Press.

Blenkiron, P. (2005). Stories and Analogies in Cognitive Behaviour Therapy: A Clinical Review. *Behavioural and Cognitive Psychotherapy*, 33(1), 45–49.

Brunning, H. (2006). *Executive Coaching – Systems Psychodynamic Perspective*. London: Karnac.

Czander, W. (1993). *The Psychodynamics of Work and Organisations*. New York: Gilford.

De Haan, E. and Graduates, (2016). *Behind Closed Doors – Stories From the Coaching Room*. Farringdon: Libri.

Diamond, M. (1993). *The Unconscious Life of Organisations*. Westport, CT: Quorum.

Freud, S. (1951). *Psychopathology of Everyday Life*. London: George Allen & Unwin Limited.

Hirschhorn, L. (1990). *The Workplace Within: The Psychodynamics of Organisational Life*. Cambridge, MA: MIT Press.

Jacques, E. (1953). On the Dynamics of Social Structure. *Human Relations*, 6, 3–24.

Kets de Vries, M., (1991). *Organisations on the Couch: Clinical Perspectives on Organisational Behaviour and Change*. San Francisco: Jossey-Bass.

Levinson, D. (1996). *The Seasons of a Woman's Life*. New York: Ballantine Books.

Mellor, K. and Schiff, J. (1980). *Transactional Analysis – Treatment of Psychosis*. San Francisco: Harper & Row.

Obholzer, A. (2006). *The Unconscious at Work: Individual and Organisational Stress in the Human Services*. London: Routledge.

Peltier, B. (2009). *The Psychology of Executive Coaching*. 2nd ed. New York: Routledge.

Senge, P., Scharmer, C. O., Jaworski, J. and Flowers, B. S. (2007). *Presence: Exploring Profound Change in People, Organisations and Society*. London: Nicholas Brealey.

Smith, J. A., Flowers, P. and Larkin, M. (2009). *Interpretative Phenomenological Analysis: Theory, Method and Research*. London: Sage Publications.

Stewart, I. and Joines, V. (2000). *TA Today – A New Introduction to Transactional Analysis*. London: Sage Publications.

Wilson, S. (2010). *Autonomy and the Growing Edge in Keeping the TA Torch Alight: Reading After Berne*. Utrecht: P & D Intact Publishers.

5 Working in the shadows

Pain and suffering in coaching and supervision

Patrick Hobbs

Meeting a life

I am introducing myself to a group of coaches. I tell them how many years I have been coaching and supervising coaches, I mention my professional qualifications and accreditations, the thousands of hours of coaching experience working with people across dozens of countries, and I name some of the global organisations where I have coached. These things I say are true, they are part of my story and the mark I imagine I make in this world, and in different ways they matter to me. I also hold a strange belief that in some way they might matter to some of the people listening to me, that these facts might lend me some kind of legitimacy or credibility.

After a pause, I continue speaking. I talk about hurt and failure. I tell them of the tropical virus I contracted when I was a student leading to some 20 years of disability, destroying my career and leaving me unable to work, dependent on ever-shrinking social security benefits. I speak of my brother, the person closest to me, a most beautifully gifted man who ended his own life, and of the painful and ultimately unsuccessful struggle to have children.

These things are also true, and they have done more to shape who I am as a person, my relationship to the world and the self I bring to my work. When I ask the group which introduction they connect with, they say very clearly that it is the second. These are aspects of human experience that do not usually come into coaching, and yet it seems these aspects hold an energy and meaning that resonate forcefully for both speaker and listener.

Coaching focusses on achieving goals and success. It does not readily embrace suffering and pain, confusion or failure, and yet this can lead to a separation of 'positive' and 'negative' in human experience, and a dualistic understanding of human beings that serves neither them nor the work we seek to do.

What happens if I continue speaking for another two minutes of what is important to me? I can speak of skiing in the French Alps, badly, perhaps dangerously, exhilarated and terrified; of being moved to tears as I listen to Vaughan Williams' *Fantasia on a Theme by Thomas Tallis*; of being mesmerised by the barn owl quartering the meadow in a hunt against the twilight sky; of taking a break between supervision sessions to dance across my office to the 'Harlem Shuffle';

or of the deep love I feel for my father as I hold him after he has collapsed with what looks like a stroke. As the stories unfold, they become harder to categorise as positive or negative, and the need and desire to do so evaporate into the day. The experiences are what they are. What happens to coaching and the supervision of coaching when we start with simply meeting a life?

A human being hearing a human being

There is little value in looking at the supervision of coaching without looking at coaching, what it is and what happens in it, because this is what supervision holds and supports.

My own belief is that coaching in its essence is a human being hearing a human being and helping that human being to connect with what matters to them in the reality in which they find themselves. When I am doing this something meaningful can happen, and when I am not doing this, I wonder what I am really doing. The role of coaching may change with the rise of artificial intelligence, but the question of what it means to be human will become more, not less, important.

Our challenge lies in the fact that in hearing a human being we need to establish some focus if we are to do effective work, and yet if we are too prescriptive in what we will listen to, we can miss so much that is vital to that person, part of their lives, affecting them and who they are, how they live, work and lead. In its focus on success coaching can miss the human experience that lies in the shadows – this may be physical illness, the loss or suffering of a person they love, the grief of childlessness masked by a successful career, bullying at work, confusion in relationships, the apparent failure of losing a job, the deceptive addiction of workaholism. I remember at one point in my coaching career I had seven executive coachees whose marriages were in different stages of crisis or breakdown, and although this was not the focus of the coaching it was part of the human picture.

It is tempting for the executive coach to imagine that these issues are confined to people's 'personal' lives, as if they cease to be persons when they arrive at the office. We know that many people are unhappy in the workplace, and there can be dark shadows in organisations. In one tragic example, between January 2008 and April 2011, more than 60 employees at France Télécom ended their own lives, several blaming stress and unhappiness at work. Sadly, another wave of similar deaths followed in early 2014. Wherever coaches are at work, part of the task of supervision is to ask into the shadows. What happens if we begin by rooting our coaching and our supervision first and foremost not in models or goals but in a shared humanity?

The American psychologist Carl Rogers, the founder of person-centred psychotherapy, reflected, "I realise there's something I do before I start a session. I let myself know that I am enough. Not perfect. Perfect wouldn't be enough. But that I am human, and that is enough" (Remen, 1989, p. 93). Perhaps our most vital gift, as coaches and supervisors, is our humanity, how we share this, how we meet it in others.

We need labels to sort and order the world of our experience, and they are a necessary shorthand, but we limit ourselves, our clients and the work if we imagine that the labels adequately describe what is there. If we focus only on those aspects of a person's experience that we categorise as positive, what happens to the rest, and the energy and wisdom it contains? How would it be if in our coaching and our supervision of coaching we could hold beauty and pain, failure and celebration, dismissing nothing, free to embrace both the fragility and the fire in human experience?

A fear of the dark

Coaching, for good reasons and with good intentions, has focussed on success. It is goal-oriented; it is about moving people forward, and organisations paying for coaching will usually want to see results they can measure. This practical forward focus is worth celebrating and extending into every area where it might help people to become more effective. However, where this focus has become exclusive it has shaped a paradigm for coaching that may discount other aspects of human experience or relegate them to the margins. Within the coaching tradition there can sometimes be an aversion to contemplating pain or failure. One of the great insights of the most enduring spiritual traditions is that they understand pain and suffering as an inescapable aspect of human existence, and the question becomes not how we avoid them but how we respond to them.

There has been some misunderstanding of positive psychology and its implications. Martin Seligman, one of the leading figures in the field, describes in his book *Authentic Happiness* the moment when he took a new direction in both his parenting and his work as a psychologist. Gardening with his five-year-old daughter, and not appreciating her anarchic approach to weeding, he yelled at her, only to have her suggest to him that if she could stop whining then he could stop grouching. Seligman had what he calls an epiphany: "Raising children, I now knew, was far more than just fixing what was wrong with them. It was about identifying and amplifying their strengths and virtues" (Seligman, 2003, p. 28). Seligman challenges both a grouching victim mindset and a preoccupation with fixing what is wrong rather than studying the qualities that can carry a person forward, and he places a clear emphasis on 'strengths and virtues.' Our strengths and virtues and possibilities do not only exist in the light, but find their roots and meaning in the shadows, and it is here that they are shaped and tested.

If we explore the dark focussed on the light that we imagine we carry we will be blind to much of what is in the darkness. If we go with an anxious need to fix or change or even eradicate the shadows, we will miss the person half-hidden there. The acceptance of the shadows is not about rescuing or correcting what is there but acknowledging it and letting emerge what wants to emerge. There can be riches in the shadows. Where there is pain or despair there is longing, and where there is longing, or any strong emotion, there will be energy. There may also be wisdom, insight, learning and other gifts. If we ignore the shadows we miss not only human reality but also human potential. When in coaching and supervision we are open to the whole of the other person, including their grief, suffering and shame, more becomes possible, because we are allowing so much more of the other person into the shared space.

The oft-repeated instruction to coaches to focus on the positive is rooted in the fundamental and hugely practical insight that we tend to move towards the thing we focus on – if I tell myself not to drop the ball I remain likely to drop it; if I tell myself to catch the ball I become much more likely to catch it. And yet if this focus becomes too relentless or too exclusive the coach may miss vital aspects of the client's experience. We can dismiss huge areas of life, and in doing so we impoverish our clients, we impoverish ourselves and we impoverish our work, reducing its relevance and thus its value.

One of the key differences between coaches who can work at a deep level and those who struggle to do this consistently is the capacity to engage with all of the client's reality, even if some of it is painful or challenging, without getting pulled in and without needing to rescue. The supervisor plays an important role here, and it takes in all three of the key functions of supervision – the management of what is actually happening in the coaching, the support of the coach in relating to their own shadows and their coachee's shadows and the development of their understanding and practical wisdom in coaching people who may be in some way hurting.

The journey for both coachee and coach is often about changing our relationship with the shadows – from being a rescuer to being responsive, from being a persecutor to being potent, from being a victim to being vulnerable, and thus creative. It is rare to find much creativity where there is no vulnerability, and it is in responding to the shadows that we can make one of our most fundamental contributions as supervisors – to support the coach's courage to stay long enough with what is, without needing to categorise it, trusting themselves and their coachee to create from what is there.

A coach brings to me a session with a coachee who is facing huge challenges in her workplace and is clearly suffering in the experience, mentally, emotionally and also physically. The client is strong, not reacting as a victim, but taking full ownership of her situation with great courage. With great warmth and care the coach is keeping a relentless focus on what she sees as positive possibilities, asking forward-moving questions. The client is going with her but not with all her energy. Looking at this from the perspective of supervision, and with the great advantage of having a recording of one of the coaching sessions, I notice that the coachee is continuing to refer to how hard the experience is, until this is acknowledged by the coach. There is good trust and rapport, and the coachee wants the coach to go with her on her journey. The coachee seems to have the resources she needs, and it is also clear that this situation she is in is very painful and taking its toll. She needs the coach to acknowledge both, allowing all of her reality into the coaching. Until the coach is able to do this, allowing all of the coachee into the work, she is not going to bring all of her energy to the new possibilities. Once the coach is able to let go of a fear of the dark and emotions she might label as 'negative,' her paradigm of exclusive positive focus and the associated filters, the coachee is able to bring all of herself to the work.

A fear of the light

We push parts of our lives and ourselves into the shadows. We live in a society with a high incidence of emotional ill health. It is probably not unconnected that we also live in a highly individualised consumerist society that holds up near-impossible ideals and dreams for personal achievement, appearance and relationships. In such a society there is inevitably a strong under-current of shame, a deeply held sense of personal and professional inadequacy. It is possible that coaching is as much a symptom of this culture as a solution. Moreover, coaching, with its emphasis on achieving goals and realising dreams, may unwittingly collude with and reinforce this sense of shame. No coach ever wants to reinforce shame, but this may happen in two ways – firstly, if coaching is over-focussed on achieving goals this can hook into the coachee's sense that where and who I am are not good enough, I need to be somewhere and someone different; secondly, if the coaching process avoids what lies in the shadows, this can strengthen the feeling that what is in the shadows is somehow unacceptable and needs to be kept out of sight.

When I began coaching I sometimes felt both curious and intimidated in meeting other coaches, because very few of them seemed ever to fail. I remember speaking with one coach who had enjoyed a stellar business career and insisted that in his experience coaching was always relevant and always effective, and he had never done any coaching work which had not been transformational for his clients. It is possible that I am a poor coach, but as I reflected, I became aware of three things – firstly, the possibility that as coaches we might be filtering our experience; secondly, the need for us to be aware of our own shadows; and thirdly, and perhaps most significantly, the shame I felt in front of other coaches because I did not have a shining corporate CV.

Our reluctance to admit or explore what lies in the dark can cause us to shy away from the light, and we hide our own story, our own reality, our own life and what it might offer. There may of course be other, very understandable, reasons for this – in a competitive market coaches feel they have to 'sell' themselves, and so we edit our stories through a filter of success. I know that for some years I hid the fact that I had spent several years disabled and on benefits, afraid that other people in the coaching industry would look down on me and I would get less work. In doing so, I left part of myself behind.

As supervisors of coaches, we need to be aware of and sensitive to how shame may come into the story of the coachee or the coach, our supervisee. If the coach comes from a paradigm that has little time for failure or any thinking which is not seen as positive, where will they take their failures and their struggles? If they are wanting to earn a living and expand their business in a highly competitive market, of which we may also be a part, how reticent might they be to speak of when coaching does not work?

In my early days as a supervisor, a coach brings to one of his first sessions a situation that troubles him, where he thinks there might be a conflict of interest in some executive coaching work he is doing. The issue is complex, but as we discuss it, it becomes clear that there is a significant tension; there are serious ethical concerns and some real risks, not least to the value of the work. I ask the coach what he thinks, and he says he can see a clear conflict of interest, but he is going to continue because he needs the income, and he needs this money because of a family situation that is both painful and precarious. I wonder whether the coach possibly knew before supervision both that there is an ethical issue and that he is going to go ahead anyway, if perhaps he is wanting me to tell him there is no problem and give him permission. What troubles me as a supervisor is that in focussing too quickly on the presenting question and not seeing the pain and anxiety hidden in the shadows, we have perhaps missed the heart of the matter. I wonder if shame has played some part in this, and I wonder how I might have handled this differently.

I take away three questions:

- *How much of my supervisee and their life needs to come into the supervision session in order for us to do the work we need to do?*
- *What is needed in the supervisory relationship so that shame does not stop us doing this work?*
- *What is in the shadows, and how do we bring it into the light in a way that feels safe?*

Being with

Carl Rogers argued that every human being has an innate desire to learn and grow and will do so when another person can be with them and offer three things:

- Congruence (being fully oneself and fully genuine);
- Unconditional positive regard (complete acceptance); and
- Accurate empathic understanding.

The word 'compassion' has been sadly misused, cheapened and reduced to a fraction of its true meaning. Compassion is something far more radical than a kind gesture or a sympathetic feeling. Coming from the Latin *cum* (with) and *patior* (to suffer), it means to suffer with another person. We need also to revisit the word 'suffer,' which in its original meaning was not associated only with pain but meant to experience or go through something – the French verb *passer*, also deriving from the Latin *patior*, means 'to happen.' So, compassion means to be with someone in what is happening to them. It does not in itself mean fixing people, yet it is an honest being with the other in their experience that facilitates a process of change, and a possibility of healing.

After the death of my brother, there was one response which brought me more strength than any other. I was speaking on the phone with a friend from university, and she said simply, "It's f★★★★ing hard." It was the only time I had heard her use such language, and yet it was entirely appropriate; I needed extreme language to honour my experience. The simple recognition and empathy contained in those words gave me strength. Two years later, when I was very ill, suffering a relapse and in severe pain, another friend took both my hands, looked into my eyes and said, "I don't know how you carry on." It was spoken with great tenderness and profound respect.

There was no rescuing, no wise question, no answers, no model or technique, but these few words did more to nurture my courage in these periods than anything else. They were in no way focussed on the positive, and yet somehow they were affirming and profoundly positive; they were not forward-looking, yet they allowed me to go forward. This was not psychotherapy, yet it was actively therapeutic. It was not coaching, yet it helped me find my own resources.

It is important to grasp what Rogers means by 'understanding' – it is not an analytic knowing and having answers, rather it is a deep hearing of what is there. Part of the compassion of the comments made to me is that neither pretended to understand, yet both reflected back in utter honesty and simplicity what they felt as they touched what I was going through. The second comment was explicit in its not knowing. We may never absolutely understand the experience of another human being, and when we think we do we are probably projecting or transferring something from our own life, thoughts or emotions, but we can hear what is there, and in this deep hearing we move to accompany them in what matters to them.

This is not about adopting special language; it is about being with a human being. I have in supervision used the words 'It's hard' when listening to a person's story because it describes something hard for the person concerned. In letting the human being in front of me feel seen and heard in their experience, I respect, value and honour them and their story, trusting and inviting them to find in themselves the resources and wisdom they need.

If the supervisor can stay with the coach in their experience and help the coach to be with themselves, they can in turn support the coachee in being with themselves. I know from my early over-zealous beginnings and mistakes as a supervisor that I am little use when I slip into trying too hard to answer the question or fix the issue, without being with my supervisee in being with their coachee.

Part of this is holding contradictions. We often recoil into confusion when faced with a contradiction when what we can most usefully do is stay there. I sometimes hear coaches troubled by contradictions in their clients, but I am curious as soon as a contradiction appears, because where there is a contradiction there is something interesting, and at the meeting point of the most potent contradictions there is often a vital energy that can be unlocked.

Before becoming a coach, I was, among other things, a poet. I sometimes see coaching at its best as a form of poetry – as with poetry its raw material is human experience and human utterance. Poetry, like all art, has no fear of the dark. It exists in the tension between the light and the dark, offering us either beauty or a way of responding to a world where beauty and joy, love and justice, and the things we long for are alive yet hard to find. Poetry, art, film and music all use imagery, metaphor and story to engage with the contradictions of human experience and in doing so reconfigure it, bringing new perspective. Supervision means seeing from a higher point, and as supervisors we can both learn from and work with the way art forms play with and reconfigure reality, allowing us and our supervisees to be with what is there and see it in new ways.

I sometimes wonder if we might perhaps bring more perspective to our coaching and supervision if we read more great literature, more poetry, listened to music that connects us to the life in us and around us. Writing this I have been listening to Sibelius' Fifth Symphony, and the opening of its third movement describing swans taking off from a lake; and Stormzy's urban grime, with its wit and fury, his yearning, his spiky masculine hunger and also his sense of grace. Both of them change how I see the world.

Being with another person in their life is not a soft option. Compassion does not rescue people from reality or responsibility. Contradiction can involve conflict, our stories can raise truths we would rather not face and the reconfiguring of our world can be a fierce and painful process. Supervision needs to be both tender and fearless, agile and at moments sharp. Sometimes the most compassionate action is the question or challenge that cuts to the reality that is there. The courage to be with what is there allows it to be both faced and reconfigured.

Here the work of supervision connects with the essence of coaching – to be with the person, not to protect them from reality but to facilitate a creative interaction with it that opens up learning, growth and possibility. We stand with what is real, we stand with the person entrusted to us and we do both at the same time, so that they can do both.

I am supervising a coach whom I have been working with for some time. I have a profound respect for the personal and professional integrity she brings to her work. She reports feeling flat after a coaching session with a coachee whose partner has been diagnosed with an aggressive form of cancer. The coachee herself has returned to work after a break of more than ten years, facing the question as to how she can continue working while giving her partner and children the support they need. Her organisation is very keen for her to stay, and she is keen to do so. She wants to focus the coaching on how to negotiate the terms of this with her employer without bringing into the coaching her partner's illness or her feelings around this. After several minutes listening and discussing, I reframe what I have heard: "So she seems to be saying 'Let's talk about life without emotion and without pain'"; and the coach responds: "Yes, and I came away from that session feeling empty . . . because that's not living." I am interested in what is happening in the coach, in the coachee and in their work together. One approach would be to see this as a simple question of staying with the coachee's agenda and ignoring what she does not want to talk about. Another approach, perhaps more readily associated with some forms of psychotherapy, would be to focus on exploring the pain and the emotion. I suggest a third way – to name the cancer, to invite the coachee to name her emotions, and let her decide where she wants to go. This approach acknowledges what is there, darkness and light; it offers her a broader map of her landscape, includes more of her reality and leaves the power and freedom with her.

Richer goals

When working in the shadows we need to take particular care around the shaping and pursuit of goals. Goals, like positive focus, have been an axiom of coaching, and the supervision of coaching, although less goal-focussed, supports a process that is overwhelmingly concerned with achieving objectives. As human beings we orient ourselves in relationship to what is important to us, our values and our aspirations. We set objectives as a way of motivating and directing ourselves in our life and work and gauging where we are, and it can be very difficult to create and complete a meaningful journey without these markers. And yet, as a coach, a supervisor and a human being, I increasingly find myself questioning the ways in which people choose, define and shape these objectives and some of the frameworks offered for doing this.

People's goals are commonly rooted in either an internal narrative or an external expectation but do not always bring the two together with sufficient depth of exploration. In some cases the internal narrative has become distorted, while the external expectations have become disconnected from a reality that truly works for people. In others the internal narrative and external expectation have combined in a toxic mix, with our pursuit of objectives connected to our shame, our sense of inadequacy, our fear of failure. There is often a sense that we are not quite where we should be, and we feel the pressure of a need or expectation to be somewhere else. We can easily end up pursuing outcomes that do not truly reflect who we are or the realities in which we find ourselves. We can be overwhelmed by our goals, and we can clutch at them too desperately. We need a greater wisdom in how we approach the process of making the changes important to us, while at the same time nurturing and protecting what we do not need to change.

I notice that coaches are sometimes more focussed on outcomes and more anxious about achieving them than the coachee. We should perhaps not be surprised at this. The coach may be judged on the apparent success of the coaching, and the success of their business may depend on this. Organisations want to know they are achieving something through their spending on coaching, typically something that will benefit them financially, and there is a never-ending quest for ways to demonstrate return on investment. Moreover, coaching is what the coach does, usually their primary work, whereas coaching is not usually the primary focus of the coachee. While it is the coachee who is responsible for their results and the greatest investment must come from them, the coach can sometimes feel they have more to lose if objectives are not met. If as a supervisor I can help the coach accept and explore their own relationship with outcomes, and how this is playing out in coaching, this frees them to explore the coachee's relationship with their own objectives.

One of the possibilities that emerges out of a reappraisal of goals is that we are ultimately more motivated or inspired by our sense of identity and our story than we are by objectives that can feel external to us. Rightly or wrongly, people may be more driven by a sense of who they are than what they seek to achieve. If this is true, coaches can hold back from seeking or pushing goals too early in the process, and coach the person rather than the objective. This will be particularly important when working with people in dark places. We embrace the desire for change, and we let the goals emerge from the person and what is important to them, who they are and the story they have to tell.

The need to root coaching goals in the coachee's story has been feeding into coaching with an increasing focus on a coachee's purpose in life and work as part of the coaching. This is important work, yet we need to go gently here, because many people will struggle to conjure a bright, shining, compelling 'elevator speech' of a purpose, and perhaps they do not need to. The reality of human lives is that for many people, including some who may have been very successful in material terms, their purpose amounts to a few fragments, wrapped in a dirty cloth and carried at the bottom of a bag – it is not complete, it does not shine and it is kept hidden, but it is theirs, and it has meaning. If coaching believes in human potential it needs to have something to offer to the person whose sense of purpose in this life, beyond survival or the next step on the career ladder, at the moment barely exists, but whose story and identity as a human being are by definition as rich as any.

The coach's work becomes a work of hearing the human being, helping them to connect with what is important to them and how this finds a place in what they do. My work as a supervisor is to stand alongside, hearing the coach and what is important to them in their work, and at the same time looking and listening with the coach to the coachee. What is their story? What are we noticing here about this person and what matters to them? Where have they come from, and where might they be going? What is the work they need to do now? At its best, this is a work of love.

A coach comes to supervision, concerned and baffled as to why a coachee, a senior executive who is self-aware, focussed and diligent in coaching, seems to be making no progress. Goals for coaching were agreed with the organisational sponsor at the beginning of the coaching, and the coachee is fundamentally in agreement with these goals. We spend some time exploring tools, models and frameworks, several of which the coach has already tried. I ask into the dynamics of the coaching relationship, and there seems to be no issue here. I go with an intuition and I ask, "What is happening at home?" The coach is silent a moment; he has no evidence he can recall, but he thinks this is worth exploring. At the next session he puts the question to his coachee, who opens up about the disintegration of his marriage, and from this point the coaching shifts. The coaching does not become coaching on his marriage; the primary focus remains his professional goals, which he adjusts, but in ending the separation of goals and story, reaching into the shadows and beginning to connect his goals to who he is, his story, what matters to him and what is important in the reality in which he finds himself, these goals can connect to his life.

In the woods near the border

Working in the shadows involves seeing what is there as part of human reality, without the need to fix and heal the pain we find, and yet working in this territory raises the question of the boundary between coaching and psychotherapy. More research and reflection are needed to explore this area, combined with an ongoing conversation between the different disciplines. At present it seems that while there are significant differences between coaching and therapy the exact boundary is porous, not clearly defined and not always easy to identify with absolute clarity. It feels like an unmarked border between two neighbouring countries – we may recognise the other country when we find ourselves in it, but the border line itself is not always clear. Sometimes we find ourselves in the woods that straddle that frontier, knowing we may be near the line yet unsure where exactly it runs. In the woods staying safe is as important as knowing where we are. If we search too hard for the border instead of looking where we are going, we may stumble. We must keep looking at the person we are with and the ground beneath our feet, while using our wider awareness to make sense of which country we are in and which way we need to turn.

Coaches will be working with people with mental health issues. In the UK 43% of adults report experiencing a diagnosable mental health issue at some point in their life, while according to the World Health Organisation, even in the most developed countries 35–50% of people with severe mental health problems receive no treatment (Mental Health Foundation, 2016). Most paid coaching happens in the workplace, and here 60% of UK employees have experienced a mental health problem in which work was a contributing factor, 31% were formally diagnosed but only 11% have discussed such problems with a line manager (Business in the Community, 2017). It seems likely that mental health issues are still under-reported, particularly in organisations. These statistics not only reinforce the importance of professional supervision for coaches but show the simple reality that supervisors will be supporting coaches working with people with mental health issues, whether declared or not. It is also highly likely that the coach will not be fully aware, particularly in the case of high-functioning executives who may be very adept at masking their struggles.

My experience as coach and supervisor suggests that growing numbers of people who may in the past have gone to a therapist are now seeking coaching, perhaps because it is seen as more aspirational. I have had several supervisees report coachees saying that they came to coaching instead of going to a therapist. In these coaching relationships there seem to be four main possibilities:

1   Coaching offers a supportive stepping-stone into therapy;
2   Coaching happens alongside therapy and with a distinct focus;
3   Coaching continues effectively, and there is no need for therapy; or
4   The coachee does not want or cannot find therapy, but the coach feels unable to continue, and coaching ends.

If I sense or hear my supervisee is working with a coachee in a very dark place or in an area where therapy may be more appropriate there are four elements to my response:

1   Ask the coach to look at the reality without diagnosing or pathologising, letting it be what it is. I sometimes use the metaphor of a physical illness – imagine you think they have broken their leg: What do you know? What

are you aware of? What is your role now? What do you need? When do you call for help?

2   Check the coach's state and resources, inviting the coach to diagnose themselves, not the coachee – What are you feeling? Where are you in relation to the limits of your experience, expertise, competence and resources? At what point do you need to refer on to a professional with specialist skills?

3   Encourage the coach to stay with what they are noticing in the coachee and use their coaching skills to generate awareness and help the coachee to make any decision they need to make for their own well-being. It is essential the coach does this without either rushing to pass the coachee to a therapist or engaging in amateur psychotherapy – the first can leave the coachee feeling rejected and dangerously isolated, and the second can be extremely risky.

4   Check what I am hearing and sensing, and support, challenge, warn or direct as needed, until the coach is sufficiently clear how to respond, and also taking this to my own supervisor.

I am speaking with my own supervisor about a coachee. I am in the woods, it is dark and I cannot see the edge. I work with the metaphor; with her help and the questions she asks I can find myself in the moment and look around me – what kind of tree is this? What do I see? What do I need? Which way do I go? I do not let go of my care, but I let go of my fear, I begin to see shapes in the dark, I check where help is available and I see a path through the trees.

The gift of imperfect lives

In his poem 'Damaged' the Scottish poet Donald Adamson reminds us that our wounds and our growth can be part of the same gift:

There's not a single tree in the wood
that isn't damaged.
Yet they grow tall and old
and when at last they fall they are noticed
not by their malformations
but by their absence, sudden blue
astonishments of sky.

Being is its own achieving.
The fabric of things
mends in spans accomplished and the joy
of particular wounds. Do not ask to be cured
nor pass your parcels of injuries
to others. You were damaged, let yourself
be changed, and grow, and live.

(Donald Adamson, 2002, reproduced with permission)

For many people, including many coaches, the word 'damaged' is highly provocative, and this is perhaps intended. The former version of the Code of Ethics of the International Coach Federation stated that the coachee is "creative, resourceful and whole." Part of the challenge for coaches and supervisors is to find their own way of living and working with the recognition that we can be both wounded and whole, confused and resourceful. As long as we can hold this awareness with wisdom and compassion and without passing our injuries to others, we can do work of great meaning. My job as a supervisor is firstly to do this in myself, and secondly to support it in my supervisees.

Adamson's poem comes from a collection he titled *The Gift of Imperfect Lives*. For a coach and a supervisor an imperfect life is perhaps the richest and most potent gift I work with, and if I work too hard with anything else I may be missing the point.

Something opens in us when we can look at more than goals and beyond the visions of success and meet with what is in people's experience. We ourselves become open to those areas of life that do not fit easily into a neat paradigm of achievement, and we become sensitive to the injustice and hurt around us and the longing and energy held within these situations. Our asking into the shadows can challenge some of our misplaced priorities and allow us to connect anew with our own and others' humanity.

What happens when we, as coaches and supervisors, come as ourselves, with open eyes and open heart and open mind, knowing our limitations, yet being more human than perfect? What happens when we meet another life, and enjoy the person not the problem, being with them in their experience without avoiding and without rescuing? Perhaps we can move into a paradigm that is about one human being meeting with another human being, and seeing and hearing and feeling and touching what is real, what is felt, and all that is possible when human beings connect with their experience and what is important to them. We will not meet every need, and at the same time we may find that some of our truest, most honest and most creative work begins in the dark.

Bibliography

Adamson, D. (2002). 'Damaged' from *The Gift of Imperfect Lives*, Kirkcudbright: Markings Publications.

Business in the Community, Mental Health at Work Report. (2017). *London: Business in the Community*. Available at https://wellbeing.bitc.org.uk/all-resources/research-articles/mental-health-work-report-2017 (Accessed 30 March 2018).

Choy, A. (1990). The Winner's Triangle. *Transactional Analysis Journal*, 20, 40–46.

David, S., Clutterbuck, D. and Megginson, D. (2013). *Beyond Goals: Effective Strategies for Coaching and Mentoring*. Aldershot: Gower.

Hart, V., Blattner, J. and Leipsic, S. (2001). Coaching Versus Therapy: A Perspective. *Consulting Psychology Journal: Practice and Research*, 53, 229–237.

Mental Health Foundation, Fundamental Facts about Mental Health. (2016). *London: Mental Health Foundation*. Available at www.mentalhealth.org.uk/publications/fundamental-facts-about-mental-health-2016 (Accessed 30 March 2018).

Peltier, B. (2010). *The Psychology of Executive Coaching*. Hove: Routledge.

Remen, R. N. (1989). The Search for Healing. In Carlson, R. and Shield, B. (eds), *Healers on Healing*. Los Angeles: Tarcher.

Rogers, C. (1967). *On Becoming a Person*. London: Constable.

Seligman, M. (2003). *Authentic Happiness*. London: Nicholas Brealey.

Discography

Byrd, B. and Nelson, E. (1963). 'Harlem Shuffle' (sound recording) performed by Bob and Earl. Los Angeles: Marc Records.

Sibelius, J. (2002). *Symphony No. 5 in E Flat* (sound recording) performed by the Gothenburg Symphony Orchestra conducted by Neeme Järvi. Berlin: Deutsche Grammophon.

Stormzy. (2017). *Gang Signs and Prayer* (CD). London: Merky Records.

Vaughan Williams, R. (1963). *Fantasia on a Theme by Thomas Tallis* (sound recording) performed by the London Sinfonia conducted by Sir John Barbirolli. London: Decca.

6 A new dimension? Using observational data creatively in supervision

Kathryn M Downing

An invitation
To experiment, and explore by
Asking others to sit with you
And observe your coaching
With kindness, appreciation, grace
Honesty, integrity and challenge.

Introduction

Reflective practice is at the heart of our continued development as coaches and supervisors. The purpose of the chapter is to stimulate consideration of occasional use of audio or video recordings in coaching supervision to formulate deeper reflective practices and increase coaching capabilities. Three methods of using recordings are explored: using a video that prompts reflection unrelated to a specific coaching session; using a video of a coaching session in which the coach is not part of the virtual supervision group; and using audio or video recordings of coaching by one of the coaches in the virtual supervision group. Any one or combination of these may be explored creatively in supervision.

I invite you to consider case studies and my own experiences using recordings as a supervisee and as a supervisor in the hopes of tickling your curiosity about the potential of utilising recordings for ongoing professional development. These cases suggest opportunities for developing greater self-awareness; seeing yourself from different perspectives; and with new insight, reflecting on how you might want to integrate the new awareness.

If you observed yourself in-the-moment utilising a recording, what more might you see, discover or learn? What if you invited others to observe recordings of your actual coaching? As R D Laing observes – we are "limited by what we fail to notice" (Seymour, Crain and Crockett, 1993, p. 53). Perhaps it's possible that recordings will provide an opportunity for you to notice something new.

Through the cases, we will look at creatively using recordings within the supervision session; the vulnerability, courage and openness required for exposing our work to observation; and how our willingness to use recordings is influenced by a number of factors, including our relationships with our supervisor, other group members and our clients, as well as our developmental maturity and experiences with feedback. Reflection questions follow each of the case studies and include the perspectives of supervisees and supervisors.

Why I extend this invitation to you

I am enthusiastic about using observational data, including recordings, for reflective practices and for continuing to develop professionally and personally. As a doctoral candidate at Middlesex University (London), I have research underway on the use of observational data, including recordings, in virtual group supervision. The early experiences of the research participants are widely variable and raise a number of fascinating questions. I interweave elements of the research into the case studies in this chapter.

I developed, early on, a deep desire for feedback to fuel my learning and development. In my coach certification programme, I found the reviews of recorded coaching sessions with mentor coaches to be pivotal points in my learning. As a practicing executive coach and coach supervisor, I have continued mining recordings. In my own practices as a supervisee I routinely bring parts recordings to my supervisors. As a supervisor, I have used recordings with small groups.

As you consider the offerings and examples I share, I encourage you to sit back and reflect on what you see and feel, what resistance is stirred, what curiosity comes forward and what you notice that might contribute to your growth and development. One of the joys of supervision is it offers a space that is designed around adult learning principles (Knowles, Holton and Swanson, 2015). The elements of adult learning include being driven and designed by the adult, based on what is important and meaningful to them, and using experiential learning in the context of one's professional development. Applying these principles in the supervision context, a supervision process that is co-created among the supervisees and supervisor is ideal.

I am not advocating that recordings are essential, nor that they would be useful for every person or every coaching case. My stance, too, is invitational – inviting you to consider in what circumstances you might be drawn to experiment with or embrace their use. I describe possible processes for bringing recordings into supervision, and ask, how would you design a process that works for you?

Bringing your work to coaching supervision

> *The range of what we think and do is limited by what we fail to notice. And because we fail to notice that we fail to notice, there is little we can do to change; until we notice how failing to notice shapes our thoughts and deeds.*
>
> R. D. Laing's quote in Seymour et al. (1993)

There are a number of ways to bring your work to supervision; overwhelmingly the preferred method is people talking about their coaching cases and relating what happened (Bird, Reilly, Wiggins, De Haan and Atter, 2014). This use of narrative, telling the story, can be in-the-moment during the supervision session, the coach sharing extemporaneously (de Haan, 2012) and trusting that learning will occur. The coach may also prepare for the session by reviewing their current clients and bringing forth a case, theme, pattern, concern or success to share, and, with one additional step, the coach may write up a brief of the case and share it in advance, using the write-up and their story in the session (Hodge, 2016, pp. 101–102). Hodge found the coach's preparation for the session, the actual session and the coach's reflections afterward enhance learning in coaching supervision. These narratives are shaped by what we remember, what we noticed, how we want to be seen and our self-awareness (Hay, 2007).

Another approach is one of emergence, trusting that what comes up in the session is just what needs to be there. For those who trust emergence, coming to supervision without a specific theme, case or situation on their mind, and accepting what emerges in the moment with their supervisor can result in learning (de Haan, 2012).

Alternatively, the coach may take time immediately following a coaching session to write down everything she remembers about the interactions between herself[1] and the client. This approximate transcript can be used as the basis for exploring the session (Ibid., pp. 91–92). Or the notes could be used to refresh the coach's memory before engaging in telling the story in supervision.

Storytelling approaches have advantages for the coach. We are biologically hardwired for stories. "Meaning making is in our biology and our default is often to come up with a story that makes sense, feels familiar, and offers us insight into how best to self-protect" (Brown, 2015). Telling our stories gives us greater control to select what we share and what we omit, and we are able to eliminate details to protect the confidentiality of the client and any facts or feelings that we find embarrassing or shameful. We can position ourselves in our stories as we prefer. For example, I have noticed in supervision that the act of sharing a story, in and of itself, becomes a tool for raising awareness about our biases and assumptions about the client's words or behaviour (Patterson, Grenny, Mcmillan and Switzler, 2002).

We know that we are inclined to view stories based on our own views and experiences. Karr (2015) is an author and memoirist who teaches about the writing of memoir. She recounts an exercise in her graduate classes where she stages a fight with a colleague and then asks the students to write about what happened. Each of the students writes their version of what happened, each from their own lens, background, beliefs and experiences, and their versions differ remarkably from each other. A month later their memories vary even more.

If we consider the limitations to storytelling, might they stir our curiosity to explore additional ways to learn about ourselves? Dunning (2005) found a number of patterns in his research on self-insight. How we experience situations and interactions is viewed through our own worldviews and framed only by our awareness of what is going on. Self-insight is difficult to come by accurately. We are unaware of many aspects of who and how we are in the world and often misjudge or misinterpret our capabilities and impact on others. Perhaps surprisingly, it is especially hard to evaluate our own competency, especially when we are less skilled. "What others see in us also tends to be more highly correlated with objective outcomes than what we see in ourselves" (Ibid., p. 5). Our inner critic and threads of perfectionism can cause us to view ourselves more harshly, and fear of judgment can drive us, consciously or not, into nondisclosures (Brown, 2012) as well as "confabulations – lies, honestly told" (Gottschall, 2012, p. 110).

This raises interesting questions about what is in our stories, as well as what is missing from them. There are a number of factors that influence what one is willing to share in supervision. A selection of these factors with reflection questions are included at the end of the case illustrations.

Observational data is sometimes used in supervision and includes bringing a recording, a transcript of the recording or both (Sheppard, 2017), or through direct observation by the supervisor during a live coaching session (Hawkins and Smith, 2013). Using recordings in coaching supervision has been described as the "gold standard of preparation" (Clutterbuck, Whitaker and Lucas, 2016), and as providing a "contrast and compare" opportunity between the actual verbal and non-verbal information in the recording, and the coach's experience (de Haan, 2012, pp. 91–92). Rogers has encouraged us to bring our actual coaching to supervision, saying, "[c]oach supervision only goes so far because essentially it is two people talking about work one has done when the other was not present. It depends critically on extraordinary levels of self-awareness and candor on both sides" (Rogers, 2011, p. 343).

Bird and her colleagues (2014, pp. 25–26) explored the use of audio recordings in one-to-one supervision, noting the following benefits:

1   An opportunity for the coach to discover or recognise feelings that may have been stirring for him or her in the session;
2   A shift in the working alliance between the supervisor and coach that was a "more collaborative, shared endeavor";
3   Recognition of patterns including energetically what was happening in the session; and
4   An opportunity to fully observe from the balcony what was happening in the session.

The use of recordings may raise vulnerability and fear of judgment to a greater extent than storytelling. Coaches have shared with me a variety of reactions to recordings. For example, having recorded, some could not bring themselves to watch or listen. In other instances, the coach watched, and noticed that her inner critic was front and centre and she hated her voice and mannerisms. In that circumstance when a coach could bring themselves to view it a second time they found it was more possible to actually observe what happened in the session. Some coaches ultimately concluded it would be inappropriate to ask their client to record because of awareness of the client's organisational setting, sensitivity to the content of the coaching, fear of impacting the relationship with the client or disclosing that the coach is in 'supervision.' Still others had clients whom they were comfortable asking for permission to record; they recorded sessions, listened and observed themselves, and then shared part or all of the recording in group supervision.

Hay (2007, p. 7) shares her reactions to listening to tape recordings of her work as a transactional analyst:

> I quickly saw the benefit of the process even though I had to steel myself to play the tapes to colleagues and my supervisor. I spent a lot of time noticing with horror how many significant aspects of the interaction with the client I'd missed. I was often shocked to realize that I had completed [sic] missed something the client had said, or I had failed to pick up at the time the tone the client used . . . I persevered and gradually learned to accept these insights and improve my competence for the future instead of beating myself up over my perceived inadequacies.

For coaches who are feeling reluctance in bringing a recording to supervision, perhaps the approach of recording a coaching session only for one's own learning and reflection is worthy of trying. Hay (2007, p. 8) describes using recordings to inform supervision in this way. The coach listens to the recording, noticing what might have been outside of his or her awareness. The coach may identify a pattern present in the interactions with this client. That pattern may also show up as the coach listens to other recordings. Having recognised a pattern either with this client or more broadly, the pattern becomes the exploration in supervision. Thus, the recording, although not brought literally into the supervision session, informs the coach's self-awareness.

Table 6.1 features reflection questions for you.

There is another possibility beyond self-recording. I invite my groups to use video recordings found online. This practice developed from my curiosity of how to balance four observations:

- Exploring ways to create safety with the use of recordings – where the stakes, for some coaches, might be lower risk than self-recording;
- Exploring opportunities for supervisees to strengthen their abilities to observe themselves in the moment;
- Developing an approach with recordings that is consistent with reflective practice as distinct from using recordings for competency assessments; and
- Using recordings as fun and playful learning elements.

Table 6.1 Reflection Questions about Recordings

Potential key factors	Reflection questions for supervisees	Reflection questions for supervisors
Client's willingness to be recorded	★Do you have a client who might be willing to be recorded? ★How might you explore this with a client? ★What assurances would you give the client? ★How would you explain the reason for your desire to record? ★Would you share with the client this is for your continuing professional development? ★How might you or the client modify their behaviour in the session if it was recorded?	★Having reviewed the recording, what do you notice in yourself as you consider the coach? ★If the coach records the client and reviews the recording as part of their preparation for the supervision session, would you want them to share with you that they had used this approach? ★What curiosities arise for you if you notice a difference between the coach's memory of the session, and the things they notice when reviewing the recording? How might you handle this with the supervisee? ★What curiosities arise for you about recording one of your supervision sessions and reviewing it either by yourself or with your supervisor? ★What expectations or principles do you have about seeking permission from a client?
Asking the client for permission to record to inform your reflections	★Would you ask verbally or provide a written Permission to Record document? ★What provisions would you make for the client revoking their permission, e.g. in the session, after the session, at a later date? ★What assurances would you make regarding the deletion of the recording?	★What else is stirring for you?

Method 1: watching the Ruby video – an infant reaching for a toy[2]

This experiment, with ways to introduce the use of recordings and build safety within the group, has been very interesting and not completely as I expected. I was introduced to this concept as an audience member when Guy Claxton, in a key note address,[3] invited the audience to watch a video of Ruby (Jane, 2013), an infant reaching for her toy. He asked us to notice what feelings we experienced as we watched. He invited us to notice if there was any congruence between the feelings that arose while watching Ruby and the feelings that might arise while working with clients. I have used this video with several of my small groups.

My approach has been to ask if the supervisees would be willing to watch the 3.5-minute video of Ruby. The group selects whether to watch it in the session or individually in advance. I invite them to notice their own feelings and stirrings as they watch. We then share our experiences. There is a lovely amount of fun, laughter, learning, lightness and curiosity with which we explore. The coaches notice any number of feelings including their impatience, their wanting to hand the toy to Ruby, their contentment in watching her strive, how she engages her full body as she learns, her lack of frustration and her determination, or the desire to be a cheerleader for her.

When we explored how these feelings show up in us, we identified some of our responses to clients. We identified areas for our potential development, e.g. more noticing of client's body language, or where we are impatient with a client. Other things that were noticed:

- Feeling judgment for not noticing everything and realising how trying to notice everything was really impacting presence in coaching sessions.
- Curiosity about one's level of cheerleading.
- Was goal orientation leading to driving clients?
- Was presence impacted by judging clients' speed of learning?
- Could the joy of watching Ruby learn be felt in watching clients learn?

This process has enabled supervisees to build their ability to observe themselves in the moment, to broaden what they might notice by hearing from their colleagues' noticing and to reflect on what they would like to cultivate in themselves.

There is a need to attend to safety in all supervision sessions. The relationships among the supervisor and supervisees in the group are an essential focus of attention given the multiple dynamics at work (Proctor, 2000): the sense of safety created by the supervisor and group participants; the sense of identity, inner critic and comparison gremlins arising in the coach; and the relationships among the coaches in the group. It is the creation of a safe space that invites supervisees to bring challenges and vulnerability into the session, providing the container for vulnerability.

As described earlier in this chapter, the use of the video of Ruby was free from the concerns of recording or sharing one's own coaching. The use of this kind of video for reflection is perhaps the safest place for most to experiment and build our skills as outlined earlier.

Method 2: using a recording of coaching by a person unknown to the group

I had imagined that using a recording of a part of an actual coaching session where the coach and client were unknown to the members of the supervision group might be a comfortable experience, more aligned with watching Ruby than bringing the coach's actual recording into a session. The group could experience reflecting on a recording without needing to bring their own work forward. You will see this is not a fair conclusion as you read the following cases.

I invited two of my supervision groups to explore the use of recordings by reviewing a YouTube session of a coach working with metaphor (TPC Leadership UK, 2012). Both agreed. One group, Group A, selected a flexible approach to watching the video, having the opportunity to watch in advance, if any member had the time, and to watch as a group in the session. The other group, Group B, selected to watch it individually, in advance.

Each group had its own characteristics, relationships and experiences; the responses of the coaches in the two groups varied.

Case study – Group A – using a segment of a coaching session recorded by a coach unknown to the group and watching it together in the session

In Group A, some of the coaches had watched in advance, and some had not. The coaches were invited to consider these questions: "What came up for you? What did you just notice? And if you watched it in advance, what, if anything, has shifted between then and today?" We watched the recording in the session. The group dynamics did not shift based on who had watched it in advance.

The coaches were curious, explored the process used by the coach on video and shared reflections on their own coaching. For example, one coach noticed:

- The coaching process – that the recorded coach asked his client to pick an image, and then at the end of the session asked her what the image had provided her. She saw this as an opportunity for the client to identify what she had learned.
- Reflections on her own coaching – she loves and uses metaphors, imagery and visuals often with her own clients.

Another coach noticed:

- The coaching process – that the client lit up with some of the coach's questions and seemed to uncover new learning.
- Reflection on his own coaching – he doesn't use metaphor, and the thought of doing so is very intimidating.

Case study – Group B – using a segment of a coaching session recorded by a coach unknown to the group and watching it in advance of the session

The group opted to use the recording by watching it in advance and as a case study. We discussed the recording as the final segment of the supervision session. As we started to explore, judgment, comparison and the inner critic entered immediately. The coaches noticed that they had a lot of judgment about the coaching session. Was it staged? Was it too easy for the client to use the metaphor? They then moved from negative judgment of the coach to judgment of themselves as they acknowledged feelings of inadequacy of their coaching. This led to a rich discussion of judgment of our clients and of our inner critic. The sense of why judgment was so front and centre in the use of this video, and not with the Ruby video, was expressed by one coach as, "put me with coaches, that is so close to what I do and how I serve the world, it feels, the word, threatening is coming up. What if they're so much better and I figure out I really suck at this?" Looking from the balcony at the whole of the supervision session we could see the inner critic and comparison gremlins threading through from the moment we checked in until we concluded.

You may notice that this group has developed a depth of safety between them, and with their supervisor, that they dared to surface fears, inadequacies and the painful voice of their inner critics in service of the group and individual learning. As one coach shared, "What I have learned from supervision is that there is learning in everything. The power in becoming the observer is how it opens up access to choice." Choice, to this coach, means the ability to recognise in the moment how she is feeling and choose how to proceed rather than reacting.

Table 6.2 features reflection questions for you.

Table 6.2 Reflection Questions about Group Dynamics

Potential key factors	Reflection questions for supervisees	Reflection questions for supervisors
Relationships within the supervision group and a sense of safety with colleagues (Proctor, 2000)	★What influences your sense of safety in the group? ★What would you need from your colleagues? ★What explicit contracting would support you regarding how the recording will be debriefed, discussed, shared? ★What are you noticing about your curiosity or about your concerns? How might this influence how you come to supervision?	★What do you notice as you consider the invitation and use of a recording in your supervision practice? ★What explicit contracting would be necessary regarding how the recording will be debriefed, discussed, shared? ★What group dynamics, if any, may need special care?

Method 3: using recordings of our actual coaching

Let's now look at experimenting with the use of recordings of our actual coaching. There are many factors that influence how each of us perceives the levels of risk, anxiety and courage necessary to bring our own work into supervision. Consider:

- Imagining the use of the recordings as a reflective practice, initiated and led by the coach, not an assessment led by the supervisor.[4]
- Impact on our relationship with the client. The relationship between the coach and the client is the most important determinant in the outcome of the coaching engagement (Rogers, 2008).
- Disclosure to clients that we are engaged in our own professional development.
- Performance anxieties and resultant impact on the way we or clients show up.
- Observing ourselves on the video.
- Shame – am I good enough? Will everyone see I am an imposter?
- Comparison and judgment to others in the group.
- Relationship with feedback.

Table 6.3 features reflection questions for you.

Table 6.3 Reflection Questions about Vulnerability

Potential key factors	Reflection questions for supervisees	Reflection questions for supervisors
Vulnerability – ability to be vulnerable and how that was shaped in our family of origin (Brown, 2012)	★What is your relationship with vulnerability ★When you were growing up how did your family view vulnerability? Who in your family, if anyone, openly showed vulnerability? What impact did that have on you?	★What are your beliefs and assumptions about the use of recordings? ★How could you imagine using recordings to inform reflective practice as distinct from a mentoring process? ★What feelings are you noticing?
Self-compassion – how you manage your inner critic, and how you cultivate self-kindness (Neff, 2011)	★What feelings, if any, of comparison and competitiveness do you notice in supervision? ★How do you cultivate self-compassion? ★How do you contextualise where you are on the learning journey towards mastery? ★How do you manage your inner critic?	★What vulnerability and self-compassion issues might you want to explore?

Two case illustrations

1 My own struggles with clients – using partial recordings as supervisee

The first case illustration looks at my own use of a segment of recordings with my supervisors. In the first one I am a coach supervisee. The second case explores the use of a full recording with a group that I was supervising.

Supervision of my coaching

I had entered into a coaching contract with an executive in a corporation who was highly motivated about coaching. Her goal was to learn to modulate her need for control as it was negatively impacting her work and family relationships. We entered the coaching relationship with a warm connection, and both expressed pleasure to be working together. My sense of her was one of openness, candour and an ability to observe herself and articulate what her feelings were in the moment.

By our third meeting I noticed I was not looking forward to working with her. I found my presence diminished in our session. I was aware that I had an emerging judgment of her with respect to one of her relationships. I brought this, as a supervisee, to my small group session. In exploring the case my descriptions were critical of the client's actions. My supervisor and the other coach wondered what these feelings of judgment were telling me about her and how they could inform our work. Was there an opportunity for her to learn about her impact on another? How might I shift my presence to move towards acceptance rather than judgment? I left the supervision session with new insights.

In our next two coaching sessions I was able to be more present, and to shift a bit out of judgment. However, I was beginning to dread working with her; my feelings were growing stronger. I took this back to supervision. We explored my 'judger' from the lens of compassion. What was going on for my client in her world? Where had my compassion gone? We had identified a potential parallel process that I was feeling inept with this client just as my client was feeling inept in one of her key relationships. I felt encouraged.

In my next coaching session with her, I had the clear sense I should not continue to work with her. Following the session, I was considering stepping back from the engagement. I called my supervisor to inquire if we could quickly arrange a one-on-one supervision session. She agreed.

I explained that I wanted to work through how to terminate this coaching relationship. I was accepting full responsibility. I brought a few minutes of the recording from my last coaching session. My client had agreed, in our initial contracting, that we would record all of our sessions, and that I could use any of these recordings in my own supervision. We agreed she could ask for any recording to be stopped, deleted or not used at any time whether in the session, at the end of the session or on reflection. I contacted her to confirm that I had her permission to use the recording of this particular session.

My supervisor and I contracted to watch a few minutes of it together at the start of the session. I knew that she would completely see why I could not work with this client based on the client's behaviour.

Something else happened. When I paused the recording, my supervisor shared that this client did not exhibit many of the behaviours I had been describing. She wondered if I had brought another client recording in by mistake. I was momentarily stunned. Feeling defensive, I took a deep breath, and then another. I felt the shame flooding my body. I may have sat silently for 5 minutes, grounding myself, letting go of my fierce inner critic and moving towards curiosity. My supervisor sat beside me, and I could feel her compassion. I was ready to move forward with our discussion.

As we explored, I came to realise that I had identified with a member of the client's family and aligned myself against my client. In feeling protective of the third party I had lost presence and unconditional positive regard. The breach I felt in our relationship and my wanting to flee the engagement were all about me. It had little to do with my client. I left the supervision session revelling in the excavation of this blindness. I was blind to two perspectives – firstly, that I was projecting on my client and her family member my own stories, and secondly, that I had aligned with a third party against her. I continued to reflect and consider the steps in this journey with the client. I could feel my heart open up to her and to myself.

Prior to sharing the recording with my supervisor, I had watched the video of my coaching session and could observe a number of things. What I couldn't notice was that my client was different than I was experiencing her. Eurich (2017) shares that we are unable to fully observe ourselves even on video. She encourages, as one step in learning more about ourselves, to seek feedback on our abilities and behaviours. For me, in this case, I was watching with the same view I had of my client in the session. It was the feedback from my supervisor, who saw the client with different eyes, that enabled me to 'see' her as she truly was.

The relationship between myself and my supervisor was honed over several years and the bond of trust between us solid. Bachkirova (2015, p. 11), in considering how self-deception may be addressed in the supervision experience, proposes a model that recognises the need for "an *atmosphere of safety* in order to feel increasingly capable to disclose any aspect of their work and thus develop greater awareness and self-understanding" (italics in original). I had that 'atmosphere of safety' with my supervisor. It may also be worth noting that shame appeared, in those initial minutes, after watching a few moments of the recording, even though I have a strong relationship with feedback and had control of the process, and a solid bond with my supervisor.

Table 6.4 features reflection questions for you.

2   Case illustration: using a full recording with the group

John, a new member of one of my existing supervision groups, shared he was eager to bring a recording. He asked the group if he could do so at the next session.

Table 6.4 Reflection Questions about Supervisory Relationship

Potential key factors	Reflection questions for supervisees	Reflection questions for supervisors
Relationship between supervisor and supervisee has been established as the most important factor in effective supervision. The level of safety that lets one bring mistakes, shadows, ethical concerns and self-judgment to allow the full exploration of one's coaching practice depends first and foremost on this relationship (Beinart and Clohessy, 2017).	★What do you notice about your level of safety with your supervisor? ★If you want to experiment with a recording, what additional contracting do you need? ★What are you noticing about your curiosity or about your concerns? How might this influence how you come to supervision?	★How do you assess and manage the ebb and flow of safety with your supervisees? ★What considerations of additional contracting elements might be useful? ★What are you noticing about your curiosity or about your concerns?
Elements of adult learning include: the level of interest in the new learning; expectation that the learning will be meaningful; and whether the new learning will assist development (Knowles et al., 2015).	★What might you learn from any resistance to recording one of your sessions? ★What might you learn using recordings? ★How might the observations of others watching or listening to the recording be useful?	★How do you view the roles of the supervisee, the supervisor and the group? ★What is the balance in the structure you provide for the group in what you initiate or require and what you invite or expect of the supervisees?
How the recording will be used needs to be within the control of the supervisee (Ibid.).	★What are your prior experiences, if any, using recordings? How might this influence you now? ★Having read the different ways of using recordings described in this chapter, what process do you feel would be most useful to you?	★What are your prior experiences, if any, with recordings and their use? How does this influence you? ★What requirement or expectations are you currently holding about how the recording may be used? ★What additional time might be required if you use recordings, and how will that be handled with respect to your contracts and fees?

When they agreed, he asked if they would be willing to listen, in advance, to a full hour session. He offered to provide a transcript. The group agreed they would strive to listen in advance. To include this preparation time was a significant addition to the group's contract. He sent a brief description of his work with the client, the recording and the transcript. He designated a few specific minutes of the recording for those who chose not to listen to the full recording.

When we came together for our group session, we had a diversity of preparation. I had reviewed the full recording and transcript, one group member had reviewed most of it, one group member had read the full transcript and listened to a part of the recording and two had not received the e-mail with the recording and transcript. John presented his case as he normally would through narrative. The discussions included some comments and reflections based on having listened or read the transcript; and some comments were informed only by the story. John reported the dialogue served his needs and reflections.

One aspect that I noticed throughout was that the participation of the individuals who had not listened contained more hesitancy and apologies for not having listened. This shifted the dynamic in the session by placing individuals in different strata – those 'in the know' and those who viewed themselves as not. This difference in strata felt to me as though it significantly diminished the presence of those who had not listened as their numerous apologies and body stance suggested diminution. It raised contracting issues, questions about committing unexpected time to prepare and questions about the different levels of communication needed when transcripts or recordings were sent in advance. This also raised the question about how many containers were needed for this one group. I use the word 'container' here to describe the boundaries around the different elements that make up the whole holding of the group within the supervision context. For example, how does the supervisor hold a container for the person bringing the recording, for the part of the group that listened, for the other part of the group that read the transcript and for the part of the group that was using the narrative description only?

This case study raises a number of lines of inquiry, including:

- How will the supervisor charge for their preparation time to review and make notes in advance of the session?
- What contracting might be required at the onset of the group and/or at the point of request by the coach?
- If the request is made after initial group contracting what inquiry might be useful about boundary management?
- Will group members be able to commit to the advance preparation and watch or listen ahead of the session?
- How does the supervisor contract with the group in anticipation that there may be different levels of preparation?
- What feelings or fears related to the process may show up in the supervision session?
- How might the supervisor and the group embrace different levels of preparation as a part of their overall inquiry – valuing the 'new' observations and the prepared thinking as both valuable in the whole?
- How might the supervisor use all available data (request, process, recordings, feelings) to hold a wider inquiry into parallel process?
- How does this experience inform our work with our coaching clients?

The case study illuminates our ongoing inquiry into how we show up fully in supervision. The disparity among the group is not limited to whether one has listened to the recording. Disparity can show up in a number of ways – for example, a less experienced coach demurring to a more seasoned coach, a case reflection based on the use of an assessment with the client that another group member has no experience with or a coach working with a team in a group of coaches that engage in one on one coaching. What can we learn about ourselves as coach in these circumstances? If we are feeling less well prepared than the client, do we lose our voice? If we are not well versed in the organisational context, do we feel 'less than' our client? If our client arrives not having done their homework between sessions, to what extent do we take responsibility?

Notice also that, in this case, the coach was new to the group. He had just joined. He brought a recording. What does that say about him and how he is in groups? About how he joins groups? About group safety? This illustrates the point that the use of recordings is very individual – our own ability to be vulnerable, our relationship to the recording and our experiences with feedback are important determinants of our willingness to bring recordings into supervision. These may be acts of vulnerability and courage; they may be the easiest way for a participant to bring himself into the group.

Our relationship with feedback

McLean (2012, p. 15) writes that learning about our self and therefore our 'self as coach' "requires us to be fiercely aware of our strengths, weaknesses and tendencies. It demands that we call forth our talents, address ever changing challenges and constantly self-correct." To know ourselves is a life-long journey that requires robust opportunities for cultivating self-awareness, observing ourselves, reflecting, learning and, as importantly, receiving feedback. Being 'fiercely aware' is a challenge to us. In my own experience, using recordings takes a fierceness in facing my own vulnerabilities and ability to receive feedback. For others, it is as natural and comfortable as it was for the coach who brought a recording to his first group supervision experience.

In planning my research project, I assumed it would be fairly straightforward to recruit coaches and supervisors who were willing to experiment with recordings in small supervision groups. I was mistaken. I encountered a great deal of resistance; it was a more difficult task than I had imagined. The most frequent reaction was of fear of exposure – that we would not be seen as the coaches we want to be. The strong waves of fear, of imagining we might not be good enough, being discovered as an imposter or being seen as less than we hope to be were overwhelming. It was asking for vulnerability that was beyond what many coaches and supervisors were able to embrace (Brown, 2012). You, the reader, may have had some of these same feelings as you considered this invitation. Others of you may be quite ready to jump in and experiment. Some of you may be on the fence, leaning to one approach or another.

It is an intriguing set of circumstances. If, philosophically, we are curious about exploring the use of recordings, how do we overcome barriers related to our own vulnerabilities and relationships with feedback? Is there a sufficient potential gift of learning about ourselves that might motivate us? How can it inform our work with our clients? What are the potential risks and harms? In answering these questions, we will open the door to learning something new.

Notes

1 Pronouns 'he' and 'she' are used interchangeably.
2 The case studies in this chapter are composites and anonymised to protect the identities of the coaches, clients and supervisors. The examples of coach supervision groups are based on actual groups comprising North American based coaches who primarily work as external executive coaches or as internal coaches for organisations, with North American based supervisors.
3 Claxton, G. (2017). *The Coach: Directive, Maieutic, Addictive or Empowering?* The 7th International Conference on Coaching Supervision May 13, 2017. Oxford Brookes University, Headington, Oxford.
4 There are a variety of positions on the use of assessment in coaching supervision from almost universal agreement that ethical assessment is required; to the downsides of requiring assessment back to the organisation which has contracted for supervision of internal coaches; to regulatory bodies requiring statements of competence by the supervisor. It may be that some coaches will want to use the recordings as a competency review with their supervisors. While this is intriguing it is beyond the scope of this chapter.

References

Bachkirova, T. (2015). Self-deception in Coaches: An Issue in Principle and a Challenge for Supervision. *Coaching: An International Journal of Theory, Research and Practice*, 8, 4–19.
Beinart, H. and Clohessy, S. (2017). *The Effective Supervisory Relationship: Best Evidence and Practice.* Hoboken: Wiley-Blackwell.
Bird, J., Reilly, C., Wiggins, L., de Haan, E. and Atter, A. (2014) *Reliving the moment using audio feedback in coaching supervision.* Available at: http://www.erikdehaan.com/wp-content/uploads/2014/08/Reliving-the-moment.pdf (Accessed: June 15, 2014).
Brown, B. C. (2012). *Daring Greatly: How the Courage to Be Vulnerable Transforms the Way We Live, Love, Parent, and Lead.* New York, NY: Penguin Group (USA).
Brown, B. C. (2015). *Rising Strong.* New York, NY: Spiegel & Grau.
Claxton, G. (2017). *The Coach: Directive, Maieutic, Addictive or Empowering?* The 7th International Conference on Coaching Supervision May 13, 2017. Oxford Brookes University, Headington, Oxford.
Clutterbuck, D., Whitaker, C. and Lucas, M. (2016). *Coaching Supervision: A Practical Guide for Supervisees.* Devon: Routledge.
De Haan, E. (2012). *Supervision in Action: A Relational Approach to Coaching and Consulting Supervision (Supervision in Context).* Maidenhead: Open University Press.
Dunning, D. (2005). *Self-insight: Roadblocks and Detours on the Path to Knowing Thyself.* New York: Psychology Press.
Eurich, T. (2017). *Insight: Why We're Not as Self-aware as We Think, and How Seeing Ourselves Clearly Helps us Succeed at Work and in Life.* New York: Crown Business.
Gottschall, J. (2012). *The Storytelling Animal: How Stories Make us Human.* Boston: Houghton Mifflin Harcourt.
Hawkins, P. and Smith, N. (2013). *Coaching, Mentoring and Organizational Consultancy: Supervision, Skills and Development.* Maidenhead: Open University Press.
Hay, J. (2007). *Reflective Practice and Supervision for Coaches (Coaching in Practice).* Maidenhead: Open University Press.

Hodge, A. (2016). The Value of Coaching Supervision as a Development Process: Contribution to Continued Professional and Personal Wellbeing for Executive Coaches. *International Journal of Evidence Based Coaching and Mentoring*, 14, 87–106.

Jane, A. (2012). *Ruby Reaches for a Toy*. YouTube Video, Available at: https://www.youtube.com/watch?v=5Q2cL-WteZk [Accessed: April 21, 2018].

Knowles, M. S., Holton, E. F. and Swanson, R. A. (2015). *The Adult Learner: The Definitive Classic in Adult Education and Human Resource Development*. 8th ed. London and New York: Routledge.

Mary Karr On Writing Memoirs: 'No Doubt I've Gotten A Million Things Wrong' (2016) *Fresh Air* [Podcast] 23 September 2016 Available at: https://www.npr.org/2016/09/23/495161071/mary-karr-on-writing-memoirs-no-doubt-ive-gotten-a-million-things-wrong [Accessed: April 21, 2018].

Mclean, P. D. (2012). *The Completely Revised Handbook of Coaching: A Developmental Approach*. San Francisco: Jossey-Bass, a Wiley Imprint.

Neff, K. (2011). *Self-compassion: Stop Beating Yourself up and Leave Insecurity Behind*. New York: William Morrow.

Patterson, K., Grenny, J., Mcmillan, R. and Switzler, A. (2002). *Crucial Conversations: Tools for Talking When Stakes Are High*. New York: The McGraw-Hill Companies.

Proctor, B. (2000). *Group Supervision: A Guide to Creative Practice*. London: Sage Publications.

Rogers, J. (2008). *Coaching Skills: A Handbook*. Maidenhead: McGraw-Hill/Open University Press.

Rogers, J. (2011). Afterword Challenges Ahead. In Wildflower, L. and Brennan, D. (eds), *The Handbook of Knowledge-based Coaching: From Theory to Practice*. San Francisco, CA: Jossey Bass Wiley.

Seymour, J. L., Crain, M. A. and Crockett, J. V. (1993). *Educating Christians: The Intersection of Meaning, Learning, and Vocation*. United States, Abingdon Press, U.S. ©1993 Abingdon Press Used by Permissions. All Rights Reserved.

Sheppard, L. (2017). How Coaching Supervisees Help and Hinder Their Supervision. *International Journal of Evidence Based Coaching and Mentoring*, 111–122.

TPC Leadership UK. (2012). *Demonstration of Coaching Using Metaphor*. YouTube Video, Available at: https://www.youtube.com/watch?v=QI3Uqtdxs3I [Accessed: April 21, 2018].

7 Attending, daring, becoming

Making boundary-play conscious

Louie J N Gardiner

Knowing before knowing I know

When an urge-to-act becomes alive in me, I have learned to get out of the way of myself and let what is becoming come in and through me. When I find myself asking if I should or shouldn't do something (under the illusion that rational processing is possible) eventually, I realise that my answer is in what I am actually (not) doing. This 'should/shouldn't' debate arises when I am lost in my head or plagued by feelings I find uncomfortable. I get stuck, fretful or panicky and may become emotionally reactive. Yet when I find myself flowing into action with ease, my response comes as a manifestation of an inner coherence arising from a process of synthesis, born of attending[1] to what is present and current, dissonant and resistant in and beyond me. I know what to do without knowing why.

I liken this to the pattern of flow in and of the cosmos which, in centring in on itself, draws in energy and, in the process, expands.[2] I find resonance too with Freeman's[3] explanations about nonlinear sense-making based on complex adaptive systems theory and with Rayner's[4] description of receptive-responsive presences and the fluid dynamics of Natural Inclusion. Polanyi[5] refers to this non-verbal knowing as 'tacit.' His term does not quite capture this state of 'coming-to-know' which, for me, arrives sometimes suddenly and always unpredictably as a deep sense of recognition about what I shall do. It comes upon me as a coherent, unshakeable, undeniable, embodied clarity. All within me comes into agreement, and I find myself moving into presenceful-embodied action. My unknowing knowing had me say Yes to my supervision group . . .

Where endings begin

In 2010, I was invited to run a coaching supervision group. Over the next two years, members of the group repeatedly requested that I teach them what I was doing. I listened but did not respond. At that time, I wasn't sure how I could. Eventually, I heeded their call, recognising this might bring us face-to-face with ethical[6] dilemmas. *How would responding to their request change our relationship(s)? What would this mean about our future supervision contract? What might be the unintended consequences of attempting to do this?* I knew we could not answer these questions ahead of time – all I could do was bring them to the fore so that we, as people in relationship, could explore them as we lived through each next step together.

In responding affirmatively, I was called to consider what I was 'doing' with them in our supervision: *Could I conceptualise my approach in a way that would make it accessible, comprehensible and transferable?* I entered a period of deep introspection,[7] reflection, inquiry – a solitary exploration and synthesising of my life experience and learning. In summer 2012, a representational form revealed itself, and it came to be known as the P6 Constellation©. Since then, I have been learning with and teaching others how to embrace it, and have been exploring the validity and efficacy of the approach within my doctoral studies.

Our emerging praxis has us experiencing and witnessing transformative shifts in ourselves, our clients and our families and friends. Our reach goes beyond coaching supervision into executive and life coaching; into community and conflict mediation; and across generations with children as young as 5, teenagers, families and adults in their 90s! We are artists, musicians, psychologists, photographers, film-makers, teachers, consultants, peace activists. Along the way, whilst learning to apply the P6 Constellation in real-time in our own lives and in supporting each other, I and three *Pioneer Practitioners* found ourselves becoming a Community-in-Practice. As our capacities to attend to what was present within and beyond ourselves grew, we found ourselves struggling to name this distinctive new praxis and state of being. Finally, the words came to us: *Presence in Action® (PIA)*.

So, what is PIA? How does the P6 Constellation work? We grappled with these questions – eventually recognising they are best answered through personal embodied experience, not words on a page. In March 2018, John Wilson of Onlinevents offered a sound-bite we rather like: "you are offering a new approach to human transformation!"

What made it possible for this to emerge? We were willing to extend beyond existing constructs, and discovered that new ways can be found, fresh frameworks and models can emerge and boundaries can be consciously and carefully re-defined. We realised that daring to move beyond what others believe is right, reputable and relevant meant risking feeling fear and shame, and potentially facing rejection and loss. And, for my unique part, I decided to embark on a PhD to bring a different kind of exploration and rigour to our praxis.

In the following text, I briefly mention my doctoral inquiry and the part it has played. I then set the scene by illuminating the paradigmatic assumptions, deeper dynamics and patterns influencing me as coaching supervisor. Later, as threads of our story unfold, I draw attention to significant developments that arose as we found ourselves in unfamiliar terrain within and beyond the originating supervision group. I share some ethical and boundary dilemmas we encountered and describe how we navigated them. None of what has evolved was predetermined.

Re-incorporating research

Since 2014, I have been examining our emerging praxis and weaving third-person inquiry[8] throughout my doctoral research. This has afforded sufficient constraint and ample opportunity through which my embodied self could meet and extend unexplored dimensions of myself. I have experimented with a new epistemological approach – subjective empiricism[9] – in which, amidst learning interventions and Community-in-Practice developments, I have been holding myself simultaneously as research subject, participant in the research and holder of it. Some fruits of my Living Theory Action Research[10] are evident herein. In the process of playing with visual and verbal ways of translating, describing, explaining and passing on to others what has emerged through me, I have come to realise my life-long quest: a simple re-incorporating[11] way (the P6 Constellation and PIA praxis) to use the entirety of myself to transform how I engage in and with life. My most humbling insights about the nature of this learning are that it is personal, relational and contextual; it needs me; it needs others individually and collectively; it needs our shared co-creating context; and no one can make any other learn on demand!

Paradigms and patterns

As I recount aspects of our story, I refer to bodies of work that have a bearing on what follows, although I do not attempt to discuss them in any depth. In so doing, I also shed light on assumptions and practices that pervade the world of coaching, coaching supervision and other similar and associated people-supporting professions.

As you read this chapter, my words will interact with all that you bring; and together something will come alive – become current in you. I cannot know ahead of time what you might get from engaging with my offering. I make this explicit because your making sense of everything that unfolds hereafter depends on recognising how much not-knowing has made what we have done possible. Our group process is held by a complexity-thinking paradigm,[12] augmented by nature's principle of Natural Inclusion[13] (see later).

Shifting paradigms: why?

If we believe we can identify, control, manipulate and manage situations and people to achieve predictable, deterministic ends, then this is what we will try to do. If we believe we can set aside aspects of ourselves e.g. our emotions, or isolate our impact from endeavours in which we are involved e.g. as researchers claiming to be objective, then we will proceed as if we can. Both tendencies are typical of linear, reductionist, objectivist thinking – the paradigm that currently dominates traditional science, management and leadership practice, coaching and other domains. The all-pervasiveness of these assumptions is not always recognised, even in academic literature on systemic coaching approaches.[14]

In contrast, we experience the world as sometimes but not always *volatile*; often, yet not wholly *unpredictable*; certainly *complex* except when things are simple; and amidst some certainties, many *ambiguities (VUCA)*. Perceiving 'reality' in this way situates us in a complexity-thinking paradigm. But merely 'thinking' this of the world is insufficient[15]; there is a deeper knowing that we access through our bodies. Yet many systems thinking and complexity scientists suffer from two crucial tendencies rooted in the objectivist paradigm dominating traditional sciences. The first is the common drive to leverage technology to identify more variables (assuming this is possible) to help us *to better predict, manage and control what happens.* The second is to exclude the first-person experience and perspective.

Two questions had become increasingly alive for me in my coaching and supervision practice:

- *What does it mean to embody and dance with complexity?*
- *How could I re-incorporate and leverage my full Self: recognising that as a researcher, supervisor, coach, leader, human being – all of me is present, always?*

My tacit embodiment of complexity principles in my practice paved the way for the representational form of the P6 Constellation to materialise. Then, in 2016, I was delighted to discover through Rayner[16] that the form, design and process of the P6 Constellation appeared consistent with the principle of Natural Inclusion[17] which illuminates the inseparability of self from our relational and wider world context. Now, let's rewind to consider what this actually means and what brought Presence in Action (PIA) and our Community-in-Practice into being.

Dancing with emergence

A colleague connected me to Sam, who wanted a supervisor to run a supervision group. It would be easy to slide into the linear causality (cause–effect) mindset of the reductionist paradigm by saying that Sam led, and I followed. Formal Ballroom dance convention has us believe that one person (usually the 'man') always leads, whilst the other (usually the 'woman') always follows. Such labelling carries us into a categorical cul-de-sac in which it is assumed that leadership resides (solely) in one person rather than in another. If we pause long enough to ponder how this assumption leaks into our social and organisational world, we can see that it rests on shaky ground. For if the caricature were true, then the world would be divided into those who initiate (leaders) and those who do not (followers). Yet the caricature persists and perpetuates through our language: *he is head of the family; she is leader; he is the captain; he is the head of the Church; she is party leader; a good leader sets direction for others to follow.* When we excavate this (il)logical conclusion, we reveal how nonsensical it is. It implies that those who follow have no endogenous agency. Now if this were true, they would forever be waiting for someone else to tell them what to do! We know from our own experience that this is not what happens – at least, not all the time. We all move to action of our own volition . . . or do we?

Let us return to the start of the supervision group: did Sam lead and I follow? How we label people and their actions depends on what came before and/or what comes next. So, if I agree to Sam's request and start making arrangements, who then is leading and who is following? I might conclude I am leading only when or if another responds to me; and yet, the instant the other exercises their agency and I respond to them, our roles are reversed. Each action, preceded and followed by another, becomes simultaneously an act of followership *and* leadership. Welcome to dancing with emergence! Rayner,[18] through Natural Inclusion, illuminates how all of life is founded on this dynamical inter-relationality[19] that manifests as a co-evolving reciprocal flow.

But who started the group? Let's expand the time container and widen the context: my colleague knew I was available and that I had experience Sam wanted. I could claim it was me. Perhaps, I opened a receptive space for Sam's responsive energy to flow towards me? Natural Inclusion transcends cause-effect thinking, enabling us to appreciate, without paradox, the reciprocal exchange between receptive-responsive presences. Thus, Sam and I responsively flowed into each other's receptive presence, simultaneously co-creating a space into which we and several others have repeatedly converged since 2010.

So, if we are in an endlessly iterative "co-creative, receptive-responsive relationship"[20] with each other, then the use of labels such as 'leader' and 'follower' which imply a fixed function or quality of a person becomes potentially irrelevant and ultimately redundant. *What might this mean for (y)our supervisor-supervisee relationships?*

Let's dive a little deeper.

Nature's invocational flow

Crucially, Natural Inclusion (Inclusionality) exposes another harder-to-reach assumption related to the conventional dance metaphor – amplified, for example, by how (in general) we perceive the sexual encounter between men and women, and indeed, the way in which we characterise the male sperm as the proactive agent in relation to the female egg. At both human and cellular scales, there is a tendency to perceive the (male) gesture as the initiating force; they are perceived as the leading, active agent, whereas the female is afforded the seemingly passive (less valued) role. Our modern world increasingly focusses on and favours thrusting, driving and controlling over receptivity. In the process we remain oblivious to nature's principle: receptivity *invokes* inward flow. Once we *let this in* (allow ourselves to be receptive to the notion!), it changes our relationship to all that plays out within and between us as living beings in a natural world. The tendency to exert force upon another goes against the flow of nature – which, Rayner suggests, is evidenced by the scale of dysfunction and destruction reaped by man across the planet.

Inclusionality

The space between defines the place of immateriality.
The thing you see is no such thing, as no such thing can be.
That which we see in time in space is concentrating energy that flows
    in form in place through space, informing receptivity.
For space imbues; embraces all without exclusivity.

(Gardiner, 2018)

Focussing on the tangible evidence of the 'action/reaction' of the 'leader/ follower' misses that space is receptive and energy responsive. How do we know this to be so? The water of a river flows into the space of the river bed; rivers flow from mountains into ocean beds; when we expel air from our lungs creating space, new air is drawn inwards to fill it; when our tummies are empty, we draw in food to fill them; when we have unmet needs, our energy flows to address them. *Receptive space influences*[21] *i.e. invokes an in-flow of responsive energy.* Space is thus the sourcing, resourcing, recycling influencer in the flow of life drawing in energy that enforms[22] the dynamically bounded (not hermetically sealed) entities of material form. Receptive space thus pervades all form and is neither closed nor passive! It is a generative, invocational[23] presence.

Responsive energy, therefore, is not a proactive driver exerting power over others, the idea of which is born of the mechanistic mindset that claims we can be masters over our dominion. So, when we let go of over-reaching and propelling our Selves into and onto what is beyond us (as if that is a mark of leadership), we return to being more in tune with the *in-fluencing* nature of Nature: receptive-responsive presences simultaneously centring, opening and inviting flow between other receptive-responsive presences.

Of all lenses I have explored, this comes closest to describing Presence in Action (PIA): being with not-knowing; letting go of attachment to outcomes and expectations; following what arises for/in the person in process; attending, moment-to-moment, to what is present and current within, between, through and around those gathered together. PIA is following what calls for our attention from the edges; it is flowing responsively into receptive space, to where what-is-becoming beckons. It is opening ourselves – inviting, receiving and responding in mutual, natural sway unconstrained by mental constructs that would otherwise have us define, split and separate ourselves from each other and life. It is how we are when we are most coherently ourselves, aligned and attuned amongst others.

How is PIA different to 'mindfulness,' 'relational presence' or 'Presencing'? Answers to this question arise through embodied experience within each of us as practitioners, when we enter the space between shifting paradigms, embracing nature's forgotten principle and attending to what is present and current, held by our congruent nonlinear representational form, upheld by our reciprocal praxis.

Surfacing knowing through interaction

Before I could know any of this, I needed to become it – to experience it from the inside; and before it could be named, it had to be experienced in and by others, so we could talk about it – find words together that resonated with our own felt-experiencing. I found my way to PIA through 50+ years of living and learning. I found my way to passing it on through the P6 Constellation.[24] That PIA is manifesting in others is not because I forced my desires and assertions upon them but because I was living it and responded to their invitational call asking more of me . . . and they responded to the receptive space I then opened to them. Accepting such mutuality changes the nature of our engagements with each other. It means surrendering to how inextricably linked we are, knowing that none of us can make anything happen without others participating. To me this is the ultimate leveller. I may appear to lead, but only when others follow of their own volition; but to be a PIA practitioner I must follow in accordance with nature's principle. I may call myself a coaching supervisor, but this means nothing until or unless coaches bring themselves to me. The Zulu principle of Ubuntu captures this. If I were to say to you *sawubona* I would not simply be saying *hello*. If you were Zulu, you would respond with *ngikhona*. What we would be conveying in our mutual exchange is that *because* you see me, I exist. In other words, *that* I am and *who* I am is made possible by who you are in relation to me.[25] I believe this to be no less true for all of us – whether or not we are Zulu!

So, our group supervision container[26] exists today. But it is no longer the only space in which we and others come together. What helps us navigate the increasing complexities that have called us into our many shared places in space? Through repeated receptive-responsive cycles over the last five years, I realised something more was materialising. It took a while to find the words to adequately convey what I believe we are learning with/through each other: "Symmathesic[27] Agency – the meta-conscious capacity to engage in mutual contextual learning through interaction in place, in space in time."[28] Simply stated this means that through PIA we are consciously learning together to attend more coherently to greater complexity.

Making it personal

Sam leaned forward with a wide grin, asking for the third time in two years, "So, when are you going to teach us what you are doing?" I noticed a shift in the quality and tone of her request and the chorus from the others. The difference had me pause long enough to consider what was being asked of me. Something began to stir. I felt excited, having been tickled into what subsequently has become an enduring, playful, absorbing exploration. *How was I being, and what was I doing when with them?* I began thinking more deeply about my praxis – delving into the roots and routes of my knowing and how this appeared to manifest in and through me.

Their invocation could carry us beyond our supervision container. *I could lose everything! It could all go terribly wrong! What if they discover I have nothing to teach them? They'll think I'm a fraud. All will be lost ... and I will have to run, hide ... become a train driver (so no one ever sees me at work again!).* I explored this in supervision, and, yet, beyond all the noise in my head, one thing remained. I was compelled to respond. Beyond rational explanation and despite my fear of criticism from peers, I dived into this broader exploration with myself. Finally freed from constraint, I found myself attuning to a different question: *what are they calling for now, and how may I best serve them?* I sought to respond responsibly and carefully, holding above all else an abiding intention – starting with me – to safeguard my own trustworthiness ... to safeguard them and those we serve. With this as my guide, I followed and flowed into this unbounded space which seemed so full of inchoate potential.

Embracing the challenge, I continued musing on my practice. Six 'elements' distilled from my MBA[29] research were clear to me; yet there was something about the way I was working with those elements that was beyond my ability to articulate: I had knowing I could not tell.[30] This generative phase drew on my capacities for both *reflective* practice – looking back to learn from past situations and actions – and *reflexive*[31] practice – a responsivity that comes from attending, with acute awareness, to what is current and calling for attention in the present moment. After years of personal[32] and professional pondering and experimentation, the P6 Constellation framework[33] (Figure 7.1) found its form.[34] In 2013, seemingly, unrelated to these developments, I secured a place to undertake a PhD. By the time I started it in 2014, I sensed that the P6 Constellation would feature but was unclear how.

Ahead of the prototype training with my supervisees, March 2013, I recognised that we were entering a new container. I prepared to contract a shift in relationship.

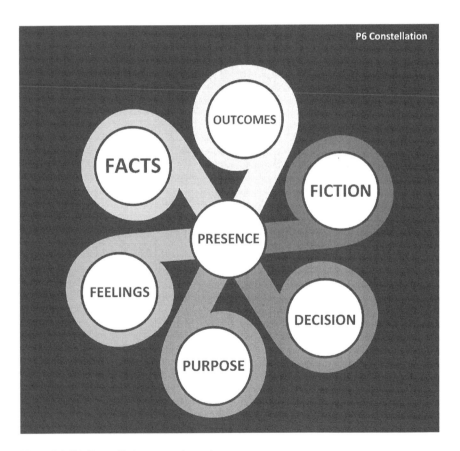

Figure 7.1 P6 Constellation comes into view

Entering new terrain

I was mindful that we as a group of practitioners were heading into unknown realms in which we were experimenting with an approach that had only just found visible form. Here was my synthesis – my way of expressing and attempting to pass on what for me was embedded, embodied practice. The P6 Constellation was a manifestation and translation of my tacit knowing represented in visual, verbal, kinaesthetic, emotional, spatial dimensions. Recognising the nature of this experimentation, I wanted to put in place safeguards to support us all. As I saw it, we were faced with a dilemma. The scientific research method shaped by mechanistic assumptions requires permissions and uses criteria such as reliability and replicability to claim validity. Such criteria are fit-for-purpose in traditional science where variables can be isolated, and cause-effect tests can be instituted; in a VUCA world consisting of complex enmeshed living systems involving human beings, this is not possible. We need new ways to bring about clarity, consistency and coherence. I wondered how, whilst being true to a complexity-thinking paradigm, I could uphold these intentions and yet also bring fit-for-complexity equivalence to what might emerge between us.

I realised we had to focus on generating *patterns* not protocols; embrace *commitments* not codes nor criteria. Informed by complexity and Natural Inclusion principles, I drew together my synthesis into a series of 'complexity aphorisms'[35] (Figure 7.2) and used these to shape a complexity-attuned alternative to

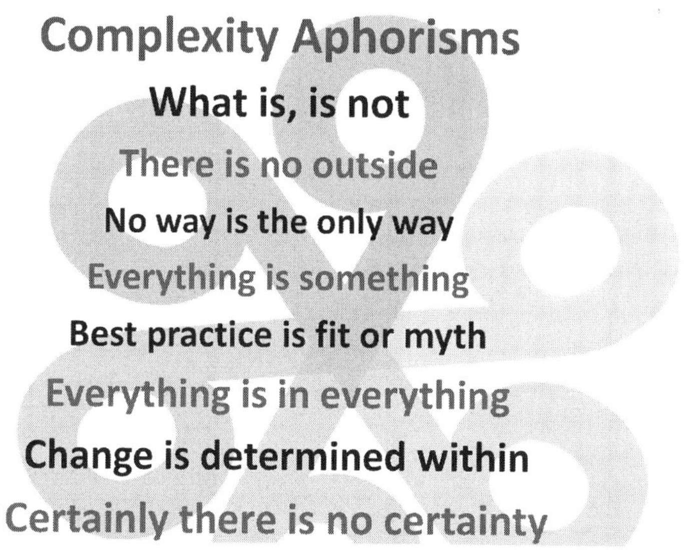

Complexity Aphorisms
What is, is not
There is no outside
No way is the only way
Everything is something
Best practice is fit or myth
Everything is in everything
Change is determined within
Certainly there is no certainty

Figure 7.2 Extract of complexity aphorisms

conventional Codes of Ethics. I introduced the first iteration of our 'Principles of My Praxis (POMP)'[36] document to the pilot cohort.

Patterns not protocols; commitments not codes

The POMP anchors our praxis. It describes the paradigm underpinning our approach and the nature of our learning exchanges. It conveys our psychological and relational commitments, expressed through Community-in-Practice behaviours that simultaneously manifest in and shape our exchanges. How these translate into day-to-day practice evolves with our shifting contexts (Appendix A).

How did our behaviours (See Box below) come to be named? I drew on CAS-based research called 'simple rules.'[37] I noticed four generative behaviours (nos. 4–7) in the originating supervision group. I included two (nos. 1 & 3) I had been consciously modelling in my supervision practice with them. Now, as insights emerge, we regularly revisit, revise and re-sign the document. This signals our renewed commitment to safeguarding our own trustworthiness personally and collectively. By way of example, '2. Engage in PIA' was recently added once we found a name for our praxis and later realised (!) that actually doing it was what supported us to access the best of ourselves.

PIA Community-in-Practice behaviours

1 Safeguard my own trustworthiness.
2 Engage in Presence in Action.
3 Attend to the wellbeing of the whole, part and greater whole.
4 Engage with courage, curiosity and caritas.
5 Follow through on promises.
6 Make more of what I and we have.
7 Celebrate and share the best of myself and ourselves.

Re-framing boundary-play

We could not have anticipated what was to emerge following the arrival of the P6 Constellation. Our supervision sessions were affected after our initial training. The group's desire to draw more from me 'as teacher' was as strong as my desire to pass on what I was discovering and learning! *Was it possible for me to hold these changing roles in a way that honoured their development, my own and whatever needed to emerge?* Time and again, I examined the ethical dilemmas in my own supervision. This helped me explore the tensions I was holding as our emerging context called us to delineate each new container, each marking an expansion and another shift in the focus, nature and dynamics of our exchanges: monthly supervision, quarterly community gatherings, café conversations, additional training sessions. With greater clarity and confidence in myself, I was able to open the conversation to include them: *how was our community space different from supervision . . . and from our training space? What were the implications for us all? Could and would we cope?* I remember early on in this transition, one of my supervisees said she did not want to hear about my personal experiences: "Supervisors shouldn't do that!" she said. She had a rule, and I was breaking it! As a group, this prompted us to reflect again on our container distinctions, recognising that in our Community-in-Practice sessions, everyone, including me, needed to be free to show up and share authentically; but in training and supervision sessions my focus needed to be on them and their processing.

By exploring these tensions, our interactions became clearer and more robust, helping us to settle into the rhythm, nature and flow of each container. The pattern we established in dealing with these tensions – being curious about our discomfort and using the P6 Constellation as our shared processing resource across all our containers – continues to serve us as our ecosystem evolves.

Our terrain became even more complex as new people attended trainings. We were engaged in something that was confronting us with an undeniable, intensifying reality manifesting in our daily lives: we were finding ourselves in myriad overlapping relational containers. We had a choice. Do we deny this reality, believing that we can keep our relationships and relationship containers separate; or do we embrace this reality and seriously commit to equipping ourselves to handle it? We chose the latter path, continuing our learning together whilst endeavouring to make the distinctions between our emerging enmeshed containers ever clearer – always starting with ourselves.

Starting with ourselves

'Safeguard my own trustworthiness'[38] grounds our mutual ethical intentionality. In embracing this behaviour, we recognise that personal trustworthiness is ours to make or break. It is founded on how we are and what we each do in *all* the spaces and places we find ourselves. It is not determined by what others do in relation to us. And it is so much more than maintaining confidentiality. It starts with doing our personal work first – always. It means showing up transparently in our community and being supported by others. None of us is exempt, not even me as the founder of the material. Often, my part is to open the way for others to process what is going on for them by going there first. Our embodied approach has us illuminate our inner machinations using the P6 Constellation. We literally 'walk the mat' using a floor-sized representation (Figure 7.3). This simple frame enables the processing of complex, unpredictable dynamics; and the experience is both revelatory and profound.

Newcomers sometimes feel wary, but they come to trust and value what this approach delivers. Experiencing their own transformative shifts first-hand and bearing witness to the swift changes in others dissolve any resistance to their stepping into the P6 Constellation. Being released from stuck and destructive

Figure 7.3 P6 Constellation – walking the mat

personal patterns more and more often in their personal/professional lives becomes too compelling a benefit to resist!

Community-in-Practice emerging

Over time, I began to express a crucial distinction arising in our work: that we were becoming a community *in* practice as distinct from a community *of* practice, which usually refers to people who subscribe to a shared body of practice. Being part of our Community-in-Practice (CiP) means we are *in* it, practising together, centring in on our ourselves to 'clean' up, get unstuck and liberate ourselves into flow-ful PIA. As our membership expands and diversifies beyond coaching and coaching supervision, our POMP is proving crucial to supporting our co-evolution.

Living our practice, held and witnessed by each other, has deepened our connections and delivered transformational shifts for all of us. My most painful learning came through losing an originating member. Those of us remaining came to fully appreciate how the future of our community and the contributions we could make in the wider world depend on all of us showing up, upholding our CiP Behaviours (See Box, p112) and facing up to ourselves first. Through the pain of losing someone dear to us from our circle, our relationships, resolve and commitment to each other and to what we are growing were strengthened immeasurably.

Often those who come on our trainings are people known to one or more of us. They come because they are bearing witness to changes in us – their friends and colleagues – and they want this for themselves. If ever there were a case for careful boundary management, this is it! By accepting and acknowledging our complex reality – and working consciously with its enmeshed nature rather than in denial of it – we find ourselves continuously developing our reflexive muscles. Despite our inevitable human fallibilities, we each are becoming ever more trustworthy in our interactions and relationships.

Following unknowing knowing

I want to pick up one more thread from our pilot training. I made an unusual request. I asked for permission to audio record and photograph our sessions. I followed that familiar, gentle, insistent urge which I have come to trust and associate with my knowing without knowing why. I sensed it was important to capture our journey from the outset but could offer no rational explanation nor give any idea how we might use the data. I shared that I sensed I was moving towards undertaking a PhD but did not know when or if I would embark upon it. My inability, at that time, to verbalise my tacit knowing fits with Gendlin's[39] developments of Merleau-Ponty's[40] proposition:

> *The body knows before we have words and concepts to express it.*

We did not explicitly contract who would have access to the recordings. Our agreement to proceed was based on the foundations of trust between us, held by our individual and mutual commitment to each safeguard our own trustworthiness. Our decision about recordings has served us well. It also established a pattern of requesting permission to record and photograph sessions – which we follow to this day – substantiated and made more explicit by what follows in this chapter.

The unteachable nature of learning

Through our CiP gatherings and supervision it became clear to us that we needed new learning opportunities to enable the Pioneer Practitioners to continue expanding the scope and efficacy of their practice. Once again, I responded to what was present, absent and current amongst them rather than reverting to defining a prescriptive curriculum. The fruits of our pioneering encounters inform the nature of the PIA learning process for those who follow, but content and focus always are generated by those involved and what manifests in the room between us.

Only once the Pioneer Practitioners declared they were ready to expand the scope of their learning (to the Group Practitioner) did we appreciate what to do with our session recordings. I had been guardian to them, yet 'knew' without knowing why that they were not 'mine' to process. I was, however, consciously guided by the autopoietic principle[41] distilled by Freeman:[42]

The self can only know and incorporate what the brain has made within itself.

This means that learning – like meaning-making – is a self-generated process and outcome. In other words, no one can make anyone else learn. No one can make meaning on someone else's behalf. This is entirely consistent with how we use the P6 Constellation – it is crucial we do not interpret what might be going on in another based on what we hear them say or see them do. Our practitioner role is as 'host' – to hold, notice, follow and reflect – with nothing added and nothing taken away. This practice illuminates the inner processing of a person *to themselves*, simultaneously transforming what is going on within them. It facilitates an internal re-configuration or shift – through nonlinear, self-organising dynamics in the brain[43] and body. Whilst this is palpable to the individual, it may or may not manifest outwardly to others.

In 2016, my unknowing knowing revealed itself: a person's process(ing) is theirs to do (not mine) . . . which meant that the recordings of their past sessions belonged to them (not me). They needed the opportunity to make sense of their own historical material. I devised a developmental reflective process to enable each person to trace, recognise and reflect on their own meaning-making and learning across the years of their involvement. Useful though this seemed, at first, I did wonder about relevance. *Given that the premise of our approach was about equipping people to attune to what was manifesting in each present moment, how would having retrospective data serve them?* Engaging in this process delivered significant unanticipated benefits – the recording data (facts) revealed the partiality and imprecision of each person's recall and directly challenged interpretations (fictions)[44] they made of themselves and each other. These insights had the further effect of loosening their attachments to their own fictions . . . recognising at a deeper, more embodied level that just because they (and sometimes others) think something does not make it factually accurate! This realisation supported their reflexive praxis when processing themselves and others on the mat.

For the Pioneer Practitioners, accessing their raw data triggered innumerable personal revelations and generative repercussions for us all. For me, it set in motion an avalanche of insights that affirmed my request to collect and hold this data until I/we knew what to do with it.

Additionally, by following through with this unknowing knowing (recording without knowing why) we have laid the ground for the first-ever longitudinal complexity-attuned Living Theory Action Research programme: tracing the creation and evolution of an approach whose reach now extends beyond its originating (coaching supervision) context. We make all this explicit with new learners when we request permission to record our sessions.

Acting with coherence – living trustworthiness

In a more traditional research project, securing permissions for non-deterministic, unbounded research purposes might have been seen to pose ethical concerns. Yet by the time we embarked on the pilot training, we had several years of trust-building behind us. We had already laid the ground and established patterns of engagement that worked for us. Each step we have taken has been incremental; in tune with the state of readiness of each person in the group; matching their pace and following their calls for progression. We acted coherently, responsively following nature's flow, engaging as receptive-responsive presences – attending and responding to what was becoming, not pulling or pushing towards what we thought 'should' be. Coherence, we have discovered, arises through engaging with what is current, awakening to past reverberations and responding to potentialities beyond conception – then welcoming what is becoming! Coherence – PIA – is a state of internal alignment, embodiment and attunement that arrives unbidden when all that is in play comes into agreement with itself. This is living trustworthiness. As PIA practitioners, we find ourselves in an expanding, more inclusive relational space in which we become increasingly able to hold and navigate the complexities of our intertwined lives. We find ourselves redefining the places and ways we play, and needing to continually re-define who and what we are, to maintain coherence with ourselves, each other and the wider world. None of what has unfolded has been driven by prescription or design.

Scope not levels; embodiment not externalised assessment

From the outset, we have repeatedly revisited whether to seek external accreditation for this emerging body of work. Early on, I recognised that our approach did not authentically align to assessment protocols born of the reductionist paradigm. On this basis, I held a line: that I would not submit the training to measures and processes that seemed antithetical. The tension experienced by some coaches in our Community-in-Practice resurfaced intermittently amidst mounting exposure from the professional bodies encouraging practitioners to 'prove' expertise by submitting their practice to externalised competency-based checks. Towards the end of 2017, my understanding transitioned through another threshold: I committed to upholding the worthy intentions of such credentialing *and* to develop a complexity-attuned approach that would be (a) congruent with our paradigm and emerging practice and (b) consistent with the role/function of the Community-in-Practice. The concept of 'Community Approved Practitioner (CAP)' materialised after several years of intermittent tension-tipping exploration with the Pioneer Practitioners. We now think in terms of 'scope of practice' rather than hierarchical 'levels.' As our PIA practice becomes more embodied, we find ourselves able to embrace and navigate greater scope and complexity. Our nomenclature attempts to convey this – i.e. CAP1 recognises self-practice; CAP2 acknowledges those hosting one-to-ones; CAP3 is for those hosting groups; etc.

The question about external validation finally found resolution with the Pioneer Practitioners (PIPs) in April 2018. Together, we explored what was activated in each of us. We agreed that using our approach on ourselves was essential and inescapable. The PIPs acknowledged that until their own PIA practice had become sufficiently embodied, they had been unable to create the conditions for transformative shifts in others. They reflected on the time it had taken them (by initially resisting their own self-practice) to cross the threshold into this non–directive, new–paradigm approach i.e. to let go of their attachment: to driving or leading clients towards desired outcomes; to protecting themselves by 'following the rules'; and to trying to 'prove' how good they were. We pondered on the challenge of trying to describe to the uninitiated '*what* we are doing' and 'how *it* works,' and recognised we could not reduce PIA into discrete skills or competencies that could be meaningfully 'measured' in isolation or tested by those who had not submitted themselves to the experience. Our conclusion? There is only one meaningful indicator: people experience insights and shifts, or they don't; and in terms of process, 'no way is the only way!'[45] We realised that our legitimacy and efficacy as PIA practitioners come from practising our practice together with others on the mat: i.e. being supported by others to process ourselves; experiencing and reflecting on our own transformational shifts; hosting others in process; and holding the space for those hosting and processing.

The penny dropped! We saw the added value of being a Community-*in*-Practice. Together, we were co-creating the context in which – through in-the-moment processing of real-life, current challenges – we were simultaneously developing and evidencing the efficacy of our PIA practice with each other. We delighted in recognising the inherent safeguards in our approach: it is simply not possible to be a transforming PIA practitioner if we do not submit wholly and wholeheartedly to the process ourselves.

Reflecting on the diversity of contexts and people in our community revealed something additionally important: whilst our approach enhances the efficacy of those of us who are coaches and coaching supervisors, its reach and impact extend far beyond these fields of practice. We concluded that – for now at least – so as not to limit how far and wide PIA might flow, we as a community needed to take charge of our own CAP learning and credentialing.

As our insights fell into place, the concept of 'Community Approved Practitioner (CAP)' shifted from an abstract notion to an accepted, internally congruent context in which we all have agency. CAP status comes to members actively engaged in practising, serving and learning in our Community-*in*-Practice. Our mutual commitment to safeguarding the trustworthiness of this growing body of work inspires us to attend continually to what is present, current and enforming within, between and beyond us. Here, we find resolution to the paradox – by centring on ourselves, held by each other, we simultaneously regenerate and extend our learning personally, collectively and contextually in place, in space, in time. Our artistry with PIA flourishes, and our Symmathesic Agency extends.

Co-evolving ecosystem

This account shows how a small, established coaching supervision group expanded beyond itself whilst retaining its core integrity. The receptivity of this group beckoned more insistently than my self-protective instinct to 'follow the rules.' My responsivity made no rational sense. Yet nine years on, here we are: still together; attending to what calls for our attention; gently co-evolving our ecosystem. Our next challenge beckons: establishing our Community-in-Practice as a social enterprise – PIA Collective – to carry Presence in Action to people, places and workplaces who invite us in. *Will we successfully navigate our next transition?* I don't know. But this I do know . . . PIA equips us better than anything else I know. *Are we up for it?* Well, as the idea came from the group not me, I guess so! *Am I up for it? Blimey, YES! Why?* Because working and playing alongside other PIA practitioners – all doing our personal work in real-time, held by each other, whilst engaged in real-life endeavours – profoundly enriches my life. It invokes a new kind of . . . BLISS . . . and I want more of it!

Acknowledgements

I am indebted to the Pioneer Practitioners: Sam Pringle, Karen Beveridge and Ro Lavender – you inspire me every day to become the best of myself, so I may better serve you and all those who come next.

Appendix A

Extract from POMP – detail of Community-in-Practice behaviours

Community-in-Practice (CiP) behaviours: our psychological and relational commitments

POPIA (four-day training) equips us to access Presence in Action in our own lives i.e. becoming a *Self-Practitioner (CAP1)*. Practising expands our scope[46] and capacity to hold and facilitate increasing complexity. Those wanting to work professionally with others can become recognised *Community Approved Practitioners (CAP): CAP2: 1–1; CAP3: Groups; CAP4: Associate Supervisor; CAP5: Associate Trainer; CAP6: Lead Supervisor & Trainer*. Only participating members of the Community-in-Practice (CiP) may gain and retain *CAP* recognition.

As Community Approved Practitioners we commit to upholding the following CiP Behaviours which have emerged amongst us in community. They illuminate how we engage, when at our best. Making them explicit enables us to express our psychological and relational commitments to ourselves, each other and the wider world. We use them to guide us in our personal and professional lives, trusting that, in so doing, we enhance our wholesome contribution to each other, to those we serve, and that we extend the reach and impact of PIA in the wider world.

By embodying these behaviours, we hope to co-create generative patterns that enhance and distinguish our praxis as a difference that truly makes a difference to the lives of those touched by it and us:

1 **Safeguard my own trustworthiness** [C]:[47] e.g. work within my *expertise and CAP status*; *uphold* the *Principles of My Practice* and align to relevant codes of practice; secure personal/professional *indemnity insurance*; credit those whose approaches/frameworks I use; practice my PIA praxis – 'go there first'; participate in at least *two CiP days per year*; CAP2–5 engage in regular *supervision*; attend to *container shifts, confidences and conflicts*; do not share P6 Constellation worksheets with those not in PIA training.

2 **Engage in Presence in Action**[48] [C, D, E] e.g. (i) use the *metaphorm* of the *P6 Constellation* (implicitly or explicitly) – always situate the 3Fs *within the whole*; (ii) *illuminate* what is present and *current* (*acuity practice*); (iii) *embrace a complexity-thinking paradigm underpinned by nature's principle of Natural*

Inclusion – PIA praxis (i.e. embodied knowing expressed through 'deep' behaviours).

3 **Attend to the wellbeing of the whole, part and greater whole** [C] e.g. *take responsibility* for my 'drops and misses'; engage in *mutual support* of/as PIA CiP members; support each other to *stay in relationship; partner* with PIA Trainers to deliver learning events; work in pairs/teams when using PIA in groups; attend to the implications of decisions/actions on myself, clients, my PIA CiP and wider realms.

4 **Engage with courage, curiosity and caritas**[49] [D, E] e.g. process my 'stuff' i.e. illuminate my personal patterns using the P6 Constellation and CiP Behaviours before *sharing 'reflective contributions'*; support others to do the same; show up, open and hold the space for *generative engagement.*

5 **Follow through on promises** [E] e.g. take on only what I am *willing and able to fulfil*; embrace and uphold *our CiP Behaviours* including personal/professional responsibilities e.g. contracts, payments, time-keeping.

6 **Make more of what I and we have** [D, E] e.g. play an *'infinite game'*[50]; share and leverage knowhow, talents, time and opportunities; partner with other PIA practitioners; proactively promote the POPIA training so we can seed Presence in Action in communities across the world.

7 **Celebrate and share the best of myself and ourselves** [D, E] e.g. speak from *first person*; *do my personal work* to liberate the best of myself; *acknowledge, celebrate and share* my and our (with permissions granted) stories of *learning, delight and impact* e.g. in case studies, blogs, social media, conversation.

Notes

1 'Attending': "by 'attending' is meant our overall experiencing of life – analysing, perceiving, relating, engaging, and embodying" (Hutchins, 2014, p. 13).
2 (Swimme and Tucker, 2011).
3 (Freeman, 2000; Piers, Muller and Brent, 2007).
4 (Rayner, 2017b, 2018).
5 (Polanyi, 1966, 1969).
6 (Varela, 1999).
7 (Varela, Thompson and Rosch, 1991; Varela and Shear, 1999).
8 (Fisher, Rooke and Torbert, 2003; Torbert, Cook-Greuter, Fisher, Foldy and Gauthier, 2004).
9 (Gardiner, PhD pending publication).
10 (Whitehead, 1985, 1989; Varela et al., 1991; Marshall, 1999; Whitehead, 2000; Marshall, 2001, 2004; Whitehead, 2009, 2016).
11 (Merleau-Ponty, 1948[2008]; Polanyi, 1966, 1969; Bateson, 1979; Bateson and Bateson, 1987; Bateson, 2016).
12 (Gardiner, 2018; PhD pending publication).
13 (Rayner, 2004a, 2017b).
14 (Tomaschek and Pärsch, 2006; Kahn, 2011; Hsia, Molvik and Lambie, 2012; Resch and Tomaschek, 2012; Whittington, 2012; Wakefield, 2014).
15 (Rajagopalan and Midgley, 2015; Hodgson, 2016).
16 (Rayner, 2017a, 2017b, 2018).
17 Alan reviewed my work, and we met in August 2016.
18 (Rayner, 2004a, 2004b).

19 (Rayner, 2018, p. 9).

20 (Rayner, 2018, p. 1).

21 The Latin origins of the word 'influence' is *in-fluere,* referring to an *inflow* of matter or 'ethereal fluid.' Between the thirteenth and sixteenth centuries this 'direction of flow' reversed to mean 'affecting the course of events externally.' The original meaning is more aligned to nature's inclusional dynamics.

22 'Enform' means to form or fashion.

23 'Invocational': act or form of calling in . . . or calling for . . .

24 (Gardiner, 2014a, 2014b, 2016, 2017).

25 This is made clearer in the Zulu folk saying "Umuntu ngumuntu nagabantu" meaning "A person is a person because of other people."

26 'Container': catch-all term for different systems/contexts/situations. CAS theory applies to living systems including human beings. CAS are subject to nonlinear interactions generated by the conditions/context. In her CDE model, Eoyang (Eoyang, 2001) suggests there are only three conditions: containers (similarities/reasons-for-being that hold us together), differences (that create the potential for change) and exchanges (the ways in which differences/agents/individuals interact). Changes in any condition affect the other conditions in unpredictable ways, generating patterns. In human beings, these manifest as patterns of thinking, behaving, doing, etc. – see Chapter 2.

27 Nora Bateson coined the term 'symmathesy/symmathesise' to refer to living, learning systems engaged in "mutual contextual learning through interaction."

28 (Gardiner, PhD pending publication).

29 (Gardiner, 2000).

30 (Polanyi, 1966, 1969).

31 I have found that by engaging in reflective practice, my capacity for reflexivity is enhanced.

32 (McMaster, 2015).

33 I use 'framework' (not tool or model) to suggest an open, supporting structure like a child's climbing frame or builder's scaffolding rather than a rigidly bounded entity which presupposes specific contents. 'Framework' implies an open, holding space with minimal 'fixed' elements and connections with, within and around which people engage.

34 The P6 Constellation is proving consistent with propositions emerging in the disciplines of neuroscience (Pellatt, 2003; Brown and Brown, 2012; Ellis, 2013), systems thinking (Rajagopalan and Midgley, 2015; Hodgson, 2016) and embodied/enactive cognition (Maturana and Varela, 1980; Varela et al., 1991; Varela, 1992; Varela and Shear, 1999; Varela, 2000; Anderson, 2003; Depraz, Varela and Vermersch, 2003; Di Paolo and Thompson, 2014).

35 Statements that distil the essence of something.

36 (Gardiner, 2013)

37 (Reynolds, 1987; Eoyang, 2010; Patterson, Holladay and Eoyang, 2013; Birch and Gardiner, 2019).

38 http://potent6.co.uk/learning-opportunities/free-learning-resources/

39 (Gendlin, 1992).

40 (Merleau-Ponty, 1945[2014]).

41 (Maturana and Varela, 1998).

42 (Freeman, 2007).

43 (Freeman, 2000).

44 'Fictions': this means 'what our mind does with . . .' It is a catch-all term for conclusions, interpretations, metaphors, myths, judgments, beliefs, values, etc.

45 (Gardiner, 2013)

46 By 'scope' we mean developing our capacity to hold and facilitate situations of increasing complexity – starting with self, then one other (1–1); then with smaller and larger groups; then being able to attend to the wider system through 'associating' then 'leading' PIA Supervision and PIA Training roles.

47 Letters in parentheses (C, D, E) refer to Eoyang's CDE model – C = container; D = differences; E = exchange. Their relevance is shared in learning events.

48 PIA delivers transformative shifts through the metalogically coherent *interplay* of its 3 constituent conditions (Gardiner, PhD pending publication).
49 Caritas = care and compassion.
50 Infinite game: download pdf of book by Jim Carse to grasp this concept: http://wtf.tw/ref/carse.pdf.

References

Anderson, M. L. (2003). Embodied Cognition: A Field Guide. *Artificial Intelligence*, 149(1), 91–130.

Bateson, G. (1979). *Mind and Nature: A Necessary Unity*. Creskill, NJ: Hampton Press Inc.

Bateson, G. and Bateson, M. C. (1987). *Angels Fear: An Investigation Into the Nature and Meaning of the Sacred*. London: Rider: Century Hutchinson Ltd.

Bateson, N. (2016). *Small Arcs of Larger Circles – Framing Through Other Patterns*. Axminster, UK: Triarchy Press.

Birch, J. and Gardiner, L. J. N. (2019). Seven Simple Rules – An Alternative Lens. In Birch, J. and Welch, P. (eds), *Coaching Supervision: Advancing Practice, Changing Landscapes*. Abingdon, UK: Routledge.

Brown, P. and Brown, V. (2012). *Neuropsychology for Coaches: Understanding the Basics*. Berkshire, UK: Open University Press.

Depraz, N., Varela, F. and Vermersch, P. (2003). *On Becoming Aware: Advances in Consciousness Research*. Amsterdam: Lonathan Benjamin.

Di Paolo, E. A. and Thompson, E. (2014). The Enactive Approach. *The Routledge Handbook of Embodied Cognition*, 68–78.

Ellis, R. D. (2013). Neuroscience as a Human Science: Integrating Phenomenology and Empiricism in the Study of Action and Consciousness. *Human Studies*, 36(4), 491–507.

Eoyang, G. (2001). *Conditions for Self-organizing in Human Systems*. Doctor of Philosophy Thesis. The Union Institute and University.

Eoyang, G. (2010). *Radical Inquiry*. Circle Pines: HSD Institute.

Fisher, D., Rooke, D. and Torbert, W. (2003). *Personal and Organisational Transformations Through Action Inquiry*. Trowbridge, Wiltshire: Edge\Work Press.

Freeman, W. J. (2000). *How Brains Make up Their Minds*. London: Phoenix.

Freeman, W. J. (2007). A Biological Theory of Brain Function and Its Relevance to Psychoanalysis: A Brief Review of the Historical Emergence of Brain Theory. In Piers, C., Muller, J. P. and Brent, J. (eds), *Self-organising Complexity in Psychological Systems*. London: Jason Aronson.

Gardiner, L. J. N. (2000). *What Are the Roots of Managerial Behaviour and How Could an Understanding of These Enable More Effective Management of Change?* MBA Dissertation. Sheffield Business School.

Gardiner, L. J. N. (2013). *Presence in Action (PIA) Community-in-Practice (CiP): Principles of My Praxis*. Edinburgh: Potent 6.

Gardiner, L. J. N. (2014a). Changing the Game of Change-making. *Coaching Today*, 12, 6–11.

Gardiner, L. J. N. (2014b). The Scottish Referendum: Complexity Perspectives. *e-O&P: Journal of the Association of Management Education and Development*, 21(2), 6–17.

Gardiner, L. J. N. (2016). Safeguarding My Own Trustworthiness. *e-O&P: Journal of the Association of Management Education and Development*, Winter, 36–47.

Gardiner, L. J. N. (2017). *Portals, Patterns and Paradigm Shifts*. EMCC 2017. Edinburgh.

Gardiner, L. J. N. (2018). *Portals to the Collective Mind*. 24th International Coaching, Mentoring and Supervision Conference. Amsterdam, Netherlands, 11–14 April 2018. Amsterdam: EMCC.

Gardiner, L. J. N. (PhD pending publication). *Re-incorporating subjective-empiricism in systemic intervention theory and practice*. PhD, Hull, University of Hull.

Gendlin, E. T. (1992). The Primacy of the Body, Not the Primacy of Perception. *Man and World*, 25(3), 341–353.

Hodgson, A. (2016). *Time, Pattern, Perception*. PhD HUBS, University of Hull, Hull.

Hsia, S., Molvik, D. and Lambie, S. (2012). Systemic Coaching: An OD Strategy Applied to Mergers and Acquisitions. *Journal of Organizational Psychology*, 12(3/4), 47–55.

Hutchins, G. (2014). *Illusion of Separation: Exploring the Cause of Our Current Crises*. Floris Books, Edinburgh.

Kahn, M. S. (2011). Coaching on the Axis: An Integrative and Systemic Approach to Business Coaching. *International Coaching Psychology Review*, 6(2), 194(2), 194–210.

Marshall, J. (1999). Living Life as Inquiry. *Systemic Practice and Action Research*, 12(2), 155–171.

Marshall, J. (2001). Self-reflective Inquiry Practices. In Reason, P. and Bradbury, H. (eds), *Handbook of Action Research*. London: Sage Publications, 433–439.

Marshall, J. (2004). Living Systemic Thinking Exploring Quality in First-person Action Research. *Action Research*, 2(3), 305–325.

Maturana, H. R. and Varela, F. J. (1980). *Autopoeisis and Cognition: The Realisation of the Living, 42*. Dordrecht, Boston and London: D. Reidel Publishing Company.

Maturana, H. R. and Varela, F. J. (1998). *The Tree of Knowledge: The Biological Roots of Human Understanding*. Translated from English by Robert Paolucci. Boston and New York: Shambhala Distributed in the U.S. by Random House.

McMaster, A. (2015). *Lifeshocks Out of the Blue: Learning From Life's Experiences*. California, US: CreateSpace Independent Publishing Platform.

Merleau-Ponty, M. (1945 [2014]). *Phenomenology of Perception*. D. A. Landes. London: Routledge.

Merleau-Ponty, M. (1948 [2008]). *The World of Perception*. Davis, O. Abingdon, UK: Routledge Classics.

Patterson, L., Holladay, R. & Eoyang, G. (2013). *Radical Rules for Schools: Adaptive Action for Complex Change*. Charleston, SC, US: HSD Institute.

Pellatt, G. (2003). Ethnography and Reflexivity: Emotions and Feelings in Fieldwork. *Nurse Researcher*, 10(3), 28–37, 10p.

Piers, C., Muller, J. P. and Brent, J. (2007). *Self-organizing Complexity in Psychological Systems*. Plymouth, UK: Jason Aronson.

Polanyi, M. (1966). *The Tacit Dimension*. New York, NY: Doubleday.

Polanyi, M. (1969). *Knowing and Being*. Chicago and London: Chicago Press.

Rajagopalan, R. and Midgley, G. (2015). Knowing Differently in Systemic Intervention. *Systems Research and Behavioral Science*, 32(5), 546–561.

Rayner, A. D. M. (2004a). Inclusionality and the Role of Place, Space and Dynamic Boundaries in Evolutionary Processes. *Philosophica*, 73, 51–70.

Rayner, A. D. M. (2004b). *Inclusionality: The Science, Art and Spirituality of Place, Space and Evolution*. Llandeilo Bridge Gallery Publishing.

Rayner, A. D. M. (2017a). Natural Inclusion and the Evolution of Self-identity. *The Origin of Life Patterns*, Springer, 45–65.

Rayner, A. D. M. (2017b). *The Origin of Life Patterns: In the Natural Inclusion of Space in Flux*. The Netherlands: Springer.

Rayner, A. D. M. (2018). The Vitality of the Intangible: Crossing the Threshold From Abstract Materialism to Natural Reality. *Human Arenas*, 1–12.

Resch, K. and Tomaschek, M. (2012). Coaching With the Kiel Counselling Model. *Coaching Review*, 1(4), 60–71.

Reynolds, C. (1987). Flocks, Herds and Schools: A Distributed Behavioural Model. *Computer Graphics*, 21(4), 25–34.

Swimme, B. T. and Tucker, M. E. (2011). *Journey of the Universe.* New Haven, CT: Yale University Press.

Tomaschek, N. & Pärsch, S. (2006). *Systemic coaching: a target-oriented approach to consulting.* Neckar, Germany: Carl-Auer International.

Torbert, W., Cook-Greuter, S., Fisher, D., Foldy, E. & Gauthier, A. (2004). *Action Inquiry: The Secret of Timely and Transforming Leadership*, 1 edition. San Francisco, United States: Berrett-Koehler Publishers.

Varela, F. J. (1992). *Autopoiesis and a biology of intentionality*, *Proceedings of a workshop on Autopoiesis and Perception.* Paris, France, 1992. CREA, CNRS—Ecole Polytechnique.

Varela, F. J. (1999). *Ethical Know-how: Action, Wisdom, and Cognition.* Stanford: Stanford University Press.

Varela, F. J. (2000). *The Three Gestures of Becoming Aware: Conversation With Francisco Varela* [Letter]. Paris, France: Sent to Scharmer, C. O.

Varela, F. J. & Shear, J. (1999). *The view from within: First-person approaches to the study of consciousness.* Thorverton, UK: Imprint Academic.

Varela, F. J., Thompson, E. and Rosch, E. (1991). *The Embodied Mind: Cognitive Science and Human Experience.* Cambridge, MA: MIT Press.

Wakefield, K. (2014). *Coaching complexity: Exploring systemic coaching in practice.* MSC. Reading, University of Reading.

Whitehead, J. (1985). An Analysis of an Individual's Educational Development: The Basis for Personally Oriented Action Research. *Educational Research: Principles, Policies and Practice*, 97–108.

Whitehead, J. (1989). Creating a Living Educational Theory From Questions of the Kind, 'How Do I Improve My Practice?' *Cambridge Journal of Education*, 19(1), 41–52.

Whitehead, J. (2000). How Do I Improve My Practice? Creating and Legitimating an Epistemology of Practice. *Reflective Practice*, 1(1), 91–104.

Whitehead, J. (2009). Generating Living Theory and Understanding in Action Research Studies. *Action Research*, 7(1), 85–99.

Whitehead, J. (2016). *How Am I Integrating the Personal and Political in Improving Professional Practice and Generating Educational Knowledge With Collaborative/Cooperative Action Research? Integrating the Personal and the Political in Professional Practice.* Bishop Grosseteste, Lincoln, Spring 2018. Manchester Metropolitan University: CARN.

Whittington, J. (2012). *Systemic Coaching and Constellations: An Introduction to the Principles, Practices and Application.* London, United Kingdom: Kogan Page Ltd.

8 Extending ourselves as supervisors

Stepping outside our cultural conditioning

Dr Sabreena Andriesz

All the world's a stage, And all the men and women merely players;
They have their exits and their entrances;
And one man in his time plays many parts, His acts being seven ages.
(*As You Like It*, Act II, Scene VII)

English is the language of colonisation and as a result is taken for granted as the language of corporations. It can, however, create contradictions in communication, especially when English is not a person's first or only spoken language. In addition, many other factors including personality, upbringing, social circumstances, life events and individual meaning-making processes are important factors to take into consideration as they inform individual ideologies and subsequent behaviour. The field of coaching points coaches to look to the future and avoid delving into the past. This can be a conundrum for coaches when they encounter a person's cultural belief system.

The intersection of these elements can have unexpected ramifications with no one the wiser as to the cause. Language and identity are central to how relationships are formed. This chapter explores the dialectic between these elements, the perceptions of talent and deviance against the backdrop of culture. The way a person is guided is discussed as a critical component of an individual's maturation. The exploration of this topic is significant for coaching supervisors in the way we approach and integrate these nuances for ourselves and the coaches and organisations we support.

Importance to supervision

The interpersonal issues we encounter in organisations are a shared experience. When there are two or more people in an interaction a dynamic is co-created by all who are involved. A person's experience of the world is crafted through the approval of those around them, and in turn applied in their own world in a similar manner. If we consider the fundamental construct of personality, an individual's experience is limited by the constraints of their society. This idea intersects with the foundations of systems theory, which espouses that a life form is not isolated; it is co-created socially, not individually (Bateson, 1999). The aforementioned notion describes the interdependence of existence and the mutuality that is displayed in collective minded communities. In Asia, it is not uncommon to hear of adults living with their parents even after they have married or have had several children. The parents take on the role of respected elders, while the adult child takes on the parental role and continues to live within the family unit. There is some similarity to the behaviour of marginalised indigenous cultures (Melton, 1995). The self is unable to extricate itself from its society as its needs are enmeshed with the communal needs and is unable to differentiate between what is mine and what is ours. In this context mine is also ours, and ours is also mine.

Me, you and together

An individual's actions are usually viewed through the lens of their own life, and subject to intrapersonal perceptions, which in turn informs their joint performance with another. When we extend this concept to coaching supervisors in relationship with their supervisee, we can see that the joint dynamic becomes a multi-layered and complex enactment, open to numerous interpretations. When cultural expectations are added to this mix, we can be confronted and confounded by unfamiliar responses and misaligned perceptions.

I recall an incident with my own supervisor that took place by videoconference. During my session, my supervisor misinterpreted my response and challenged whether I was truly 'present' in the session. I experienced her directness as rude. In that moment, I became silent, agreed, apologised, and we continued with no further mishap. What remained unresolved was the feeling I took away from the episode, which was one of unfairness. In hindsight, I realised I had not represented myself in the way that I wished. What had actually happened was an intermittent distortion of sound and time lag in what I was hearing. I felt emotionally hi-jacked, and unconsciously fell into an old emotional pattern. I shut down, disregarded my experience and privileged my supervisor's perception. Deeper inquiry revealed that the joint performance I was in with my supervisor was based on the cultural rituals, rules, norms and beliefs that formed the social conventions of my own background (Goffman, 1956). In Asian cultures it is considered disrespectful to challenge the thinking of your 'elders,' and if a person speaks displeasingly they are reprimanded or even punished. It was a surprise to me that I still adhered to this formality.

In my mind, the word 'supervisor' or to be supervised already conjures a relationship where I 'look up to' rather than face my supervisor squarely and as an equal. Layered with my Asian cultural conditioning, I had reverted to regarding my supervisor as a teacher instead of my equal. As I sat with this revelation, I realised there are some underpinning societal constraints that keep me in this master/student relationship. Although the education system is designed to nurture new knowledge, it also depends on the teacher's personality to the extent a student's ideas are encouraged. The power distribution between a student and teacher is already substantially unequal. A teacher is seen as the holder and imparter of knowledge instead of an enabler of re-invention of knowledge (Freire, 1970). Thus, the student/teacher relationship will be influenced by the degree of power held or granted to the teacher, and they in turn will have their own bias in the way they interact with a student. If we supervisors hope to create a container of mutuality with our supervisees, then we need to be attuned to the subtle dynamic of power over mutuality that we create in relationship with our supervisees.

The multiple forms of self are a function of contemporary culture "best understood as a collection of convenient masks, a variety of characters one might play" (Stevens-Long, 2011, p. 224). This concept is described as 'protean' as it seeks to adapt and flow while remaining rooted. Although this puts a positive spin on the protean self, if not integrated and unified in the self it can manifest in conflicted ways that may be problematic to the individual. As a result it is imperative that in the work we do we must be in inquiry with ourselves and our belief systems and not be afraid to challenge our deep-rooted cultural biases.

Why now

The growth of world trade has enabled the rise of Asian economies of which Asian countries, such as China and India, are notably the new geographies to watch. The increase in prominence of Asian countries amplifies an urgency to understand local issues from a global perspective. Eastern countries are more accepting of unequal power distributions than Western nations (Bakerma, Chen, George, Luo and Tsui, 2015). In societies influenced by Confucianism, the teacher is viewed as the Master, and to challenge the Master would reflect poorly on a student as well as their family. This type of inequity is common in meritocratic political structures where knowledge is bestowed through the teacher. This structural dynamic is a limitation that varies between people and can be a factor for unfairness to prevail.

It is common in collectivist cultures such as Asian societies to orient towards group needs. Thus, the pressure to conform is much greater than in an individualist culture (Hofstede, 1980). An adult is most likely to believe that the collective needs of the group are far greater than his personal needs. As a result, a person's mindset would orient the individual towards the larger community instead of the self. For example, the concept of humility is valued highly in Asia as it is associated with honesty, modesty, empathy and integrity (Oc, Bashshur, Daniels, Greguras and Diefendorff, 2015). It is especially evident in groups as an instrument that maintains societal harmony. However, the process of minimising their individuality because it is culturally appropriate can undermine innate creativity and authentic expression.

Unspoken rules of conduct in collective cultures discourage a person from standing out (Hofstede, 1980). An individual who thinks or does things differently and is naturally innovative is less likely to have credibility and may be even distrusted for their revolutionary ideas. This theme is particularly prominent in the Asia Pacific region. During a coaching assignment in Hong Kong, the Chinese Regional Sales Director of a pharmaceutical company shared that his culture had taught him to be quiet and value the input of his elders. It was considered a sign of humility. This type of cultural silence is a commonly held belief in Asian societies because speaking up might be detrimental to a person's reputation.

Deviance or talent

Although every culture has limits to its self-expression, Asian cultural traditions discourage individuals from the expression of original ideas about topics considered taboo or traditional. Not exhibited is the abolishment of irrelevant practices and introduction of more relevant norms. A person who challenges societal structures with uncommon approaches that are considered violations of societal norms is considered a deviant by traditional cultures (Oxford Dictionary). A study of teacher perceptions of deviance was correlated to the extent students were academically successful and took into account how well the students built interpersonal relationships with their peers (Ball, 1962). Students who thought or behaved differently were labelled as a threat to the group and perceived as nonconformist. However, the aspect of a person who endeavours to be different is not the same as the individual who puts forward a more efficient alternative. In the education system, the way a teacher encourages and enables a student is critical to this development. A significant omission in the study on teacher perceptions is the lack of inquiry into a teacher's ethnocentricity and esteem needs. In other words, the perception of 'deviance' is benchmarked by an institution's gate-keepers when someone tries to put forward an alternative. If we interchange the word 'teacher' with 'supervisor,' it behoves us to consider how we express and fulfil our needs in the supervisor-supervisee dynamic.

Foundational to the development of our awareness is to consider the influence of our education. The primary aim in mainstream education systems is to regulate and standardise learning. Tests and exams are used as tools to inform teachers on a student's behaviour and progress. However, the system does not generally, or easily, take into account a person's differences or cater to individuals who have special needs from conditions such as attention deficit disorders, dyslexia or autism. This applies to cultural behaviours exhibited in mainstream classrooms. Even the word 'disorder' suggests that it is not normal for an individual to have an alternative type of attention span. These people may be naturally gifted and creative and if improperly handled will not fulfil their talent. As a result, talented people may fall through the cracks of the education system due to the inability to do regular tests and exams. They are likely to be perceived as 'failures,' labelled as 'stupid,' 'lazy' or 'deviant.'

We see this type of sorting and coding of people happening within large organisations. In the pursuit of maximising profit, the production efficiency model breaks down every action into easily replicated parts, and the people responsible for the specific steps can be pressured to perform like emotionless machines. During a coaching assignment at a local university, a leader in a government agency confessed that the staff relied on being told what to do. They were scared to take on more responsibility due to the fear of adverse consequences if they did not succeed. A person's sense of security is a primary source of empowerment (Kohlrieser, 2006). A secure base is formed in the early years of an individual's development, and when those safety needs are unmet we are liable to limit our potential (p. 70). This emphasis on the importance of secure bases is particularly pertinent in organisational settings as each individual's mind will selectively assess and determine how it chooses to respond. In Asia, a secure base is attained when aligned to the collective needs, and harmony has been achieved. Thus, as supervisors it is critical to pay attention to how our own secure base guides the way we supervise and also be aware as to how our supervisee maintains their secure base. If one actor in the relationship has an individualistic worldview and the other a collective worldview it will require the supervisor to hold both in his or her awareness and develop the ability to flex between the two frames of reference.

Cultural implications

The management of consent usually appears as rules and regulations maintained by the dominant elites in a country. In India, this power is bestowed to the governing body as well as spiritual 'gurus' who might influence how people think towards the governing body. In China and Singapore, this status is earned through meritocracy. "Meritocracy has become a code for elitism" (Bell, 2016, p. 126), and through the sorting and culling of a country's best minds since birth, the most intelligent are selected to be elevated to the highest posts in the country. Each country will legitimise structures and processes for the establishment and maintenance of hegemony. In Asia, a foreign education is considered the privilege of the wealthy upper-income bracket of society unless a student receives a scholarship. These individuals are educated to replace and eventually continue the meritocratic legacy. This type of inequity is common in meritocratic political structures such as China and Singapore, where knowledge is bestowed through the teacher. This structural dynamic is a limitation that varies between people and motivates unfairness to prevail.

Although every culture has limits to self-expression, Asian cultural traditions discourage Asian born people from the expression of original ideas about topics considered taboo. For example, political leaders in Asia are not publicly seen to provoke orthodoxy, admit to mistakes, challenge known boundaries or stand for innovative ideas even if there is the risk of being misconstrued. These are not characteristics commonly seen in Confucian-type meritocracies (Bell, 2016). Needed are those 'loyal soldiers' who become responsible custodians and ensure the legacy of the prevailing system.

Concepts from examining the rituals of a prison system (Foucault, 1984) shed light on how group behaviour is formed and embedded. Foucault noticed that observation of prisoners by their wardens with full knowledge that they are observed teaches self-discipline and eventually regulates a person to abide by the rules and regulations. 'Good' behaviour according to the warders means the prisoners follow the rules, and over time are rewarded with a degree of leniency. On the other hand, 'bad' behaviour will have negative consequences and is punishable. This format could be seen at each level of the prison and would apply to the prisoners as well as in the way the warders self-organise themselves.

It appears that societal cultural values are crucial to the way behaviour is regarded. In comparison, although Western democratic societies are far from perfect, they do offer diverse educational settings and fewer societal constraints for an individual's creativity to thrive. A testament to the reserve of talent that exists in Asia is the unique Oriental arts and crafts that pay homage to innate creativity. However, familial and societal expectations in Asia tend to privilege and encourage a science-based education instead of the arts. There is a key assumption that a person's education can be manipulated or encouraged (Freire, 1970). Although the historical imprints of a person's upbringing remain, the ongoing development of an individual, if facilitated correctly, can be an avenue of empowerment.

Communication, culture and change

Adults learn in the way children learn and create through discovery and reconstruction (Bateson, 1999). As a result, improvisation occurs on an individual level and collaboratively with others, and these patterns are replicated over and over again. It becomes more complex in the context of globalisation, where adaptability needs to be exercised across dimensions of social and cultural differences. The recent prolific adoption of the acronym VUCA describes current global conditions as considered volatile, unstable, complex and ambiguous. Change is now a constant in society. People are at different stages of learning and must learn to improvise much faster in order to survive. Thus, professional services expect and rely on quicker performance, and the scripts that inform these impromptu acts closely replicate past sequences. Realistically, the human condition will have a range of speed. For example, an innovative person may be much more adaptive and able to improvise faster, while a more introverted, reflective person may take a longer time. These sequences are part of our everyday reality in all professions; a bank teller will use the same procedure with customers, teachers replicate syllabi with their students, therapists use certain phrases with their clients and nurses use particular processes with their patients. As I recall my professional performances, I see there are aspects like the introductions and closing of a supervision session that I replicate over and over again with slight adjustments depending on my supervisee's profile.

Even without verbal language, a joint performance through non-verbal shared understanding can be co-created and given meaning through improvisation. A parallel can be drawn to the parent-child relationship where this shared performance occurs through mirroring or imitation (Piaget, 1973). Just as unfamiliar situations will be addressed through an improvisation of elements from the past, parental skills are based on creative applications of past experiences from a person's upbringing. New ways and meanings are created from the old ways of knowing, and games from our childhood like peek-a-boo and hopscotch are lessons derived from repetition of a sequence; that allows for a new format that occurs through deconstruction and reconstruction.

Social creativity is based on the idea of harmonious relations with others (Bateson, 1999). The art of getting along relies on the various nuances that appear in unison; they may create resonance or disturbance. Etiquette and conventions between individuals from dissimilar backgrounds have deteriorated, and new forms need to be created. This is especially true in an era of increased digitisation, where cyber etiquette has become an issue. These rituals will eventually become the foundations of societal norms. It appears culture is a strong influence on this formation (Goffman, 1956). Bateson points out that "colliding systems of meaning, however propose segmentation, whereas unfamiliar contexts require improvisation" (p. 169) and are probably caused by fusion and fission. This process could be responsible for the ways of knowing and the ways meaning is created between relationships.

Societal rituals such as mourning, marriages and engagements have expected sequences that have parallels with religious rituals. Interesting to note that in Western cultures such as the United States, spontaneity is a sign of authenticity (Guignon, 2008). It is a reminder that in China spontaneity and high enthusiasm are generally distrusted and may even be considered inauthentic when viewed through a Confucian lens. Central to this notion is the idea of 'ren,' which is the perfection of man through being ethical and humble, speaking quietly with a calm mind and having a respectful attitude. This is diametrically opposite to the Western humanistic perspective of authenticity which sees an individual as innately capable. Humanists approach the recognition of human potential through the dynamic of unconditional regard and innate wisdom that exists in each person. So, we have these differing approaches to self-actualisation rooted in the action of doing and being.

Although multinational corporations appear to embrace diversity and inclusion, what we see is that performance is measured against Western-constructed definitions. For example, the International Coach Federation (ICF) definition for direct communication is based on a Western ideology that excludes the Asian sentiment need for dignity through the rituals of 'saving face' (Goffman, 1956). Even though families are known to have a variety of idiolects and behaviours, Western originating organisations still appear to orient towards a competency model devised in their culture with an assumption that it is universally applicable (Wasti, Tan, Brower and Onder, 2007). The maintenance of harmony is a highly valued trait in Asia, whereas difference and discussion are admired and encouraged in the Western context.

Self-reflection

At the centre of supervision is the ability to empathise and 'be' with our supervisees. Our ability to reflect and act in the moment is a key skill to our own self-mastery. Here are a few questions to provoke your thinking about your own inprints:

1   *What familial and societal norms affect how you show up as a supervisor/ supervisee?*
2   *What cultural influences from your side contribute to the dynamic with your supervisor/supervisee, and in what way do these influence the process between you?*
3   *How do you set up your supervision partnership so that your supervisee is empowered to speak up and challenge you if needed? How effective has this been? How do you know?*

Summary

Cultural conditioning is like the roots of a tree and not evident to the naked eye. Our backgrounds are levers to our behaviour and the ways we see ourselves in the world. For coaches and supervisors, these roles include the encouragement of alignment within the self as well as with others. The discovery that others do not have the same modus operandi can be uncomfortable and lead to separation instead of connection. Anecdotal client experiences prove that confidence and self-esteem increase when there is greater self-awareness of who we are in the world and have a positive impact on the existential question 'who am I?' As mentioned the protean self is the ability to be rooted yet flex like the branches of a tree exposed to the elements of nature. Strong branches bend with the wind but do not break. Thus, we may surmise that the capacity to master one's environment is dependent on a person's level of maturity. The ability to know how and when to bring forth the different parts of self in any given situation can be seen at higher stages of human development. From this perspective, and central to the attitude of cultural conditioning, is the notion of self-reflection as key to raising awareness on how we as instruments of our work impact our supervisees. "Knowledge only emerges though invention and re-invention, through the restless, impatient, continuing, hopeful inquiry human beings pursue in the world, with the world, with each other" (Freire, 1970, p. 53). It is from this stance of inquiry that we are able to simultaneously partner transformation in our supervisees as well as our own.

References

Ball, J. C. (1962). The Teacher, Student Deviance, and Personality. In *Social Deviancy and Adolescent Personality: An Analytical Study With the MMPI.* Lexington, KY: University of Kentucky Press, 87–101, Chapter xv, 119 Pages. http://dx.doi.org.fgul.idm.oclc.org/10.1037/11185-007

Bakerma, H. G., Chen, X., George, G., Luo, Y. and Tsui, A. S. (2015). West Meets East: New Concepts and Theories. *Academy of Management Journal*, 58(2), 460. Available from https://fgul.idm.oclc.org/login?url=http://search.proquest.com.fgul.idm.oclc.org/docview/1680986673?accountid=10868

Bateson, M. C. (1999). Ordinary Creativity. In Purser, R. E. and Montuori, A. (eds), *Social creativity*, Vol. 1. Cresskill, NJ: Hampton Press, 153–171.

Bell, D. A. (2016). *The China Model: Political Meritocracy and the Limits of Democracy.* Princeton: Princeton University Press.

Foucault, M. (1984). *The Foucault Reader.* New York: Pantheon.

Freire, P. (1970). *Pedagogy of the Oppressed* (1996 ed.). Translated by Myra Bergman Ramof. New York, NY:: Penguin Books.

Goffman, E. (1956). The Nature of Deference and Demeanor. *American Anthropologist*, 58(3), 473–502.

Guignon, C. (2008). Authenticity. *Philosophy Compass*, 3, 277–290. doi:10.1111/j.1747-9991.2008.00131.x

Hofstede, G. (1980). Motivation, Leadership, and Organization: Do American Theories Apply Abroad? *Organizational Dynamics*, 9(1), 42–63.

Kohlrieser, G. (2006). *Hostage at the Table: How Leaders Can Overcome Conflict, Influence Others, and Raise Performance.* New York: John Wiley & Sons.

Melton, A. P. (1995). Indigenous Justice Systems and Tribal Society. *Judicature*, 79, 126.

Oc, B., Bashshur, M., Daniels, M., Greguras, G. and Diefendorff, J. (2015). Leader Humility in Singapore. *Leadership Quarterly*, 26(1), 68–80. doi:10.1016/j.leaqua.2014.11.005

Oxford Dictionary. Available at https://en.oxforddictionaries.com/definition/deviance (Accessed 28 July 2017).

Piaget, J. (1973). *To Understand Is to Invent: The Future of Education.* New York: Grossman Publishers.

Stevens-Long, J. (2011). The Prism Self Revisted, the Matter of Integrity. In Pfaffenberger, A. H., Marko, P. W. and Combs, A. (eds), *The Postconventional Personality: Assessing, Researching, and Theorizing.* New York: SUNY Press, 221–232.

Wasti, S. A., Tan, H. H., Brower, H. H. and Onder, C. (2007). Cross-cultural Measurement of Supervisor Trustworthiness: An Assessment of Measurement Invariance Across Three Cultures. *The Leadership Quarterly*, 18(2007), 477–489.

9 Moving from frozen code to live vibrant relationship

Towards a philosophy of ethical coaching supervision

Kees de Vries

Introduction

I am not a writer. I am a free-time philosopher, a hard-thinking thinker who listens and likes to question established ideas in conversations with others. My thoughts, ideas, theories and insights don't translate well into the written word. I struggle to capture what I think in written language. As a result, it's been quite a journey not only agreeing to and engaging with a chapter asking me to do what I am uncomfortable doing – writing – but also the writing itself has been challenging. Simply writing down what I think, on my own, without interaction, without a reply or input from the other is, for me, like dry swimming, swimming without water. I tried, believe me, I tried. It didn't work. Then it struck me. Why not do what I do best and find my way forward through conversations, in dialogue using relationships.

In dialogue I am not the 'ugly duckling' fighting for identity, but I am like a fish in water, moving, curious, in the present and dancing with the flow of the river. I find myself and my thoughts in community – with and alongside others. My new plan for creating the chapter was simple: I would set up dialogues with a number of people and let these conversations both fashion my own thinking and allow the written chapter to emerge in its own way.

I asked ten individuals who are involved in coaching supervision ethics to talk with me about their understanding of ethics. It wasn't intended to be an interview where I would glean from others their philosophy of coaching supervision ethics. Rather it would be a conversation, a "thinking together in relationship" as Isaacs defines dialogue (Isaacs, 1999), where together we would think, reflect, ponder, discuss, agree, disagree, probe and generate new ideas.

And so, my explorative, challenging writing process started. It was in setting up and involving myself in these dialogues that I discovered what eventually would be the heart of this chapter. I learned in my dialogues that I used the same method (open conversations, trusting each other, being open to the emerging truth, staying in the here and now, letting go of my prejudices and assumptions, trusting in the relationship and trusting each other, listening intensively) here as I did in making ethical decisions.

Ethics comes alive in relationships. Ethics is about how we treat and deal with one another (even when the other is absent). It concerns itself with how we see the 'other,' and we make ethical decisions dependent on that perception. Ethics is not something we choose to have or not have. We have it – it's a given. But we do choose how we make ethical decisions and what we allow to influence us in making those decisions.

Allowing compassion and empathy to impact ethical decisions makes a huge difference to simply making ethical decisions rationally and logically. Me-centred ethics will judge what is right and good insofar as it affects me.

Other-centred ethics will look to the welfare of others, even if we limit who those others might be (my group, my community, my family, my society, etc.). The guiding principles that emerged for me in my ethical dialogues and now are central to how I understand ethics are:

- Open conversations where we share in dialogue;
- Trusting each other;
- Being open to what truth emerges and being prepared to change in the light of that new truth;
- Staying in the here and now;
- Letting go of my prejudices and assumptions (insofar as I can); and
- Being faithful to my relationships.

In brief, what does this relationship I am in (coaching, supervision) ask from me that contributes to the welfare, wellbeing, growth and learning of the other person or persons in this relationship?

Ethics is dialogue

Ethical dialogue is the basis of supervision. Dialogue is the leading form of conversation in supervision itself. Dialogue is relationship in motion in the present.

It's not one person imposing rules on another or dictating how another should live. It's not a debate or a discussion, or a monologue, or an argument. It's an open and honest conversation with self, with another, with a team about the best way forward – always in the context of relationship and fidelity to that relationship. In dialogue you park your own truth for a while as you engage with another: you are open to the emerging conversation and its conversions. In dialogue you often 'murder' your best ideas and surrender them for a new truth found in the conversation. In dialogue you don't start with the destination – you begin the journey, and the destination appears. And the focus on that dialogue is the welfare and learning of the supervisee.

Ethics is the same: you don't start with the givens and the endings and knowing where you are going: you change as you go along or as someone once put it – 'you build the bridge as you are crossing it.' How different is that than having a book of instructions (or a Code or Framework of Ethics as we call it) to guide you. Books of instructions are fine for machines or finding your way around a territory – but don't help when humans journey together in relationships. Ethics can never really be captured in words on pages. Ethical codes can.

Words are dead; they too easily finalise. Too many ethical codes and tomes rest on practitioners' shelves that remain what they are – words. Words finalise, freeze and have set purposes. Dialogue frees from the pressure of a set result. There is too much pressure/stress on results – results that are predetermined, ahead of time, already knowing what's going to happen or what it's going to look like. Could this in itself be unethical – to know the ending before you have begun the journey? How often we learn ethics detached from relationship when, like agony aunts, we dissect an ethical problem in order to solve it.

Dialogue means we make and create the ethical conversation together in the present here and now. Ethics is not something we impose on the conversation or we come back to when an 'ethical dilemma or problem' appears. It's there all the time.

Every conversation is itself an ethical conversation because it's built on a relationship and the kind of relationship involved will colour and influence the ethical decision made.

If books of instructions are ponds of stagnant water, then an ethical dialogue is a river, a stream of different opinions, thoughts and ideas. A dialogue enables me to bring out new insights and knowledge through the relationship with the other. A river is open and free, and always in motion. The river also has no concrete goal other than feeding the sea. It's not a journey planned as a trip, from start to finish, with a preconceived destination and outcome. It's a journey as a trek that has a beginning and a direction but not a plan or route. It has an open end or a non-specified destination. It is like a generative dialogue with no solution at some end, but a resolution to continue.

Ethics is not about dealing with what goes wrong. Strangely enough in ethics we know what we 'don't want to do.' 'What we actually do' is open to question and depends on a number of factors. Codes tell us what we don't want to do, and it's unethical if we do so. Ethics on the other hand is a constant challenge in learning what we will do in this situation with this person. In supervision there is an ongoing dialogue, even if not a conscious dialogue. There is always a sub-ethical context where supervisor and supervisee are asking one question: 'how can I give the best service possible to this client/coachee/supervisee within the relationship I have with him or her?'

A dialogue is like a relationship in continuous motion; it never stops moving and changing (like the river). 'Temporarily' saying goodbye to your own truth and discovering new truths seems too close for comfort for some and makes others curious for more. And many would rather see the flow of meaning, that is, the river, as a quiet bath in which they can float around and do nothing wrong. All this takes place within the security of the banks with their dikes and water level checks. So often we mistake ethics for the solid and safeguarding bank rather than for the flowing waters of the river, like the child that mistakes the wrapping for the gift.

Dialogue is about assuming others have a piece of the 'answer,' looking for new possibilities and opportunities, listening to understand and find a basis for agreement or indeed disagreement. It means being open to be changed by what you hear, bringing up your assumptions for inspection and discussion, learning from mistakes and personal biases and non-violent communication and social change.

Going back for a moment

For too long our ethical codes have dictated the lowest common denominator – what I must do to avoid falling under the ethical line. Stay above that line and you are ethical and safe. Ethics can so easily become looking back in your rear-view mirror rather than observing what is now and what is to come. Often when asked what they would do in a given coaching situation, coaches and supervisees reply that they would 'address the issue or the problem or dilemma with their supervisor.' There is a hint that the supervisor will have the answer, or if they do not have that right at hand, they can find it. There is an ethical solution out there waiting to be found and once found can be applied to the problem at hand. This two-dimensional way of thinking leads us to the conclusion that if we can devise the right code, then we all have a ready reckoner to what is right and wrong in coaching and indeed in supervision.

Knowing what is right and wrong in advance is the domain of fundamental-ism, and for too long we have been fundamentalist ethical thinkers, knowing there are right answers of which we are certain. Certainty rings the death knell of relationships, dialogue and ethics. As soon as something is a rule, it establishes the social minimum.

Many supervisors feel pressured to find the right answer to the ethical ques-tions asked by their supervisees. We call this 'problem-solving ethic' as if on the one hand there is a problem that needs to be solved and on the other hand an answer must necessarily be given. It then becomes a mathematical formula that results in the correct answer. Of course, the formulas are contained in ethical codes. But ethics is not a problem to be solved: it is a relationship to be lived. However, the answers can be found across all our ethical manuals and codes for coaching and supervision:

- Do not ever break confidentiality.
- Do not touch customers.
- Keep the relationship professional.
- Take care of yourself.
- Keep notes of coaching sessions.

And many others. We forget (as Schoen (1983) keeps reminding us) that there is a gap between principle and practice and the solution is using reflection to discover what fits best for this client in this situation. Touching could be the worst thing to do for client A and a life-saver for client B. But how will I know what the difference is if I am not acutely aware of the relationship, the person, the context, and the source and impact of my behaviour.

As soon as the word 'ethics' is mentioned there is almost immediately thought of problems, of good or bad, right or wrong, of criteria drawn from experiences, from the past, and often also an essentially rather defensive reaction.

Ethics and the river

A leading metaphor I have already mentioned that helps me understand ethics and the relationship between ethics and codes and frameworks of ethics is that of 'water in a river.' In his book *On Dialogue* Bohm (2004) describes dialogue as "a stream of meaning that flows between us and among us and through us." That describes ethical dialogue to me as the river that flows from a source of not-knowing, swirling, dancing and wandering through the landscape to the ocean of the unknown.

Some features of the river that resonate within ethics are the following:

- A river consists of a bed and water that flows through it. It never stops flowing. A river runs slower as the bed becomes wider and deeper. Our ethical alertness and watchfulness ensure that we monitor the flow of relationships, and as they deepen, we become more aware of how sensitive we need to be to what is happening.
- A river flows and moves, changing constantly, like relationships. When water stops flowing and moving it becomes a pond or a pool. A pond could become a puddle, and muddy. We need 'river ethics,' not 'pond ethics.' Dead relationships are like stagnant pools.
- We channel rivers for different purposes. Sometimes it has been canalised to keep the power under control. Bridged, tunnelled, an inserted dam, straightened, cut off are all actions we perform on water. However, one element that does not change through all of this is the water of the river. When there is water, there is always a possibility of life. And where there is life, there is relationship and therefore ethics. Ethics too needs to be managed. Sometimes we use reason, sometimes emotion, sometimes both. Sometimes we wait; sometimes we move quickly. What doesn't change is the constant flow of the relationship.
- The water flows through the river bed, surrounded by banks, sometimes finding stones and rocks, and rapids, and deep channels and pools on its path to the ocean. It's never the same, constantly changing as it faces new challenges. Our relationships face new ethical challenges as we open up to one another and vulnerability enters our lives. We need to stop and look again at the relationship: is it still fit for purpose?
- Ethics and dialogue are like flowing water, as a process that moves through the entire coaching supervision session as a continuous stream. Ethics keeps the dialogue clean. Ethics monitors our lives, our intentions, our interactions. It keeps them clean.
- Sometimes the river is calm and peaceful; sometimes it's babbling along with gentle energy and sometimes a little stronger, and sometimes it's

torrential, sweeping everything in front of it. Sometimes it's wild, and sometimes it overflows the banks. Ethics adapts and, like good supervision, is flexible. It bends when it needs to and challenges when necessary. Ethics doesn't stand still.

- An emerging truth is like the river you walk along today that will be different when you walk along the banks tomorrow. It's the same river, but it's not the same water. It might be the same bank, but things have changed.
- Coaching and supervision take place in the flowing relationship of the river, not on the banks. That doesn't mean we don't need banks and that we don't need to spend time on the banks. Quite the opposite: they work together. However, they are two sides of ethics. When a supervisory relationship moves onto the banks of the river, the participants are in an I-It relationship – more rational and logical: when they are in the river there is an I-Thou relationship (Buber, 1923) at work. As in the Netherlands, when there is a storm, we lower the barrier in the river to protect Rotterdam and surroundings to stop the flood coming in, as in London with the Thames barrier.

What does the image or metaphor of the river add to and teach us about our understanding of ethics?

Like the river ethics is concerned about the here and now. Ethics is now. Ethics is not something in the past, but it is something I create in the present, in the moment, now in the relationship. The past will influence that. One ethical decision builds on the one before it.

Ethics lives and breathes within individuals, couples, teams and organisations. Ethics is something between people, not above them or beneath them or even around them. It's a relational concept, like love. As with those who would describe and write of love, it's not the professionals who capture it best – it's the poets, the visionaries, the artists. Like the river, it won't be captured. Lift out a pail of water and you don't have a piece of the river. Ordinary words are illusive when it comes to such concepts as love and ethics – they often lead us astray as they freeze what is actively living.

Yet we have to say something about ethics in written formats if we are to communicate to wider audiences. Too often, when we try to capture in words what belongs in relationships, we lose something. It becomes formulaic, ritualist, sets of rules we are meant to adhere to. With the best will in the world we make ethics unintentionally a set of dictates outside of ourselves to guide our ethical stances when we engage in supervision of coaches. If ethics is the free-flowing river, then codes and frameworks are the banks of the river that contain it and help it flow to the sea.

You don't teach rivers, as with ethics. It's giving a child a rulebook to help them walk or talk. Children never learn rules through written words. They learn them in relationships with others who walk beside them, encourage them to keep trying, pick them up when they fall and rejoice when at last they stand and walk on their own feet and talk with their own words. We catch ethics from others not in what they say, but in what they do. We don't learn ethics from reading books. We learn ethics in the same way as children learn to talk and walk – with and alongside others whose values we imbibe and whose principles and personal characteristics worm their way into our lives and our work spontaneously. Actually, 'child ethics' like 'Don't do that!' and 'juvenile ethics' like 'You'd better not do that' move effortlessly, we hope, into the adult ethic of 'so what will I do now in this relationship?'

Ethics is not a story from the head. Ethics is about the whole body, head and heart. Ethics is about what I do, not about what I did. Ethics is about the present, not about the past. Ethics is about me and the other. Ethics is about relationship. Ethics is about trust, and about fidelity. Ethics is about me and you, I and Thou. It's too easy to turn it into an I-It relationship (Buber, 1923) or even an I-I relationship which is about the supervisor.

Ethics and relationship

The supervision relationship, and ethics in coaching supervision, is like a dance between equals, like a Jive. When we dance, we move in freedom together. The Jive is a lively and uninhibited variation of the Jitterbug, a form of swing dance. It has to flow. You have to notice where you go for guidance. Taking responsibility for the dance comes from both sides. That doesn't mean there is no leadership or leading at times, but the roles in the relationship and the responsibility for the roles often differ. I lead; you follow. You lead; I follow. Like all relationships, the dancing relationship has one who starts.

Trust is vital in moving together. Dancing is initiating, having a relationship and having faith. There is rhythm, movement and discovering together, having fun taking turns according to the music. It starts with a cautious foxtrot. You feel the other person with you; you feel what he or she wants.

Words are not used, but sensing, intuition and emotional resonance communicate between the dancers. The dancer challenges, appreciates and lets the other discover their individuality in the movement together.

When you dance, knowledge resides in the body, not in theory. Not knowing is the essence of dancing. Not knowing ignites curiosity that keeps you moving together. That creates space for discovering more possibilities and new moves and breakthroughs. Dancing is a journey of discovery together, about each other, about trust, about being vulnerable and about learning together in relationship (the same definition that Isaacs gave to dialogue). Dancing is about togetherness and learning by moving together: you could say it's a dialogue without using words. Just as the river has a bank where the river can be discussed, so dancing has its stop moments when we reflect on the dance and what we need to do to improve ourselves. Few dancers learn without stepping on each other's toes.

The relationship we have with others defines our ethical stances. Relationships entered the world with the arrival of mammals, who had limbic brains as well as reptilian brains. Reptiles don't have relationships or emotions and obviously have no moral codes or ethical stances. Mammals do have both relationship and emotions (take a puppy away from its mother and watch what happens). But they too don't have an ethical take on life and relationship. With the arrival of the human or executive brains comes reflection, and now humans have relationships, emotions, rationality, reflection and conversation. Put those together and our ethical thinking emerges. People are the only ones who practice ethics. Ethics and relationship are inextricably linked. Only when another person comes into play is there ethics.

Relationship is key. No relationship, no ethics. Ethics is all about relationship. It is in being true and faithful to the relationships we form in coaching and supervision (and, of course, in life itself) that our ethics plays out. What is this relationship asking from me so that the welfare and wellbeing and growth and learning of the other takes place? From a practical point of view this means we ask 'how can you and I enter a relationship called coaching supervision where I promise to do what is best for you, and your welfare? How much support, how much challenge, how much reflection will be involved is yet to be decided. But the fundamental relationship principle is in place: that the emphasis is on your well-being, your welfare, your learning, your progress. My ethical task as supervisor is – can I be vigilant in keeping you safe and free?'

One dimension of relationship that is crucial and an ethical foundation is the issue of power and how it is exercised and expressed in relationships. Power is resident in all relationship, and we know from recent events how easy it is for power to become abusive, especially in what we call asymmetrical relationships (those where power is not evenly divided e.g. manager-employee, parent-child, priest-parishioner). Supervision starts asymmetrically, and in creating dialogue as the format for our conversations, we begin to share power so that power moves 'within' the supervisee. That doesn't mean supervisors give up their power: they still hold it but move backwards so that the supervisee can take on more and more power. Such movement challenges the relationship, and supervisors are alert and watchful for moments when they go onto the bank of the river and discuss what is happening between them.

Dialogue says I'm leaving my power over here and I'm meeting you here as an equal and we're going to begin to talk. I am not going to insist my way is right, and you're not going to insist your way is correct. We'll disagree; we may even fight. That's not bad. But you will have a voice, and I will have a voice.

Relationships are also about contracts. Inevitably both parties bring their relational histories with all the probabilities and possibilities that may occur. A contract needs to account for this and address the question 'how we will be together?' It needs to account for the fact that whilst the relationship has a mutual basis, the roles are asymmetric, and the supervisor is seen as the 'helper' and the supervisee as the one coming for help. Each has different tasks to attend to (Cornell, 1986).

So, contracting, for me, rather than a formal outcome-focussed agreement, is ongoing ethical attention to issues of consent, permission, trust, and games and enactments. We are not only going to include ethics the moment something goes wrong. Ethics will be an ongoing dialogue, even if not a conscious dialogue;

subconsciously underneath there is a sub-ethical context where all the time we're asking one question, 'How can I give the best service possible to this client, within professional boundaries, within this relationship?'

Ethics, trust and fidelity

Trust is the heart blood of relationships as it is of ethics. Trust is about predictability: my knowing and believing that you will keep your word and your promises. When coaching supervisors are asked, 'Why should I trust you?' it's interesting how they answer:

- Because I am fully qualified as a coach.
- I have an MA or a doctorate.
- I subscribe to a Code of Ethics.
- I have never had a complaint made against me.
- I go for supervision regularly.

Trust is learned, and it becomes a matter of faith and risk taking. We take a chance on each other, and as we work and learn together, we build trust. Inevitably it will be tested, as it should be. And the test will be passed and trust strengthened when supervisors monitor the relationship carefully and address any impasses or interruptions to the relationship. We talk about relationship together, we come clean when we have disappointed or let down our supervisees (and we do) and we apologise when we get it wrong (and we do). Trust builds on vulnerability that is acknowledged and open. Supervisors are human and make mistakes, and my experience is that supervisees love supervisors who accept that and share with them (at appropriate times) their vulnerabilities.

Supervisees need to know, not necessarily through word but often through experience, that their supervisor gives the best of themselves in the present in the service of the relationship with them as a supervisor, the coach. Above all, supervisees learn that 'you are safe here in supervision with me and can now be open to experimenting, and discovering, and reflecting in open and transparent ways.'

Trust emerges when there is predictability in the relationship and I know my supervisor will put my learning first and be dependable and reliable in holding the boundaries. I trust my supervisor when he or she will review the relationship and repair it when there are breakages or impasses or tears in our togetherness. I need my supervisor to be alert and vigilant so that nothing creeps into the relationship to destroy the learning togetherness. And when there are problems and issues in the relationship, I trust my supervisor to bring them up and engage in dialogue with me about them. Sometimes supervisors apologise for getting it wrong – that strengthens the relationship and is a sign of vulnerability and strength.

Trust's first cousin is fidelity. From the very first instance, as supervisor I am faithful to this relationship. That doesn't simply mean that we are true to the minimum. Most of our partners would not be elated if we told them we were faithful to them by not having sex with someone else. Faithful means much more than that: we have looked intently at the relationship, made efforts to keep it alive and energetic, and are involved in ways to ensure it stays fresh and important.

Ethics and responsibility

"From a systemic perspective, I can only bear the ethical responsibility for what I do and do not do, for what I say and do not say, and never for its consequences . . . Ethics has to do with me with actions and behaviour and a lot less with principles" (Hoebeke, 2004, p. 84). Responsibility for ethics in the coaching supervision relationship is mutual and reciprocal and lies on both sides. Responsibility starts on one side, usually first on the side of the authority, in this with the coaching supervisor.

Responsibility is caring for the relationship and managing the power in the relationship appropriately. That's why I think it's up to the supervisor to take that responsibility primarily. The ethical supervisor is responsible for monitoring and caring for this fragile relationship, ensuring it remains safe and boundaried, that it is both compassionate and challenging. The coachee/supervisee is also responsible for maintaining the relationship. As in dancing, each partner takes responsibility for leading and following.

The supervisor is responsible for creating the ethos of the relationship just as parents are for doing the same with their children. This helps supervisees grow in responsibility and take up their own power (power within). I think there are two kinds of responsibility in coaching supervision: the supervisor's responsibility for servicing the relationship and being an effective and mature supervisor and then responsibility of the supervisee to be open to learning and working in partnership with the supervisor. It's a growing relationship of trust where both take risks in being open to the I-Thou (Buber, 1923) learning involved in being together.

Responsibility 'for what, for what area?' How is it divided in the relationship, or how is it split? Or shared? Demand is that the relationship and the communication are open.

When there is something felt but not spoken to then the first germ of distancing in the relationship is sewn – if it is only and always the supervisor who mentions feelings like 'I sense something is changing, or different in the air or shifting or just happening, and I feel that in my body.'

And the supervisee never says anything or remotely something like that the relationship between the supervisor and the supervisee tends to turn into an I-It relationship (again), seeing the supervisor as the one with the answers, the 'authority' and the 'power.'

And so . . .

This chapter has been investigating what a 'philosophy of ethics in coaching supervision' might look like and has not concerned itself with the details of ethical codes and frameworks. It's an attempt to 'get right' in our heads what is at the heart of ethics in this domain. In conclusion I want to summarise that philosophy as I understand it and connect to the practical issue of how we go about making ethical decisions in the here and now.

My first point is that ethics is a relational concept like love or shame. It happens between and amongst people and concerns itself with how we deal with our relationships, both local relationships and wider ones. How we view 'others' is the bedrock of our ethical stances in life and will have huge impact on what we actually do to them and how we treat them. The ideal supervisor relationship is the one described by Buber as the I-Thou relationship. If our relationships are the ethical river in which we swim and work and play together, then trust, fidelity and responsibility to and for that relationship are the ethical areas we look to and monitor to ensure that the relationship is healthy. Ethical responsibility means we put our clients and their wellbeing and welfare first. The client is the ethical focus, and what is good for them (not always what they say they need) has right of way on the ethical roundabout.

Relationships are driven by conversations, and again the best ethical conversation for supervision is dialogue (meeting and talking together in relationship).

I presented two metaphors to describe this philosophy. One was the flow of the river, which connects both bank and river, and the other the art of dancing. For me the water in the river is the active, flowing place where ethical work takes place. The banks are the containers (the codes, the books, the frameworks) and direct the waters and keep them doing their job.

These two images also suggest that while we come with a past, ethics takes place in an evolving, changing relationship, and it's always difficult to know in advance what will be the best ethical decision to make. Predetermined ethics lives on the banks. In the water you have to make present decisions that may change from client to client and from time to time and from context to context. I don't know what I will do in advance if I am in my ethical home. The here-and-now situation, with the here-and-now relationship, forges my ethical decisions. If you already know what you are going to do, you are a 'fundamentalist' where the same rules apply in all situations, regardless of whether individuals, diversity or relationships play a part. True ethics has nothing to do with fundamentalism and banishes it forever. Relationships and ethics die when bogged down in the certainty of knowing what to do.

Rules and frameworks are necessary but subservient to the relationship and what that relationship needs. I see these rules and codes as a beginning, the minimum, something like traffic signs, necessary to be able to structure and maintain order in the streets. But they do not offer a solution.

Solutions come from within the relationship and my faithfulness to what that means. In the last analysis that is the focus of ethics – the needs of the other as paramount. Ethics really lives with us, moves with us; it is part of not only how we treat each other, but how we are with each other.

Rumi puts this well:

> Out beyond ideas of wrong doing, and out beyond ideas of right doing, there is a field, I will meet you there.

(Barks, 2004, p. 36)

Acknowledgements

My thanks to Michael Carroll for reading and commenting on the first draft of this chapter.

Also, my thanks to Fiona Adamson for the many challenging dialogues, her ever attentive listening ear, her unwavering support and trust.

References

Barks, C. (2004). *The Essential Rumi: New Expanded Edition.* San Francisco: HarperSanFrancisco.
Bohm, D. (2004). *On Dialogue.* London and New York: Routledge Classics.
Buber, M. (1923). *I and Thou.* Translated by Ronald Gregor Smith. London: Scribner Classics.
Cornell, W. F. (1986). Setting the Therapeutic Stage: The Initial Sessions. *Transactional Analysis Journal,* 41, 4–10.
Hoebeke, J. (2004). Verantwoordelijkheid in Netwerken: Paradoxaal en toch werkbaar. *Article in: M&O Tijdschrift voor management & organisatie,* 58(4/5), juli–oktober, 84–97.
Isaacs, W. (1999). *Dialogue and the Art of Thinking Together.* New York: Bantam Doubleday Dell Publishing Group Inc.
Schoen, D. (1983). *The Reflective Practitioner: How Professionals Think in Action.* San Francisco: Jossey-Bass.

10 Supervision for internal coaches

Katharine St John-Brooks

Introduction

As recently as 2001 internal coaching was described as "flying under the radar" (Frisch, 2001), but it is now mainstream, and for the past decade it has been growing at speed (Lambert, 2008; CIPD, 2015; Sherpa, 2016). Many large organisations in the UK have said that they are likely to invest more in their internal than external coaching resources going forward (Ridler, 2015), and the number of internal coaches is said to exceed the number of external coaches in some countries (Moral et al., 2017). So what is internal coaching?

Two helpful definitions are:

> Internal coaching is a one-on-one developmental intervention supported by the organisation and provided by a colleague of those coached who is trusted to shape and deliver a programme yielding individual professional growth.
>
> (Frisch, 2001, p. 242)

> The internal coach is comparable in every sense to the external coach, with the exception that the internal coach is an employee of the same organisation as their coachees.
>
> (Carter, 2005, p. 7)

Key features are that internal coaches have a formal coaching identity within the organisation and receive specialised coach training – usually leading to a recognised coaching qualification. To be clear, managers using a coaching approach with their own staff are not considered to be internal coaches. In the prevailing model in the UK, internal coaches deliver coaching sessions to two to three clients at a time, outside their managerial chain, on top of their 'day job.' However, this disguises a wide spectrum of activity that includes coaches who may only have one client at any one time and coaches who work in an organisational development or learning and development role who may be coaching internal clients for 50% of their working week.

Like external coaches, once their initial training has been completed internal coaches need to continue to develop their skills and competence. The most enlightened organisations provide continuous professional development and professional supervision.

> Those organisations that scrimp on the careful selection, training and supporting of internal coaches run serious risks.
>
> Hunt and Weintraub (2006, p. 4)

This chapter explores the nature and function of supervision for internal coaches; the degree to which it is actually happening; what the alternatives are; in what respects the role of supervisor may be a little different for internal coaches; and some of the challenges peculiar to internal coaches that may be brought to supervision.

What do we mean by supervision, and is it happening?

Michael Carroll offers a down-to-earth definition of supervision: "Supervision is a forum where supervisees think about their work in order to do it better" (Carroll, 2006, p. 4). The simplicity of this definition highlights how a supervision session – whether group or one-to-one – is basically providing a space for guided reflection. The European Mentoring and Coaching Council (EMCC) guidance on supervision (EMCC, 2018) draws on Hawkins and Smith's (2013) model identifying three different functions of supervision:

1   The *Developmental* Function Concerned with development of skills, understanding and capacities of the coach/ mentor.
2   The *Resourcing* Function Providing a supportive space for the coach/mentor to process the experiences they have had when working with clients.
3   The *Qualitative* Function Concerned with quality, work standards and ethical integrity.

When considering what support employers provide for their internal coaches, it will be helpful to bear these three functions in mind as some common types of support serve one or two of these functions as opposed to all three.

The idea that it is best practice for external executive coaches to receive regular supervision from a qualified coach supervisor has become well established and is supported by all the coaching professional bodies. While in 2006 only 44% of UK coaches were receiving supervision (Hawkins and Schwenk, 2006), follow up research in 2014 (Hawkins and Turner, 2017) saw a significant increase to 92%. They found that many organisations expect the external coaches that they hire to receive regular supervision, and a small number even require evidence.

However, supervision for internal coaches is not so well established. In 2006, Hawkins and Schwenk found that while 88% of organisers of coaching believed that coaches should have regular ongoing supervision of their coaching, only 23% of organisations were actually providing it. Roll forward to Hawkins and Turner's research in 2014 and this figure had only risen to 40%. St John-Brooks' research (2010a) showed wide disparities in practice, typified at the two ends of the spectrum by the experiences of these two internal coaches:

> [My organisation] funded my attendance at Academy of Executive Coaching Masterclasses, NLP diploma, Gestalt workshop, supervision sessions.
>
> Coach A

> There is no provision for internal coaches but I have my own supervision arrangements and my own CPD which I fund myself as it is a disgrace that none is provided.
>
> Coach B

So why are many internal coaches not receiving professional supervision? In 2006 the reasons organisations gave were difficulty in finding supervisors, cost and a lack of 'need.' In the UK, availability really should no longer be an issue. The following organisations have directories on their websites of members who are qualified to coach supervisors: Association of Coaching Supervisors (AOCS); Coaching Supervision Academy (CSA); Association for Professional Executive Coaching and Supervision (APECS); European Mentoring and Coaching Council (EMCC UK); International Coach Federation (ICF UK); Association for Coaching (AC). However, the other reasons still hold:

* *Lack of budget* – it is common to hear from lead coaches that they fought successfully to get the funding for training up an internal coaching resource but that getting funding for supervision for the coaches proved to be a bridge too far. Anecdotal evidence suggests that some organisations that require their external coaches to be in supervision (which is of course paid for by the coaches themselves) often do not fund supervision for their own internal coaches – which is an irony, to say the least.
* *Lack of understanding* – it is not always understood how important professional supervision is in developing coaches' skills and in 'quality assuring' the coaching. Coaches themselves may believe that support from their peers is sufficient until they come up against a really tricky issue. It is not unusual for the development of the coaches to be taken one step at a time and for supervision only to be introduced three or four years down the line when the need for it begins to be recognised.

Further considerations are whether, when supervision is made available, the coaches themselves understand the benefits sufficiently to make the time for it or whether, as reported by Butwell (2006), they are "nervous about spending too much time on something that, though they saw it as a 'necessity', might be seen by their line manager as a 'luxury'" (p. 51). A minority of organisations make attending supervision and CPD sessions a condition of the coaches being allowed to continue to practice, but it is much more common for it to be positioned as a voluntary activity. It is perhaps surprising that more organisations do not make it mandatory given Hawkins and Schwenk's (2006) finding that while coaches themselves see the main benefit of supervision as being further development of their skills (so the 'developmental' function in the aforementioned definition), organisers of internal coaching put more emphasis on quality assurance (so the 'qualitative' function), thus minimising the organisational risk potentially posed by unethical or unprofessional practice.

Something to think about

Should supervision be a privilege or an expectation i.e. voluntary or mandatory?

When is supervision not supervision?

Organisations can mean a variety of things when they answer yes to the question 'do your internal coaches receive supervision?' Some of them will indeed support 1:1, group or peer supervision with trained and qualified coach supervisors, but others, when questioned what form their supervision takes, tell a different story when you get underneath. For example:

- "Our internal coaches meet regularly as a group and 'supervise each other'" – but when asked if the coaches use a particular theoretical supervision model the answer is no. What the coaches are actually doing is co-coaching, and there may or may not be an appropriate level of challenge or holding to account.
- "Our lead coach, who is very experienced, supervises the coaches" – but when asked if that person is a qualified supervisor the answer is no. Probably what the lead coach is doing is mentoring the coaches.
- "Twice a year we ask our coaches to set aside an entire day and we offer CPD in the morning and supervision groups in the afternoon run by trained supervisors." This is certainly development, and may be excellent, but it is questionable whether participating in a supervision group at six monthly intervals really constitutes supervision (which involves building trusted relationships over time).

None of this is to deny the value of all these activities. What they all share is that they provide that essential reflective space that coaches need to develop their skills and competence. L&D professionals are resourceful: if they don't have the budget to employ qualified external supervisors they look to provide a mix of other opportunities for their coaches to reflect on their practice. A full list would include mentors for the coaches i.e. more experienced coaches mentoring less experienced ones; formal action learning sets for the coaches; buddy groups of coaches led by an experienced coach; co-coaching circles; and training in reflective practice – the idea of "developing an internal supervisor on your shoulder" (Childs, Woods, Willcock and Man, 2011). Or a mix of supervision and these other varieties of support might be provided.

An approach to internal coaching supervision at the University of Birmingham

In 2014 the University of Birmingham set up a Coaching Academy and in the first two years trained up 40 internal coaches (four cohorts) to ILM5 standard. Around half worked in HR, and most of the others worked across professional services. There was some 'supervision' in the first two years of the Academy's formation, but it was more CPD focussed and happened infrequently with no calendar of activities scheduled for the year.

A new OD director joined the university early in 2016, and conducted a comprehensive review of the Coaching Academy i.e. policies, processes, CPD, supervision, branding, etc. He appointed a PA early on who would go on to administrate the coaching academy process and build strong working relationships with all the coaches. The OD director also had support from an OD consultant, in particular around setting up processes for evaluating coach and coachee feedback, with a view to continuously improving the operating model and quality of the coaching provision. In his first year he put together a Code of Conduct that included the expectation that all the internal coaches would need to commit to 5–10 hours per month (including any CPD and supervision). Ten of the less committed coaches left the Academy in the first 12 months under the new leadership. Considerable investment was put into developing a further cohort of coaches to ILM5 level plus developing some of the existing more experienced coaches to ILM7 level, and fast tracking a small number of senior director level colleagues onto ILM7, to help build greater advocacy at this level. By the end of the year there were 35 active coaches including ten with the ILM7 qualification. In his second year, the OD director increased the volume of supervision: a mix of group supervision and 1:1 supervision. Avoiding a 'one size fits all' approach, coaches who had several clients at any one time and were coaching regularly were offered 1:1 supervision. Six 'buddy groups' – working like action learning sets – were also set up and led by experienced coaches who worked in the OD function. Their mandate was to build greater confidence, capability and reflective practice amongst the coaching pool and to support the coaches in between supervision sessions. Buddy groups ran once a term, and the leads identified thematic coach development needs, which were then met through CPD events.

Supervision and attendance at CPD events was not mandatory, but the OD director monitored attendance annually, to inform future decisions about membership of the Academy. Feedback was also sought from coaches as to how best to schedule these sessions to maximise attendance. His expectations of his external supervisors were that they provide thematic feedback to him to help shape future CPD for internal coaches and address any pressing issues that might present (some issues more OD in nature to be discussed more broadly at HR leadership team level).

By the end of the OD director's second year the coaching pool had started coaching more senior staff and academics. Looking to the future, his vision was of his coaches taking on an increasing number of coaching assignments at senior levels within the university – up to but not including the university's Executive team.

Lessons learned:

- Understanding the importance of developing demand as well as supply from the outset when setting up an internal coaching resource – and the importance of branding and visible senior level leadership.
- Considering what administrative resource you require to run the internal coaching pool professionally. Be clear about your expectations of your coaches.
- Considering a broad mix of supervision and CPD interventions, and how these can be effectively scheduled to ensure high levels of participation. Monitor and review levels of commitment and attendance at CPD and supervision events.
- Investing in different supervision modes of delivery and ensuring coaching supervision requirements are aligned to the number of coaching hours completed by individual coaches.
- Using external supervision to act as a catalyst to build the confidence and capability of internal coaches. The volume of supervision offered relative to the number of coaching hours undertaken by coaches was high; however, these sessions also acted as CPD sessions – identifying relevant thematic areas to explore, utilising the knowledge, skills and experience of the external supervision providers.
- As the Coaching Academy evolved and coaches gained more experience, it was important to consider how the supervision model needed to evolve too to focus more on specific aspects of the supervisee's coaching practice, and the specific organisational context in which they operated.

What are the options for professional supervision?

Different types of internal supervision

Organisations may use 1:1, group or peer supervision or a combination of all three. There are distinct advantages and disadvantages to each approach.

- *1:1 supervision* sessions can be expensive to fund (though telephone sessions tend to be cheaper) and can set up a dependency (Hawkins and Schwenk, 2006). Set against that: there are benefits in a longitudinal relationship through which coach development can be tracked and illuminated; for the coach the sessions are very time-effective as they have the undivided attention of the supervisor; and 1:1 sessions offer privacy for experimenting with new models, role play, etc. and allow the opportunity to address deep-seated issues that might feel uncomfortable to share in a group session.

- *Group supervision* sessions provide cheaper 'per person' supervision, but each coach receives less individual attention, while probably devoting half a day to each session. Ideally the membership of the group should be constant so that trust is built amongst the participants. When a supervision group really works, each coach gets the added value of insights from all the people in the room, not just the supervisor, so the learning is richer. They also benefit from hearing about the other coaches' challenges, being able to benchmark their practice against the others and feeling connected into an internal network. On the other hand, sometimes a focus on the group dynamics can take over the process, leaving inadequate time to address individual participants' supervision needs. Butwell's (2006) research with a supervision group that only met quarterly found that the participants did not get to know each other well enough to let down their guards entirely. One participant reported: "I've got working relationships with half the people around that table . . . Has that held me back in any way? It might have done" (p. 49). There can be fears around too much self-disclosure.
- *Peer supervision* is very cost-effective. To work well – with the coaches properly holding each other to account (the 'qualitative' aspect of supervision) – all the coaches in the peer supervision group need to receive training in a specific supervision model; be comfortable with having others discuss their practice; be prepared to give challenging feedback in front of others; and understand "how to invite someone into better, or more ethical, practice without shaming them" (St John-Brooks, 2014, p. 225). A risk with peer supervision is that there is scope for participants to become collusive.

Training internal supervisors

A strategy that some organisations adopt is to train one or more of their more experienced coaches to be supervisors themselves. This has the benefits of being cost-effective; the supervisor may be more readily available to coaches wanting a quick word about an ethical dilemma that has emerged; the coaching practice of the supervisor will be enhanced by broadening the range of lenses that they use to consider issues; building supervision skills sends a message to the business that the coaches are serious about their development; and a lead coach can play a more active stewardship role if they are also supervising the coaches (Long, 2012).

However, there are complexities involved in being an internal supervisor, particularly if they are running the coaching pool too, arising from four main features:

- The supervisor is part of the same system as the coaches. This can result in common blind spots and shared assumptions that can go unchallenged.
- The supervisor's working relationship with coaching colleagues can potentially get in the way e.g. of the coaches providing honest feedback on the effectiveness of the supervision.
- The supervisor's knowledge, in some cases, of the coaches' clients has the potential to compromise confidentiality and boundaries.

- The supervisor is responsible to both the coaches (and their clients) and the organisation, and it can be difficult to strike a balance between the quality assurance role and providing a 'safe space' where coaches can be completely honest – particularly when the supervisor is also managerially accountable for the quality of the coaching that the pool delivers.

In relation to the last point, Thomson (2011) writes interestingly about the inherent conflict for supervisors between discharging (a) the 'developmental' and 'resourcing' functions of supervision which generally involve a client-centred approach offering unconditional, non-judgmental positive regard and (b) the 'qualitative' function where the supervisor is "holding a responsibility to ensure the quality of a coach's work and to monitor the coach's compliance with a relevant code of practice," arguing that "their acceptance necessarily becomes judgemental and their positive regard becomes conditional" (p. 107). The point that he makes applies in principle to external supervisors too, but any conflict will be more keenly felt by an internal supervisor: credibility for internal coaching pools is something that is hard won, and the last thing a supervisor wants is to risk the pool's reputation as a result of an under-performing coach. On the other hand, if they were to discharge their 'quality assurance' responsibility to the organisation by, for example, suggesting to a coach that they stop practising as a coach until they have improved in some aspect, what might the impact be on other coaches in terms of their preparedness to be completely honest about weaknesses/anxieties in supervision sessions?

When it comes to external supervisors, anecdotal evidence suggests that it is very rare for organisations' contracts with them to include an element of feedback when it comes to the competence of the coaches. Regularly feeding back generic themes that have arisen in group supervision sessions to contribute to organisational learning is, however, more common.

Something to think about

What should an external supervisor do if they are concerned about an internal coach's practice?

Case study about boundaries, confidentiality and role conflicts

Jane is Head of L&D for a telecoms company. She is a trained coach and four years ago persuaded her CEO of the value of setting up a cohort of internal coaches to focus principally on raising the quality of leadership in the organisation. There are now 24 coaches actively coaching at all levels. She failed to get sufficient budget to source external supervision for her internal coaches so gained a supervision qualification herself and runs three supervision groups. Between supervision sessions coaches sometimes come to her to discuss client issues. In addition to leading the coaching pool and her other L&D responsibilities, she has six coaching clients including the CEO. Because she plays a role in matching clients to coaches, she becomes increasingly uncomfortable with some of the discussions in the supervision groups because she often knows whom the coaches are talking about (so the confidentiality clause is technically being breached). A recent example concerned a problem that a coach brought to the group about a client who he suspected was behaving unethically, and he wanted to discuss how to deal with it. Jane feels conflicted because she knows from her sessions with the CEO that the employee in question is a personal friend of his and is going through some complex personal issues at home. She is also finding it hard to be completely non-judgmental in her supervision sessions because she gets anxious about the reputation of the coaching pool – which is her responsibility – when she hears the coaches confessing to having dealt poorly with something in a client session. She realises this can't go on.

Lessons learned: Jane decides to make some changes: (a) she gets 1:1 supervision for herself – to supervise both her coaching work and her supervision practice; (b) she delegates the matching process completely to her team so that she doesn't know who is coaching whom; and (c) she changes the confidentiality contract that her coaches use with their clients to reflect the fact that they may sometimes bring an issue to her to discuss. These actions resolve the confidentiality and boundary issues, and she works hard with her own supervisor to work out how to manage the quality assurance aspect of her role as coach supervisor. Where she spots a common weakness she arranges for some CPD for the coaches to address it.

What's different about supervising internal coaches?

The nature of supervision for internal coaches can be different from that provided to external coaches for two main reasons: firstly, internal coaches by and large do much less coaching – it is not uncommon for a coach to have only one client at a time, and even those who are considered to be very active may only have three clients at a time. Secondly, internal coaches operate in the same system as their clients, and this has a myriad of consequences, from challenges around confidentiality, role conflicts and holding boundaries to coping with whatever emotions are in that system. Internal coaches bring some issues to supervision that are simply much less likely to arise for external coaches.

Implications of the fact that internal coaches do less coaching

Internal coaches generally coach on top of their day jobs, so they build up their experience more slowly than most external coaches would. There are exceptions – a small number of organisations employ full-time internal coaches who build experience quickly, and, conversely, for some external coaches coaching is only a small part of a much broader portfolio, so they build experience slowly too. The norm for internal coaches is to have no more than two to three clients at any one time, and this has implications for their speed of development in terms of both their competence and their confidence. It is not unknown for internal coaches to have a spell when they don't have any clients at all, and this can lead not just to a dip in confidence but to actual deskilling. This very gradual accumulation of coaching experience can mean that the supervision stays in the 'tools and techniques' developmental space (see Clutterbuck and Megginson's (2011) concept of 'coach maturity') for longer than would be the case if they were gaining experience at a faster pace.

Another consequence is that there will be less client work to discuss, which may put the supervisor more in the role of (a) building the coach's capacity and developing their skills rather than helping them to reflect on actual coaching experiences and (b) addressing confidence issues. One leader of an internal coaching resource said that he was beginning to wonder whether this model could actually work. He said that he would prefer to have a smaller number of coaches in his pool who could commit to one day a week than more coaches who could only devote eight hours a month. He pointed out that it was difficult to 'build the coaching muscle' with only two to three coaching sessions a month. However, there are also many experienced, mature, internal coaches working in organisations very effectively.

Frequency of supervision

One tricky issue is deciding how often internal coaches should receive supervision (or some other form of support). What should the appropriate interval be between supervision sessions or the appropriate ratio of supervision hours to client hours? It is not uncommon for the expectation of internal coaches to be to deliver a minimum of 30 hours of coaching per annum. If one were to use the common rule of thumb of a ratio of 1:35 (one hour of supervision to 35 hours of coaching), then twice a year might seem ample. But is it? Perhaps CPD to keep their skills fresh is genuinely the bigger need. On the other hand, given that internal coaches are more likely to encounter ethical dilemmas (St John-Brooks, 2010a), surely they should be given more frequent access to supervisory support than twice a year. The solution used in the preceding university case study of professional supervision interspersed with buddy group meetings is one way of addressing this conundrum.

Implications of the fact that internal coaches are part of the same system as their clients

Internal coaches operate in a more complex world than external coaches, swimming as they do in the same pond as their clients and negotiating a web of interlocking relationships and networks. As Frisch wrote in his seminal article on the emerging role of the internal coach (Frisch, 2001), the role of external coach is "cleaner" (p. 244). This complexity has consequences for the sorts of issues that internal coaches bring to supervision and what supervisors need to look out for.

Psychological aspects

- It can be difficult for the coaches to stay impartial when the client is talking about an aspect of the organisation they both work for. The coaches may fail to test their assumptions under the mistaken impression that they know what the client is thinking and feeling. One coach wrote: "It can be hard to disassociate your own experiences and your own feelings towards a business situation or structure that a client is describing, as you help them work through their challenges, and remain neutral" (St John-Brooks, 2014, pp. 25/26).
- The scope for an unconscious parallel process to operate is augmented when coach and client are working in the same system (and even more so if the supervisor is too).
- There can be 'emotion contagion' between coach and client, particularly when there are upheavals within the organisation, such as a restructuring, which equally affect coach and client. Coaching a number of anxious clients, while feeling distressed themselves about what is in the system, can put the coaches' emotional resilience to the test. One lead coach in a high pressure organisation, when asked what – with hindsight – she would have changed, said she would have paid more attention to "how coaches self-regulate" (St John-Brooks, 2014, p. 207).
- The coach, having built a close rapport with a client, may unwittingly find themselves in a 'drama triangle' (Karpman, 1968) with the coach perceiving the client as 'victim,' the organisation as 'persecutor' and themselves as 'rescuer.' The supervisor may need to remind the coach of the need to maintain objectivity and their dual responsibility to the client and the organisation.
- Where internal coaches are in supervision groups, issues within the organisation – which the coaches are picking up from their clients – are amplified given that the coaches are in the same system. The supervisor cannot ignore that emotion, but nor can they allow it to drag everyone down. It is necessary to get any angst about 'what's wrong with the organisation' out in the open and then out of the room before the coaching supervision – focussing on the clients and on the coaches' own development – can really start.

Practical aspects

Working in the same organisation as the client can present coaches with some practical complications. For example, it is not uncommon for a client to begin to talk about a colleague whom the coach knows. Unless the coach acknowledges this quickly, they can find themselves in a false position. Once they know something about a colleague from their coaching client they can't 'unknow' it, and it can toxify their relationship with that colleague. Plus they may allow their knowledge of that person to skew how they focus their questions. One coach cited the example of a "client discussing the negative impact a colleague's behaviour is having on them – the colleague is a personal friend of mine" (St John-Brooks, 2014, p. 40). The supervisor needs to be alert to a possible need to help the coach devise a strategy for such situations.

Supervisors of internal coaches often find that they are spending time on helping their coaches resolve actual or potential ethical dilemmas. There is evidence (St John-Brooks, 2010b) that internal coaches most commonly encounter ethical dilemmas relating to confidentiality, boundaries and role conflicts.

- *Confidentiality:* The concept of confidentiality is fundamental to coaching relationships but is put to the test more for internal coaches as they have so much more formal and informal interaction with managers within the organisation than an external coach commonly would. They have to work out a tactful way of dealing with, say, a chance question put by a senior sponsor in a random encounter in a corridor about 'how the coaching is going,' and as Carter (2005) points out: "innocent questions answered round the water-cooler . . . can lead to serious breaches of confidentiality" (p. 13). Supervisors may have to deal with coaches' frustrations about maintaining confidentiality in situations where they don't think it is in the organisation's interests to do so. One example: "A client was referred and it turned out that she had been bullied and was clearly suffering emotionally and confidence wise. I encouraged her to speak to her boss about it and took it to supervision. I kept asking the question about whether I could get involved in blowing the whistle on the bully but in the end had to accept the person's choice not to take it further" (St John-Brooks, 2014, p. 50).

- *Boundaries:* Internal coaches can run up against a number of boundaries. A common one is a blurred line between the roles of the coach and the client's boss. As one coach said: "A lot of people want to be coached on a specific short term problem, something to do with their current workload, and I think you have to remind them that this is more appropriate for their line manager, not a coach" (St John-Brooks, 2014, p. 46). Another is the boundary between the client's work life and personal life. Organisations can be very unclear about what they expect of their coaches. St John-Brooks' research found that 91% of internal coaches surveyed answered yes to the question "Are you content for a coaching conversation to go beyond work issues?" (2014, p. 41), and examples included family situation/relationship issues; work-life balance; bereavement/illness/fertility treatment; anxiety/ low self-esteem; and giving up smoking/losing weight. Some organisations might feel that they had trained their coaches to spend time on issues very directly related to performance at work; others would take a broader view. A third boundary is that between coaching and mentoring. Internal coaches can encounter considerable pressure from clients to act as mentors rather than coaches (particularly when the coach is senior to the client), and supervisors may find themselves needing to help coaches to maintain that boundary.

- *Role conflicts:* Another challenging boundary can be between the coach's role as a coach and their function in their day job – it comes up sufficiently frequently to merit special attention. Where a coach works in the HR or OD function they are particularly liable to encounter such role conflicts. Sometimes it is a matter of having some insider knowledge such as: "Where a client has shared that they are going for a promotion or intending to leave the organisation and I have knowledge regarding the situation which could influence their decision" (St John-Brooks, 2014, p. 38). This kind of situation is uncomfortable for the coach as they feel that their authenticity is compromised. Or the coach may be tempted to 'fix' a client's problem like this coach: "You want to rescue the individual and have to keep checking with yourself 'Are you sure you're not on your White Charger?'. There's a tendency to want to save the individual as there *are* levers that OD could pull" (St John-Brooks, 2014, p. 39). Or there may be some very direct conflict such as this coach found: "Where a line manager wanted to get advice about one of her members of staff that she was having problems with, and did not know that I was that person's coach (as the person had self-referred)" (St John-Brooks, 2014, p. 37).

Conclusion

The phenomenon of training employees to be internal coaches is still growing. A trained cohort of internal coaches offers too many organisational benefits for the trend to be reversed anytime soon. This chapter has explored the challenges that are peculiar to internal coaching and argues for the importance of the coaches being offered support in the form of professional supervision and regular CPD. Those challenges might suggest to some that being an internal coach presents insuperable difficulties. This is not so, but they are the reason why internal coaches should be given access to supervision. As Hawkins and Schwenk wrote way back in 2006:

> If you don't provide supervision for internal coaches . . . the sustainability and return on investment of your coaching initiative is in jeopardy.
> Hawkins and Schwenk (2006, p. 17)

References

Butwell, J. (2006). Group Supervision for Coaches: Is It Worthwhile? A Study of the Process in a Major Professional Organisation. *International Journal of Evidence Based Coaching and Mentoring*, 4, 43–53.

Carroll, M. (2006). Key Issues in Coaching Psychology Supervision. *The Coaching Psychologist*, 2, 4–8.

Carter, A. (2005). *Providing Coaching Internally: A Literature Review.* HR Network Paper MP43. Brighton, UK: Institute of Employment Studies.

Chartered Institute of Personnel and Development (CIPD). (2015). *Learning and Development Annual Survey Report.* Chartered Institute of Personnel and Development, London. Available at www.cipd.co.uk/knowledge/strategy/development/surveys

Childs, R., Woods, M., Willcock, D. and Man, A. (2011). Action Learning Supervision for Coaches. In Passmore, J. (ed), *Supervision in Coaching: Supervision, Ethics and Continuous Professional Development.* London: Kogan Page, pp 31–43.

Clutterbuck, D. and Megginson, D. (2011). Coach Maturity: An Emerging Concept. In Wildflower, L. and Brennan, D. (eds), *The Handbook of Knowledge-Based Coaching: From Theory to Practice.* London: John Wiley & Sons.

European Mentoring & Coaching Council. (2018). *Guidelines for Supervision.* Available at www.emccouncil.org/quality/supervision

Frisch, M. (2001). The Emerging Role of the Internal Coach. *Consulting Psychology Journal: Practice and Research,* 53(4), 240–250.

Hawkins, P. and Schwenk, G. (2006). *Coaching Supervision: Maximising the Potential of Coaching.* London: Chartered Institute of Personnel and Development.

Hawkins, P. and Smith, P. (2013, first edition 2006). *Coaching, Mentoring and Organizational Consultancy: Supervision and Development.* Maidenhead: Open University Press/McGraw Hill.

Hawkins, P. and Turner, E. (2017). The Rise of Coaching Supervision 2006–2014. *Coaching: An International Journal of Theory, Research and Practice,* 1–13, Online.

Hunt, J. and Weintraub, J. (2006). *Coaching on the Inside: The Internal Coach.* Available at www.babsoninsight.com

Karpman, S. (1968). Fairy Tales and Script Drama Analysis (Selected Articles). *Transactional Analysis Bulletin,* 7, 39–43.

Lambert, A. (2008). What's New in Coaching & Mentoring? An Update. *Corporate Research Forum,* October.

Long, K. (2012). Building Internal Supervision Capability in Organisations. *The OCM Coach and Mentor Journal,* 12, 2–6.

Moral, M., Guerand, A., Desroches, J., Reveneau, C., Levy, M., Benoit, O. R. and Muh, E. (2017). *How to Best Organise Supervision in a "Strong Coaching Culture" Environment?* Presented at 23rd International Mentoring and Coaching Conference, 2 March 2017, Edinburgh, Scotland.

Ridler & Co. (2015). *Sixth Ridler Report: Strategic Trends in the Use of Executive Coaching.* London: Ridler & Co. Available from www.ridlerandco.com/ridler-report/

Sherpa Coaching. (2016). *The Executive Coaching Survey.* Available at www.sherpacoaching.com/pdf%20files/2016_Executive_Coaching_Survey_PUBLIC.pdf

St John-Brooks, K. (2010a). What Are the Ethical Challenges Involved in Being an Internal Coach? *International Journal of Mentoring and Coaching,* VIII(1), 50–66.

St John-Brooks, K. (2010b). Moral Support. *Coaching at Work,* 5(1), 48–51.

St John-Brooks, K. (2014). *Internal Coaching: The Inside Story.* London: Karnac Books.

Thomson, B. (2011). Non-directive supervision of coaching. In: J Passmore (Ed.), *Supervision in Coaching: Supervision, Ethics and Continuous Professional Development* (pp. 91–116). London: Kogan Page.

11 Guidelines for team coach supervision

Dr Alison Hodge and Prof David Clutterbuck

Team coaching emerged very swiftly after the advent of coaching as a concept in the 1850s. Initially a directive form of tutoring for Oxbridge students, the term was soon applied to rowing, then tennis. The modern, non-directive model of coaching evolved in the early 1970s from the work of tennis coach Timothy Gallwey (1974), but the transfer of this approach into team coaching, even the world of sport, has been relatively slow. The literature on team coaching – at least in the English language – has emerged only in the past 20 years. It is not surprising then that the literature on *supervising* team coaches is even thinner (Clutterbuck and Hodge, 2017; Hawkins, 2014, 2017; Moral, 2011; Hodge, 2017). To fill this gap, in 2017 we conducted a scoping study to identify issues in team coaching supervision. This chapter draws upon both that study and our own experience, to suggest practical guidelines for both team coaches and team coach supervisors.

Summary of the research results

Until now, there is little research-based evidence (Carr and Peters, 2013) and dedicated literature to inform our appreciation of the complex range of methods and skills team coaches now require that enable them to facilitate this fascinating, challenging and arguably *new* practice of team coaching.

Based on findings from an online global survey that we conducted in the early part of 2017 there are several key tasks or elements involved in the practice of team coaching that include:

- Establishing goal clarity and purpose;
- Contracting;
- Multi-stakeholder engagement;
- Group and team learning;
- Group development;
- Managing the impact of the wider organisational system;
- Coaching the team (as distinct from one-to-one coaching);
- Managing the interpersonal dynamics within the team as well as between the team members and the coach themselves; and
- Temporal issues.

From our experience, often coaches believe they can do this work because they are highly able 1:1 coaches and imagine that their coaching skills alone are transferable.

However, borne out by the findings from our research, what is evident in fact is how challenging and demanding this work can be for the team coach. They are likely to be drawing on knowledge and skills from an extensive and diverse range of change interventions that may include a combination from any of the following disciplines: organisational development, executive coaching, group facilitation, process consulting, adult learning, systems and constellations, and family therapy.

The overall conclusion from the survey was that the majority of team coaches both need and want supervision to support them in this complex work. They are looking for support and challenge that enables them to gain awareness of what might be happening within the whole client system (not just with one individual coachee). They seek insights from the supervisor about how to balance the purpose and tasks of the coaching while managing the psychological aspects of the team dynamics and relationships. Supervision provides the container for the team coach to offload, process and gain clarity around what is happening at any one stage in the assignment as well as gaining support for the impact this may be having on their own confidence to stay grounded in the work.

With the right support that includes supervision, this work can be great fun, given that the team coach is equipped to work within the constantly changing layers of complexity.

So, how does this play out for the team coaching supervisor?

From our research, together with feedback from our clients and anecdotal evidence from the wider coaching field, it is clear that supervisors require extensive capacity and knowledge to create the appropriate container to support the coach (Clutterbuck and Hodge, 2017). These include:

- Experience and expertise in both 1:1 and team coaching;
- Strong academic and/or psychological background;
- Professional qualification in supervision (not necessarily coaching supervision);
- Strong grounding in group process and group facilitation;
- Ideally experience of actually working in and leading a team;
- An understanding of organisational structures including across cultures and remotely; and
- An appreciation of the scope of team coaching and how it extends to HR, Finance, IT, L&D, OD and any other corporate functions.

At this stage, several of the professional coaching bodies (AC and EMCC) are working on developing competency frameworks for team coaching and subsequently supervision of this practice. The Association of Professional Executive Coaches and Supervisors (APECS) has established criteria (2017), but the task of defining team coaching supervision practice is in its early stages.

Given that the team coach supervisor is able to meet some or all of the coach's needs and expectations, they face some key challenges in this work. At the core is the sheer complexity and unpredictability of any team coaching intervention. It is vital for the supervisor to stay outside of the client system and avoid getting hooked themselves into the parallel process (Casey, 1993) that might result in them enacting what may be happening in the client system and relationships. Challenges include the following.

Agreeing what is realistic in the supervision

- A willingness of both coach and supervisor to commit an appropriate amount of time to the supervision (45–60 minute sessions are unlikely to be adequate to explore and unravel what might be happening in the work that results in clarity for the team coach);
- Keeping themselves up to date as supervisors with the emerging literature, research and learning around team coaching and associated supervision; and
- Developing a clear framework to explore the knowledge and skills that the team coach needs to learn, develop and/or sustain.

Understanding of group dynamics and systems

- Appreciation of the complexity and different levels of conscious and unconscious awareness in the client system and with the coach;
- Holding a systemic perspective of the multiple relationships and group dynamics;
- Drawing on their own personal experience of the challenges of working with teams or groups in diverse contexts and how this may inform what is happening in their supervisee's systems; and
- Balancing the needs for self-awareness and development of the coach alongside the stages of team development towards meeting the purpose of the coaching.

Holding the supervision boundary

- Resisting the urge to coach the team rather than supervise the team coach;
- Holding the whole system in mind;
- Keeping sight of the purpose of the supervision (needing ongoing re-contracting);
- Holding full attention in the supervision and not getting sucked into the team's system;
- Focussing on the whole team rather than one specific individual;
- Developing the coach's capacity to work with groups;
- Committing sufficient time to explore an assignment in depth; and
- Providing continuous support to the coach as they may be swirling around in the turbulence of their client system and the work.

Establishing a theoretical model for team coach supervision

The development of theoretical models and definitions tends to be an iterative process. There will be a variety of definitions of team coaching elsewhere in this book, but we can be content for the purposes of this chapter to posit that an intervention is team coaching if it (a) focusses on an entire, bounded work team and (b) employs a level of reflective practice that can be considered to adopt a coaching style of dialogue.

One of the distinguishing features of supervision and of the more mature levels of coaching, we propose, is having a portfolio of different models to draw upon, to help coaches take different perspectives on the issues they bring to supervision. Single model or limited model approaches carry a number of risks, including groupthink, preoccupation with process rather than content and context, and myopia in the formative aspects of supervision. Our survey revealed that supervisors draw upon a wide range of models to inform their insights into team coaching (e.g. Katzenbach & Smith, Clutterbuck, 2006; Lencioni, 2002; Hawkins, 2014, 2017) but did not elicit any models of supervision.

To begin the construction of a theoretical model of team coaching supervision, we have started with what team coach supervisees say they do, as described earlier. Thus, what do we as team coach supervisors do to support the coach?

We can look at the complexity of the supervision context. In supervising one-to-one coaching, Hawkins' Seven Eyed Supervision model is widely accepted as a pragmatic method of exploring different perspectives of the coaching intervention. In the more complex context of team coaching, there are at least two other perspectives to consider, relating to the relationships between team members and the relationship between team members and the team leader. Other models include Clutterbuck's seven conversations, which deconstruct the coaching intervention into mainly unspoken conversations that may consciously or unconsciously affect the spoken conversation (2007).

In team coaching, we can add several more approaches that may also suit the development of the supervisor:

> Six Step Model (Hawkins, 2014): Here we see a guide to the steps that are involved in a team coaching assignment along a continuum. This may provide a skeleton structure and shared 'menu' for both coach and supervisor.
>
> Full Spectrum Model (Murdoch, Adamson and Orriss, 2006): Here we see that at the heart of this work is the relationship, and in the case of supervising team coaching, this enables both the coach and the supervisor to explore the work through the relational dynamics that are constantly arising with all those involved.
>
> Systemic Supervision with Constellations (Moral, 2011; Whittington, 2016): Taking a systemic approach enables the coach to explore beyond the individual team members into the wider systems and multiple contexts that may be impacting on the work.

Three Pillars of Supervision (Hodge, 2016): Given the dynamic, relational complexity of a team coaching assignment, the supervisor needs a solid base from which to provide containment and safety for the coach to dive down into what may be happening at any given time without losing sight of the overall learning and change objectives they are facilitating.

Case study

With all this in mind, let one of us (Alison) share a personal experience as a team coaching supervisor.

I was approached to provide supervision for a group of four team coaches who were already engaged in a major change project. The coaches wanted to explore the issues that were arising for the three teams engaged in team coaching and at the same time consider the project within the context of the wider change initiative. We agreed a series of monthly 90-minute telephone supervision sessions. My proposal for longer sessions was declined on the grounds of time/coach availability and existing commitments.

Based on the initial briefing and contracting sessions with the coaches, what struck me was a number of key elements:

- *Multiple relationships between the client organisation employees;*
- *Multiple relationships between the client and the coaching team;*
- *Stress in the client system, also evident in the coaches' system;*
- *Pressure to deliver results for both; fear of failing;*
- *Different levels of client engagement; and*
- *Multiple relationships within the coaches' team and with me.*

I found the following questions recurred for me in this supervision assignment:

- *How would I hold the space and determine how to address each coach's needs as they were constantly changing?*
- *How could I clarify and establish my role and responsibilities as I engaged with a group of highly experienced coaches, with established patterns of working with each other?*
- *Given the time constraints as well as both the implicit and explicit pressure, how could I support our agreed purpose in supervision?*
- *How could I manage and contain the sheer volume of data about the client organisation, the purpose and progress of the team coaching assignment, the specific issues that the coaches wanted to address at any one session?*

It was only once we started that it became patently clear how complex, 'messy' and pressured this project was for the coaches, let alone what may have been happening in the client system. At the time, our focus was very much on what was happening and what was needed in the client system. It became evident to me, however, that we needed more time than was available for supervision, to allow us to explore both the coaching group's needs as well as the individual practice issues for each coach. What also became clear was that there was stress for everyone involved. Client employees, the external coaches, all being asked to get results, usually involving complex, difficult development work alongside hard strategic work. This work can be challenging and pulling people together to get it all done, pushing it along and then finding space to reflect on it all . . . In this twenty-first century, it calls for real compassion all round.

After three supervision sessions, I was informed that the team coaching assignment within the change project had been cancelled. I was not entirely clear why this had come about, but, based on the issues that were emerging in the team-based interventions, my understanding was that the priorities within the organisation were changing and the teams needed to adjust their focus. As a result of the team coaching being cancelled, so too was the supervision. As the coaching supervisor, I was left with a number of questions that may contribute to our thinking about the demands and challenges of team coaching supervision:

- *Can this work be done realistically and effectively by one supervisor in such a complex project with the number of coaches involved?*
- *What assumptions did we each and all make about how supervision could and should work? What is the supervisor's role and responsibility to establish and meet our purpose, given the demands of the client system on the coaches?*
- *How can a supervisor be prepared for something like this? What other contracting would have made it more effective?*
- *How as supervisor do we build safety and individual/group learning in a constantly changing supervision group doing team coaching with constantly changing participants?*
- *How do we use the supervision as the basis for inquiry into what is happening in the client system to inform how to proceed with the client project?*
- *What is realistic for the supervision in such a context? When and how does the supervisor say 'No' instead of taking on such an assignment?*

Factors to consider in team coaching

It was partly as a result of this assignment, together with ongoing learning and reflections about this work, that Alison developed the map that appears here in Figure 11.1: factors to consider in team coaching. Whilst this is not a model of team coaching supervision, it is intended to offer a visual representation of the key elements that exist in an assignment and that both coach and supervisor may focus on at any given time in supervision. The aim here is to demonstrate how diverse are the perspectives while attempting to acknowledge the breadth and depth of this practice. What is difficult to capture

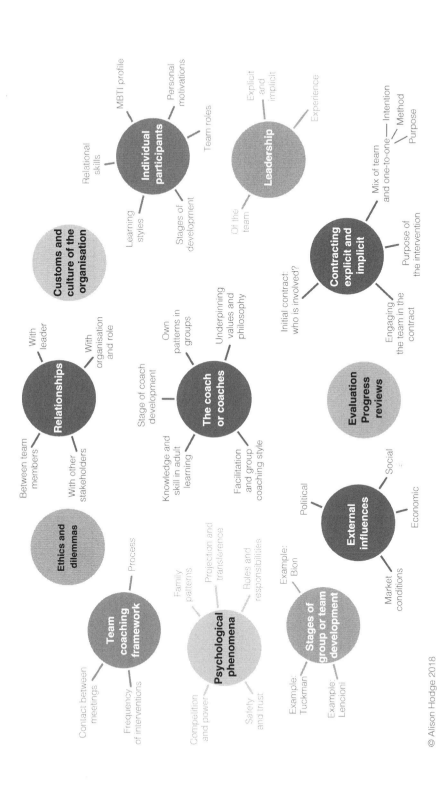

Figure 11.1 Factors to consider in team coaching

© Alison Hodge 2018

Individual participants
- MBTI profile
- Personal motivations
- Team roles
- Relational skills
- Learning styles
- Stages of development

Leadership
- Explicit and implicit
- Experience
- Of the team

Customs and culture of the organisation

Relationships
- With leader
- With organisation and role
- Between team members
- With other stakeholders

The coach or coaches
- Own patterns in groups
- Underpinning values and philosophy
- Stage of coach development
- Knowledge and skill in adult learning
- Facilitation and group coaching style

Contracting explicit and implicit
- Mix of team and one-to-one — Intention
                            — Method
                            — Purpose
- Purpose of the intervention
- Initial contract: who is involved?
- Engaging the team in the contract

Ethics and dilemmas

Evaluation Progress reviews

Team coaching framework
- Process
- Contact between meetings
- Frequency of interventions

Psychological phenomena
- Family patterns
- Projection and transference
- Rules and responsibilities
- Competition and power
- Safety and trust

External influences
- Social
- Political
- Economic
- Market conditions

Stages of group or team development
- Example: Bion
- Example: Tuckman
- Example: Lencioni

and communicate in a static diagram is the complexity (and at times chaos) of how the factors interconnect and interact in a living, relational process. This is resonant with Bateson when she describes "alive-inbetweenness" (2017) in liminal leadership.

Let us now discuss the different factors.

The coach

In Figure 11.1 you will see that at the heart of team coaching supervision is the team coach (or, if working as a dyad, the coaches) themselves. We can start by considering their level of knowledge, skill and capabilities in coaching and group facilitation practice. An important factor also here is the coach's own patterns and responses in groups. We need to consider how they develop their capacity to work with complex relational and organisational systems.

With the coach as the focus in team coaching supervision, together we can explore and reflect on a team coaching intervention through any one and all of the following lenses with no one factor more important than another (see Figure 11.1). What is challenging for both the coach and the supervisor is how to attend to and/or hold all these factors in mind during the supervision. Figure 11.1 may be seen as a 'constantly moving constellation' with different factors coming into the foreground at any one time while also impacting on any and all the other factors. Perhaps one way to attend to this in supervision is to visit each factor over a series of sessions rather than attempting to work through each one in any given session.

However, by holding the coach at the centre of our attention, we can avoid the pitfall or temptation as supervisor of getting involved in the team coaching itself (research findings 2017). Each of the following factors includes at least several elements and is constantly changing, ebbing and flowing in terms of significance and relevance, and impacted by all the other factors.

Individual participants

- Relational skills;
- Personality profiles (e.g. Hogan, MBTI, Enneagram);
- Team roles (e.g. Belbin);
- Stage of adult development and emotional literacy;
- Learning styles; and
- Personal motivations.

Leadership

- Of the team;
- Experience of the leader;
- Role and responsibilities; and
- Explicit and implicit leadership.

Contracting – explicit and implicit (Carroll, 2005)

- Purpose of the intervention;
- Initial contract – who is involved;
- Between the team leader and the team, between the team leader and the sponsor;
- Agreeing the mix of team and one-to-one coaching (intention, purpose, method); and
- Engaging the team in the contract individually and collectively.

Stages of group or team development (some examples)

- Bion (1968);
- Lencioni (2002); and
- Tuckman (1965).

Psychological phenomena

- Competition, power and authority;
- Family patterns – how individual participants show up;
- Projection and transference;
- Roles and responsibilities; and
- Safety and trust.

Relationships

- With the leader;
- Between team members;
- With other stakeholders; and
- With organisation and each participant's role.

Customs and culture of the organisation

- 'This is how we do things around here.'

External influences

- Political;
- Economic;
- Social; and
- Market conditions.

Ethical issues and dilemmas

Evaluation and progress reviews

A step by step process for team coaching supervision

Another perspective is to see team coach supervision as a *process*. From this perspective, we can identify six sequential elements:

1   Preparation. Establishing realistic expectations of how the team coaches will reflect on their client experiences, create an agenda for supervision and give the supervisor time to prepare.
2   Case or issue presentation. A case relates to a specific client team; an issue to a recurring theme, such as working with teams that have ineffectual leaders. A construct we find helpful in presenting cases is:

   a   What is the context of this team (the purpose, internal and external dynamics)?
   b   What are the challenges for the team? (Clutterbuck's five pillars of team performance can be helpful here: Purpose & Motivation, Relationships, Internal Processes, External (Stakeholder) Processes and Learning Processes; 2009.)
   c   What are the challenges for you as a team coach?

3   What have you learned so far, from your reflections on this team and your interactions with it?
4   What do you need to feel more confident in working with this team? (What do you need from *me*?)
5   Exploration. Looking at the issue(s) through different lenses.
6   Affirmation. Building confidence; acknowledging learning and new insights.

Preparing for team coaching supervision: a coach perspective

One-to-one coaches get more out of the session if they have prepared for it (Hodge, 2016). Given the greater complexity of team coaching, preparation is even more important. We can break this down into two elements: (i) immediately after a team coaching session and (ii) immediately before supervision.

i   Immediately after a team coaching session, the coach needs to find a congruent way to capture the key elements of what happened, the progress (or not) of the team and what they consider may be influencing this. Equally, they need to reflect on and record the impact of the intervention on themselves, what worked, what may not have worked, how is the group/ team affecting them, how are they managing themselves in this process. This information need not be conclusive, but rather be viewed as 'data' that informs what is happening and how the coach might proceed.
ii   The supervision dyad may agree in advance some sort of framework to support the coach in their preparation for sessions so that they get the

most out of it. At the same time, both parties need to be open to what may emerge unexpectedly during a supervision session that gives rise to greater clarity, insight and 'aha moments.' In preparation, the team coach is likely to review their notes from (i) and notice what is in the foreground that they want to explore during the supervision dialogue. Likewise, they may identify the key questions they wish to address in supervision that will support their preparation for subsequent client engagement.

Content to bring to supervision

Based on the survey findings and coupled with our own experience of supervising this work, there are a number of key issues or themes that team coaches consistently seek to work on in supervision:

- How to manage their feelings of stuckness or self-doubt by what is or isn't happening within an assignment, especially when the team does not appear to be moving.
- Monitoring and responding to the team's individual and collective commitment and capacity to engage with the declared or intended purpose and not losing sight of the overall purpose.
- Holding the unpredictability of the project, especially with the ever-changing relationships within the team, with the sponsor, with the coach themselves.
- Creating the container and conditions that enable the team members to disclose more of themselves with the intention to improve interpersonal relationships that enable the purpose of the work and the team to progress.
- Contracting issues that persistently arise in any team coaching assignment and in supervision the coach is able to regroup and identify when or if the purpose and/or project design and approach need to be revisited. Without exception, every team coaching disaster brought to us has involved a failure of contracting, with the team, the leader, a sponsor or all three.
- Supervision provides the container for the coach to explore any 'dysfunctional' elements within the client team, particularly where trust may be in question (Lencioni, 2002).
- Coaches may feel a cumulative sense of frustration and impotence that affects their confidence when their attempts to coach the team to succeed appear to lack impact or result.

When not to coach a team

In our experience one of most important functions a supervisor can offer is to help the team coach determine when not to take on an assignment. Self-confidence can take a very hard knock if a team coaching assignment goes badly wrong. Supervisors' restorative role should, we argue, include prevention, helping the coach to recognise, and thus protect themselves, against a 'poisoned chalice.'

When not to coach a team:

1   When there is no compelling rationale for being a team – for example, when members of a group have little interdependence.
2   When it is too large to be a real team – above eight, it will become harder to gel as a team; above 12, social loafing and other dynamics will be a major impediment to performance.
3   When only the leader wants team coaching to happen.
4   When the team leader is weak – for example, unable to deal with dissension. In such circumstances, the team coach can easily find themselves in the role of surrogate leader.
5   When the team expects you to rescue them, or for you to find the solutions to their problems instead of working things out themselves. If they won't take responsibility for the process or the outcomes, you are liable to become the scapegoat when things don't work out.
6   When the team has no prospect of acquiring the resources it needs to succeed.
7   When you are a stakeholder in the team – any real or potential conflict of interest can undermine your effectiveness.
8   When you have close relationships with some members of the team, but not with others.
9   When the team's problems are pathological – deeply unhealthy teams will find it impossible to engage with the team coaching process.

The added complexity of team coach dyads

Recommended good practice in team coaching is increasingly to work in pairs (Moral, 2011), with at any time one person leading the coaching dialogue and one observing the group dynamics. The benefits of doing so include:

- Sharing the parallel tasks of facilitating the group and observing the group dynamics;
- Each coach having frequent breaks from intense engagement with the team, so they remain fresh;
- Being able to step in when a colleague is stuck (for example, pointing out a group dynamic and asking the team what they would like to do about it); and
- More effective debriefs than when one coach reflects on their own.

In supervision, the coaching dyad is also a team, so the supervisor must be aware of the added complexity of whether and how to act as coach to this team, demonstrating good practice. A critical question to the dyad is 'How do you coach and supervise each other during and after each team coaching intervention?'

   Supervisors can help these coach dyads prepare by asking them to reflect upon questions such as:

- How do you complement each other?
- How do you role model being a (two-person) team?
- What dynamics are played out between you in front of the team you are coaching together? (For example, what happens when one of you rescues the other?)
- What is your process for co-learning?

Group supervision

The value of supervising team coaches in a group setting is firstly that there is a wider spread of team situations and dynamics to learn from. At the same time, the greater level of anxiety and vulnerability that team coaches often experience compared to one-to-one coaches means that they may need higher levels of affirmation – which group supervision can provide.

Mixed 1:1 and team coaching supervision

In some instances, coaches opt to engage in 1:1 supervision for their 1:1 coaching assignments. They then commit to dedicated team coaching supervision (often in group) for these projects where they can attend to the multiple layers and complexity not always evident in individual coaching.

Our research was inconclusive in terms of team coaches' preference for 1:1 or group supervision; however, there was some indication that participating in group supervision gave the team coach greater insights as the supervision group often manifested elements of what might have been happening in the client system (parallel process). Likewise, members of group supervision bring diverse perspectives that may add to the coach's deliberations and reflections.

Further research

Based on our experience the findings from our survey provided a very broad perspective to give us some indicators of how this practice of team coaching is emerging and thus how supervision makes what is evidently a vital contribution to support the team coach.

At the same time, it would seem that we have more to discover and learn about the core competences of a team coach. This in turn suggests that we need to explore more deeply how a team coach and/or supervisor develops the complex range of knowledge and skills alongside the personal qualities to provide supervision in this context.

Conclusion

In this chapter, based on the findings from our survey and coupled with our experience, we have identified some of the many dimensions involved in team coaching. We have then explored what team coaching supervision offers to the development of the discipline and the practice of team coaches. Clearly, team coaching supervision is also in its early stages of development, and we have a need to recognise and appreciate the challenges and complexity that we need to learn to work in this field effectively.

Bibliography and further reading

APECS guidelines. Available at www.apecs.org/apecs-accredited-executive-team-coach-category-description (Accessed September 2017).

Bateson, N. (2017). Liminal Leadership. *Kosmos Journal*, Fall/Winter. Available at www.kosmosjournal.org/article/liminal-leadership/ (Accessed 16 June 2018).

Bion, R. (1968). *Experiences in Groups*. London: Tavistock Publications.

Brown, R. (2000) *Group Processes*. Massachusetts: Blackwell Publishing.

Carr, C. and Peters, J. (2013). The Experience and Impact of Team Coaching: A Dual Case Study. *International Coaching Psychology Review*, 8(1), 80–98.

Carroll, M. (2005). Psychological Contracts With and Within Organisations. In Tribe, R. and Morrissey, J. (eds), *Handbook of Professional and Ethical Practice for Psychologists, Counsellors and Psychotherapists*. Hove: Brunner-Routledge.

Casey, P. (1993). *Managing Learning in Organisations*. Buckinghamshire: Open University Press.

Clutterbuck, D. (2007). *Coaching the Team at Work*. London: Nicholas Brealey.

Clutterbuck, D. (2011). Using the Seven Conversations in Supervision. In Bachkirova, T. Jackson, P. and Clutterbuck, D. (eds), *Coaching and Mentoring Supervision*. Maidenhead: McGraw-Hill Open University Press, 55–66.

Clutterbuck, D. and Hodge, A. (2017). *Team Coaching Supervision Survey*. Available at www.emccbooks.org/book/book/research-conference (Accessed July 2017).

Corey, M. S. and Corey, G. (1997). *Groups – Process and Practice Pacific*. 5th ed. Grove, CA: Brooks Cole Publishing.

Critchley, B. (2010). Relational Coaching: Taking the Coaching High Road. *Journal of Management Development*, 29(10), 851–863.

Drake, D. (2011). What Do Coaches Need to Know? Using the Mastery Window to Assess and Develop Expertise. *Coaching: An International Journal of Theory, Research and Practice*, 4, 2 September, 138–155.

Gallwey, T. (1974). *The Inner Game of Tennis*. New York: Random House.

Gray, D. E. and Jackson, P. (2011). Coaching Supervision in the Historical Context of Psychotherapeutic and Counseling Models: A Meta-model. In Bachkirova, T., Jackson, P. and Clutterbuck, D. (eds), *Coaching and Mentoring Supervision: Theory and Practice*. Berkshire: McGraw-Hill.

Hawkins, P. (2014). *Leadership Team Coaching*. 2nd ed. London: Kogan Page.

Hawkins, P. (2017). *Leadership Team Coaching*. 3rd ed. London: Kogan Page.

Hawkins, P. and Shohet, R. (2000). *Supervision in the Helping Professions*. 2nd ed. Buckingham: McGraw Hill.

Hawkins, P. and Smith, N. (2013). *Coaching, Mentoring and Organisational Consultancy*. 2nd ed. Berks: McGraw Hill.

Hay, J. (2007). *Reflective Practice and Supervision for Coaches*. Maidenhead, Berkshire: Open University Press.

Hodge, A. (2016). The Value of Coaching Supervision as a Development Process and Its Contribution to Continued Professional and Personal Wellbeing for Executive Coaches. *International Journal of Evidence Based Coaching and Mentoring*, 14(2), 87–102.

Hodge, A. (2017). The Hidden Dimensions of Team Coaching Supervision. *Coaching Perspectives*, Issue 15, pp. 21–23, October 2017. Available at http://edition.pagesuite-professional.co.uk/html5/reader/production/default.aspx?pubname=&edid=f4a86d08-ed2c-4d50-9d8d-375eabf033ac

Katzenbach, Jon R. & Smith, Douglas K. (2001). *The Discipline of Teams.* New York: Wiley.

Kantor, D. (2012). *Reading the Room.* San Francisco: Jossey Bass.

Lencioni, P. (2002). *The Five Dysfunctions of a Team.* San Francisco: Jossey Bass.

Moral, M. (2011). A French Model of Supervision: Supervising a 'Several to Several' Coaching Journey. In Bachkirova et al. (eds), *Coaching and Mentoring Supervision.* Berkshire: McGraw-Hill.

Murdoch, E., Adamson, F. and Orriss, M. (2006). *Full Spectrum Model.* https://coachingsupervisionacademy.com/full-spectrum-model/ (Accessed 1 August 2017).

Proctor, B. (2000). *Group Supervision.* London: Sage Publications.

Ringer, T. M. (2002). *Group Action.* London: Jessica Kingsley.

Thornton, C. (2010). *Group and Team Coaching.* London: Routledge.

Tuckman, B. W. (1965). Developmental Sequences in Small Groups. *Psychological Bulletin*, 63(6), 384–399.

Turner, E. and Hawkins, P. (2016). Multi-Stakeholder Contracting in Executive/Business Coaching: An Analysis of Practice and Recommendations for Gaining Maximum Value. *International Journal of Evidence Based Coaching and Mentoring*, 14(2), 48–65.

Von Bertalanffy, L. (1968). *General Systems Theory.* New York: George Brasilia.

Whelan, S. A. (2005). *Creating Effective Teams.* London: Sage Publications.

Whittington, J. (2016). *Systemic Coaching & Constellations.* 2nd ed. London: Kogan Page.

Yalom, I. D. (1985). *The Theory and Practice of Group Psychotherapy.* New York: Harper Collins.

12 Supervision's oasis for leaders and people practitioners

Elaine Patterson

Introduction

Looking back I now wish that I had stumbled upon supervision when I was in my teens instead of my 40s! I have had the honour of leading wonderful people in amazing teams delivering transformational change but always felt the need of a 'super-vision' and 'super-seeing' of me to help me to honour my own golden threads of WHO I am, WHO I am becoming and HOW this impacts HOW I work.

I studied for the Coaching Supervision Academy's diploma in coaching supervision in order to deepen my own executive coaching practice – not to become a supervisor. However, I came to love supervision and the art of reflective practice – and could see its power not just for coaching supervision but for leaders and people practitioners – in essence for people who work with people. I also came to coach in a supervisory way and came to experiment with calling this Leadership Supervision or later Executive Reflection. This prompted me to complete my own MA research between 2011 and 2103 with the research question 'What are leaders' experiences of reflection?' where I discovered that ultimately reflection is an act of creativity – of either reshaping what already exists or bringing the new into the world (Patterson, 2015). This then led me on to work with Jackie Arnold and Alison Hodge to complete an action research inquiry between 2016 and 2018 into 'What is the value and relevance of Executive Reflection in a global, diverse and virtual world?' which will be published in 2019.

This chapter is a reflective essay on how I feel an organic holistic supervision, which attends to the development, support, resourcing and wellbeing of people who work with people, is now mission critical in today's VUCA world

Our world of work: living our questions

As Albert Einstein wrote:

> Problems cannot be solved from the consciousness which created them (Einstein, 1943).

Change and challenge are everywhere. What is now new and different is the scale, rapidity and intensity of the changes. At no time in our human history has the human race faced so many changes on so many fronts which are challenging the very essence of WHO we are, HOW we think, HOW we relate and HOW we work.

HOW we choose to live the questions as the waves of societal, economic, business, organisational, technological and ecological changes and uncertainty sweep through us, our families, our communities and our organisations will determine our fate: our ability to sink or swim in the tides of unceasing change and transformation.

I feel that Otto Schamer captures the extent of the challenge with his key statistics of 1.5; 8; and 800,000 where:

- 1.5 is that currently our world consumes the resources of 1.5 planets.
- 8 is the number of billionaires who own as much as half of us combined.
- 800,000 is the number of people who commit suicide each year – a sum which is greater than the numbers who are killed in war, murder or natural disasters combined (Scharmer, 2018).

Leaders, coaches, supervisors, HR, OD, people professionals, social entrepreneurs and development practitioners are all working on the frontline of these seismic shifts. Leaders and professionals are noticing in the myriad of conversations which we hold is that what got them – and their clients – to where they are in their professions or in their organisations is not what is going to keep them there; and more of the same is no longer enough. This is evidenced by some key pieces of research which indicate that:

- Only 15% of leaders sampled showed a consistent capacity to innovate and successfully transform their organisations (Torbert, Rooke and Fisher, 2000).
- Only 30% of CEO's are confident that they have the talent needed to grow their businesses (PWC, 2012).
- Thirteen per cent of employees are actively engaged (and twice that number would actively sabotage their employer) (Harvard Business Review).
- Fifty-eight per cent of new executives fail within 18 months of taking up their post (Gavett and Berinato, 2013).
- Only 8–12% of those who attend formal training translate their new skills into measurable performance (Skiffington and Zeus, 1999).
- Seventy-five per cent of organisations report that they struggle with overwhelmed employees (Finkelstein, 2004).

A bigger response and a bigger conversation with all of life and work are urgently needed.

The invitation

Definition of a leader

Anyone who holds her or himself accountable for finding potential in people and processes

From Brene Brown's *Daring Greatly Leadership Manifesto* (http://brenebrown.com/wp-content/uploads/2013/09/DaringGreatly-LeadershipManifesto-8x10.pdf)

This means that we are all leaders now. Leaders and people professionals also carry a double burden. It seems that never before has the responsibility been greater for us to live with our own excitements, uncertainties and anxieties as we support and resource others to do the same over the long haul.

Super-vision of ourselves with a supervisor can provide us with our own life support system as we reach out and BE the change that we want to see in the world – and as we lead, enable and role model for others to do the same.

Supervision is no longer a luxury but a necessity and an ethical duty for people who work with people to bring their best selves in service of their work.

When what we know is no longer enough

In times of turmoil the danger lies not in the turmoil but in facing it with yesterday's logic.

Peter Drucker (Drucker, 1995)

Technical competence and yesterday's logic are no longer enough as we need to create anew. As Reg Revans wrote, in times of change, learning needs to be equal to or greater than the rate of change (http://ifal.org.uk/action-learning/origins-of-action-learning/). As Barrett C. Brown notes in an IBM Global CEO Survey (Brown, 2013):

the great majority of CEOs expect that business complexity is going to increase, and that more than half doubt their ability to manage it. The sheer difficulty of keeping a corporation afloat in such turbulent economic, political, and social water is beyond most leaders' experience and mental capacity.

We are starving in a land of overload, busyness and unrelenting pressure.

One leader I was working with summed it up when he said:

I am so twisted out of shape I do not know myself or what I am supposed to be doing.

This is not unusual, as it seems many are craving:

- More headspace;
- More creativity;

- More re-sourcing; and
- More humanity.

For John Naisbitt (Laloux, 2014):

> The most exciting breakthroughs of the twenty-first century will not occur because of technology but because of an expanding concept of what it means to be human.

This means that we need to find ways – both individually and collectively – to:

- Reflect and creatively learn, unlearn or relearn from all of our experiences;
- Remember what it means to be human, to reconnect through our shared humanity and nurture our innate human capacities of care, courage, curiosity, connection, compassion, creativity and contemplation; as we
- Develop new and deepening levels of awareness and consciousness of ourselves in our world.

Supervision can now step forward to help us with our personal and professional journeys of discovery.

Supervision's oasis

Supervision needs to shake off the shackles of its old image and associations as the province of only therapists or line management supervision, command and control.

Supervision needs to reach beyond its traditional confines and reframe itself as a living, breathing profession which can provide a safe haven and oasis for busy leaders and people practitioners to come home to themselves, and from that home renew, refresh and refuel themselves for what lies ahead.

Supervision is a co-created learning partnership between the supervisor and supervisee which provides a uniquely creative, reflective and supportive space where the supervisor as compassionate witness and journey companion can super-see, support and attend to the ongoing personal and professional development of the leader or practitioner.

In super-vision we can uniquely ask for and receive the calibrated support and challenge to see what we cannot see, explore what we cannot see, touch the depths of our not knowing, engage with our vulnerabilities and from this process discover new insights for wise action in our work and lives. Supervision is an oasis because it creates the trusted relationship, safe container and reflective mirror for this powerful reflection, which then becomes a seedbed for creativity – and for bringing the new into the world.

Michael Carroll helpfully defines supervision as (Carroll, 2011):

> a way of looking at, and how with super-vision – new eyes, new perceptions, new visions, – we can see things differently. Supervision is a new

way of looking, a super way of visioning. With new visions, come new perspectives and new meanings. Supervision is always about the quality of awareness and what I choose to give my attention to. As I step outside my comfort zone and take an open stance, without blame or assumption and am open and indifferent to the outcome, what would I allow myself to think and reflect upon? Can I look beyond, beneath, above, below, against, for . . .?

For Fiona Adamson supervision is a safe space and place where (Adamson, 2010):

we can step back from the action, reflecting, pondering, analysing, trying out new ways of working, getting feedback, exploring where we are vulnerable, sharing our mistakes, understanding the part that unconscious processes play in our work, learning to hold the creative tension, attending to the intuitive and imaginative parts of ourselves . . . being playful and experimental, allowing creative leaps and non linear transformations to emerge from the apparent chaos of the moment.

This is further developed by Geraldine Holton when she writes (Benefiel and Holton, 2010):

Supervision provides a safe environment where both the practitioner and client are held. Supervision creates a container or transitional space for the emergence of a health selfhood, where all aspects of self – physical, spiritual, intellectual, personal and professional – are explored, reflected upon and integrated. It is the place (or a place) where personal and professional identity is formed and transformed. Supervision provides a safe holding environment where through wise conversation and creative attentiveness individuals and groups can co-create a deeper perspective and wisdom that can lead to transformation and effective practice.

My definition of supervision in this space is:

Super-vision is a bigger conversation inquiring into WHO you are when you practice in the bigger landscape within which you practice to enable you to do more, achieve more and be more. You will be accompanied by a skilled supervisor – who is your guide and companion – to enable you to escape the myopia of the present and to see new vistas and perhaps scale new heights. The conversations enable you to get in touch with your colour, vibrancy, elegance, dignity, humanity and vulnerability in order to better relate to yourself, to others and to your world to free you to craft a strong vision, strategy and direction for yourself, your team and your organization for the good of all. You come away with a super-seeing super-vision of yourself – and this is where your soul meets your role. This will enable you to find the wise source of your full leadership power, presence and humanity to both shine in your own uniqueness to inspire others to shine in theirs *and* to deliver the day to day whilst daring to create the future.

Supervision works because it is a relational practice working in the relationship and in the conversation in a parallel process to how leaders and people professionals also work with their clients or teams in their own workplaces. Supervision is the oasis where people professionals have the opportunity to turn data into wisdom. This is because as Bill Critchley writes: (Critchley and Sills, 2017):

> Change happens in the crucible of relationship.

And Fiona Adamson writes (Adamson, 2011):

> A relationship that truly attunes and resonates for both parties is transformational because it allows us to meet another at a soul level, free from the constraints that fear evokes in us, constraints that block our creativity and capacity to learn.

Supervision both mirrors and at the same time provides a mirror to the practitioner to see their brilliance and also their blind spots. The leader or practitioner works in the relationship and in the conversation to achieve learning, shift and change. Leadership and 'people work' ultimately exist both *in* and *as* a relationship with self, others and the world. This is because in order to connect with others, leaders and people professionals need to first relate and connect to themselves and to the heart of WHO they are. Our own human hearts are our organ through which we love, connect and relate to others, and as Vaclav Havel said as president of the Czech Republic to the Joint Session of the US Congress in March 1990 (Havel, 1990):

> The salvation of this human world lies nowhere else than in the human heart, in the human power to reflect, in human meekness and in human responsibility. Without a global revolution in the sphere of human consciousness, nothing will change for the better in the sphere of our being humans, and the catastrophe toward which the world is headed – be it ecological, social, demographic or a general breakdown in civilization – will be unavoidable.

Supervision: where role meets soul

Supervision is the place where our evolving roles meet our evolving souls: where our outer meets our inner landscape and where we can find out what is in our hearts so we stay true our own wider purpose. As David Whyte wrote in "Working Together" (Whyte, 2007):

> We shape our self to fit this world and by the world are shaped again.

In our work we have power to cast both light and shadow: the light of hope, joy, potential and possibility and the shadow of our own egos, triggers and unconscious behaviours. In our people work we use ourselves as our own instruments for our work. Our impact is shaped by what we intend and what we choose to pay attention to – and as Bill O'Brien, CEO of Hanover Insurance, is cited as saying (Scharmer, 2013):

> The success of any intervention depends on the interior condition of the intervener.

As leaders and people practitioners we therefore need to remember to remain humble in the face of our shared humanity as we work with fellow travellers. Love is the most transforming force we have. For Parker Palmer (*Leading from Within Poetry that Sustains the Courage to Lead*):

> Our lives (as people practitioners) both deserve and demand reflection. We *demand* reflection because we must know what it is in our hearts, lest we do more harm than good. We *deserve* reflection because it is often challenging to sustain the heart in work. If you decide to live an unexamined life please do not take a job that involves other people.

Exploring the relational heart of people work

Supervision's oasis supports the inquiry and discovery of our evolving selves. Given in the following text are some reflective questions for you to explore your own ground and horizons. As Parker J Palmer writes (*Leading from Within Poetry that Sustains the Courage to Lead*):

> Work is a constant conversation. It is a back and forth between what I think is me and what is not me; it is the edge between what the world needs of me and what I need of the world. Like a person I am committed in a relationship, it is constantly changing and surprising me by its demands and its needs but also by where it leads me, how much it teaches me, by how much tact, patience and maturity it demands of me.

As Hilary Owen wrote (Owen, 2000):

> People cannot be molded to be the same. Becoming a leader (or people professional) is an individual process and fundamental to the process is 'learning'. However, the learning is not through 'training' alone, but through personal experience and learning from that experience. When learning from experience occurs, it involves looking inwards at who we are. It means a deep awareness of who we are and the sort of human being we want to become. Once we know this, it can be expressed in our relationships and actions at work.

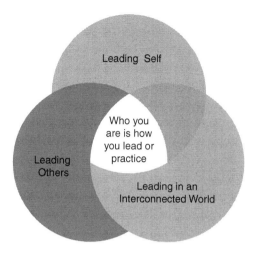

Figure 12.1 Supervisions' Three Lenses

Here are three lenses with questions for each lens to help you – or you with your clients – to explore the relational heart of supervision (see Figure 12.1). They are divided into three parts:

> First lens: for relating and leading yourself
> Second lens: for relating and leading others
> Third lens: for Relating and leading in the world

Supervision's three lenses

First lens: for relating and leading yourself

Learning to lead and work with people is first and foremost a radical act of learning to lead ourselves. In order to connect with others we must learn to connect with ourselves. Here are some question prompts to nurture the inquiry.

- *Who am I?*
- *Who defines me?*
- *Who am I when I lead?*
- *Who am I in my life?*
- *What am I afraid of?*
- *What energy am I transmitting?*
- *What, who or where are my triggers and blind spots?*
- *What are my passions and deepest desires?*
- *What is calling me?*
- *What is core to me, which I am not expressing?*
- *What am I not asking myself?*

- *What have I forgotten?*
- *What do I need to be more aware, and what do I need to learn?*
- *How do I best learn?*
- *How can I become a better version of myself?*
- *How do I keep my heart and my mind open?*
- *What am I holding onto which is no longer serving me?*
- *How do I feed, centre, resource and nourish myself?*
- *What help do I need?*

Second lens: for relating to and leading or working with others

Learning to lead and work with people is also a radical act of invitational hosting and co-creation to enable a collection wisdom to emerge. Here are some question prompts to nurture the inquiry.

- *How am I/we creating the invitations to ask the difficult questions of ourselves and of each other?*
- *How am I/we inviting, hosting and holding the courageous creative conversations which we need to have to create shift?*
- *What am I/we seeing and not seeing?*
- *What am I/we paying attention to, and what do I/we intend?*
- *What are the unintended consequences of our actions or inaction?*
- *What are the conversations we need to have which we are not having?*
- *WHO are WE when we are together?*
- *What is calling us?*
- *What is our deeper purpose together?*
- *What am I/we afraid of, and what might we be avoiding?*
- *Are we awake or are we sleepwalking?*
- *How are we aligning our purpose with our values, behaviours and action?*
- *How do I/we invite feedback?*
- *What is my/our approach to risk, errors and/or failure?*
- *How am I/we investing and nurturing our relationships and building trust?*
- *Do I/we invite multiple perspectives?*
- *How am I/we embracing difference and diversity?*
- *How do we free inspiration, creativity and best thinking to get the job done?*
- *What energy are we transmitting?*

Third lens: for relating to and working in the world

Learning to lead and work in the world is a radical act of sensing and not knowing in our VUCA world in order to create different or new futures in service of health and wellbeing. Here are some question prompts to nurture the inquiry.

- *What is my/our relationship with the unknown and not knowing?*
- *What is my/our ability to sense and see what is wanting to emerge?*
- *What am I/we paying attention to, and what do I/we intend?*
- *How do I/we create rather than control the future?*

- *What do I/we trust ourselves in this?*
- *What is calling us?*
- *What is my/our bigger purpose?*
- *What impact am I/are we having?*
- *How do I/we act with integrity in the world?*
- *What is our contribution?*
- *What is my/our legacy?*

I now coach in a supervisory way. Here is a case study of working through these three different lenses.

Case study

R. was an executive director on a board working in a highly complex and politicised environment. Despite huge material success and a happy family life she was struck feeling a strange and indescribable emptiness along with a sense that she was not fulfilling her full potential, which would not go away. Feeling typecast, stereotyped and sidelined she felt undervalued, bored and uninspired. Her question was "why am I feeling this way?" "How can I be more, contribute more and achieve more?"

We started by working through the first lens of *relating to and leading self.* Who was she when she was leading? What gifts, strengths, values and passions were being ignored by the short-term day to day pressures to deliver? What vulnerabilities and inner fears were old scripts which were now no longer appropriate and which could be re-written. What was her deeper purpose, and what conversations was she not having with herself, her chief executive, board and team which she needed to have and which would both push her out of her comfort zone and move her towards achieving more of her potential.

This work also needed to be put in the context of the second lens of *relating to and leading others.* Here it became clear that in order to release herself from the burden of operational detail she needed to work and relate differently. That by stepping forward as host she could create different kinds of conversations, which released her own, individual team members and the team's collective creativity engagement, participation and commitment. That through the process of becoming more comfortable with not knowing and exposing her potential vulnerability she was able to ask the simple but difficult and beautiful questions both in her 1:1s and in her meetings, which constructively challenged old paradigms and enabled them to innovate their way into the future.

This process was also fed and nourished by attending to the third lens, *relating to and working in the world.* The dropping of old masks, identities and stepping into not knowing meant that it became easier to read and act on the patterns found in the emerging seeds in the present to better shape the future. This process shifted the organisational culture from 'I' to 'we' and from 'ego' to 'us together' to achieve what was needed.

All three lenses were needed to shift awareness, impact and performance.

Summary

Supervision provides an oasis, mirror and haven for leaders and people practitioners to come home to themselves, know themselves and others, and emerge refreshed, renewed, reinvigorated and purposeful for skilful, wise and elegant action. Super-vision helps us to build the relational, creative and reflective capacities we need to work effectively, as Carl Jung wrote (Jung, 1953), with:

> the miracle of another living soul in front of you

Supervision has come of age and needs to move centre stage as a powerful intervention of choice for busy leaders and people practitioners who know that more of the same is no longer enough.

A final thought: I see supervision as the antidote and the answer to John O'Donohue's "Blessing for Work" – extracted here – in which he wrote (O'Donohue, 2008):

> May the sacredness of your work bring light and renewal to those who work with you and to those who see and receive your work.

References

Adamson, F. (2010). *Definitions of Supervision.* Unpublished. CSA Diploma Student Handbook.

Adamson, F. (2011). The Tapestry of My Approach to Transformational Learning in Supervision. In Shohet, R. (ed), *Supervision as Transformation – A Passion for Learning.* London: Jessica Kingsley Publishers, 90.

Benefiel, M. and Holton, G. (2010). *The Soul of Supervision – Integrating Practice and Theory.* New York: Moorhouse Publishing, 4.

Brown, B. C. (2013). *The Future of Leadership for Conscious Capitalism. MetaIntegral Associates.* Available at www. https://associates.metaintegral.org/ . . . /future-leadership-conscious-capitalism (Accessed 15 December 2013).

Carroll, M. (2011). Supervision: A Journey of a Lifelong Learning. In Shohet, R. (ed), *Supervision as Transformation – A Passion for Learning.* London: Jessica Kingsley Publishers, 22.

Critchley, B. and Sills, C. (2017). A Relational Approach to Executive Coaching. *Association of Coaching Global Bulletin,* January.

Downloaded 21st February 2018 from http://brenebrown.com/wp-content/uploads/2013/09/DaringGreatly-LeadershipManifesto-8x10.pdf

Downloaded 21st February 2018 from http://ifal.org.uk/action-learning/origins-of-action-learning/

Drucker, P. F. (1995). *Managing in Times of Great Change.* Abingdon, Oxon, p. 25 and cited in Hutchins, G. (2016). Available at https://thenatureofbusiness.org/2014/05/28/a-new-logic-beyond-the-illusion-of-separation/

Einstein, A. (1943). Quote cited in The Real Problem is in the Hearts of Men. *New York Times Magazine,* June 23, 1946. Available from http://icarus-falling.blogspot.co.uk/2009/06/einstein-enigma.html (Accessed 25 May 2016).

Finkelstein, S. (2004). *Why Smart Executives Fail: And What You Can Learn From Their Mistakes.* New York: Portfolio Trade, an imprint of Penguin Group.

Gavett, G. & Berinato, S. (2013). *The Sad State of the Global Workforce Engagement*. Harvard Business Review Blog Post, Watertown, Massachusetts, USA. https://hbr.org/2013/10/map-the-sad-state-of-global-workplace-engagement. Accessed 31st October 2017.

Harvard Business Review. Available at https://hbr.org/2013/10/map-the-sad-state-of-global-workplace-engagement/ (Accessed 26 April 2016).

Havel, V. (1990). Speech Delivered to a Joint Meeting of the US Congress. From *The Art of the Possible by Vaclav Havel*. Tranlated by Paul Wilson et al. New York: Alfred A. Knopf, Inc. 1997, 17–18.

Jung, C. G. (1953). *Psychological Reflections*. New York: Pantheon Books. Sands, Frederick. Good Housekeeping. "Why I Believe in God" (Interview with Carl Jung, 1961).

Naisbitt, J. quoted in Laloux, F. (2014). *Reinventing Organizations: A Guide to Creating Organizations Inspired by the Next Stage in Human Consciousness*. Belgium: Nelson Parker, 43.

O'Donohue, J. (2008). *To Bless the Space Between Us: A Book of Blessings*. New York, USA: Sounds True Inc, 146.

Owen, H. (ed.). (2000). *In Search of Leaders*. Chichester: John Wiley & Sons Ltd.

Palmer, P. J. Pp xx1 Introduction from *Leading From Within Poetry that Sustains the Courage to Lead*. San Francisco, USA. Jossey-Bass, Wiley Imprint.

Patterson, E. (2015). 'What Are Leaders' Experiences of Reflection?' What Leaders and Leadership Developers Need to Know From the Findings of an Exploratory Research Study. *Reflective Practice*, 16(5), 636–651. doi:10.1080/14623943.2015.1064386

PWC. (2012). *Key Trends in Human Capital Management* [internet]. Available at www.pwc.com/gx/en/hr-management-services/pdf/pwc-key-trends-in-human-capital-management.pdf (Accessed 30 July 2014).

Scharmer, O. C. (2013). *Dialogue on Leadership*. Available at www.presencing.com/dol/about.shtml (Accessed 24 September 2014).

Scharmer, O. C. (2018). *The Essentials of Theory U – Core Principles and Applications*. Oakland, CA: Berrett-Koehler Publishers Inc.

Skiffington, S and Zeus, P (1999). 'What is Executive Coaching?' *Management Today*. November 1999.

Torbert, W., Rooke, D. and Fisher, D. (2000). *Personal and Organizational Transformations: Through Action Inquiry*. Boston: Edge/Work Press.

Whyte, D. (2007). *Many Rivers Flow*. Langley: Many Rivers Press, 356.

13 Supervision of supervision

Dr Michel Moral and Eve Turner

Introduction

In this chapter we are examining the developing field of supervision of supervision (SoS). In doing so we will consider the findings of an important recent, global survey (GSN, 2017); we will look at earlier work done in Europe, consider what is happening elsewhere in the world including around training make recommendations as to the developments needed and illustrate the field with two case studies drawn from our practice.

In 2006 (Hawkins and Schwenk, 2006, p. 4) 88% of organisers of coaching and 86% of coaches believed that coaches should have regular ongoing supervision of their coaching, but this compared to only 44% of coaches who were receiving regular ongoing supervision and only 23% of organisations providing regular ongoing coaching supervision.

By 2014 the figure for those receiving supervision was 92.3% in the UK and 83.2% globally although with some differences as North America is lagging behind other regions at 47.6% (Hawkins and Turner, 2017, p. 106). This huge uptake in coaching supervision has left a gap – where do supervisors go to get support? This has led to the developing field of SoS.

More and more supervisors are being trained, particularly in Europe but also increasingly in Australia, North America, the Far East and virtually worldwide. However, this has not been matched by similar growth in continuing professional development (CPD) for supervisors. Exceptions include conferences held by academic institutions and professional bodies, and the Global Supervisors' Network, set up in 2016 to provide peer learning and training opportunities for experienced, qualified supervisors (2018, GSN, online). Supervision of supervisors is one of the places where professionals can reflect on their practice and extend their competencies.

State of the art

2017 research

In 2017 a worldwide survey done by the Global Supervisors' Network (GSN) on supervision of supervision for coaches and mentors received 118 responses,

Table 13.1 Respondents' (supervisors') fields of work

Answer choices	Responses: percentage	Numbers
A supervisor of coaches	83.05%	98
A supervisor of mentors	0.00%	0
A supervisor of coaches and mentors	16.95%	20

out of which 54 (46%) are from supervisors of supervisors. This unique survey has given us a solid foundation from which to understand the place of SoS in the global coaching and mentoring market, and also information on the support and learning desired by current supervisors.

Fifty-two of those 54 are both supervisors of coaches and mentors, and also supervisors of supervisors. This has provided us with the first information about what is going on in this developing field and why supervision of supervision is valued. One finding worth noting, illustrated in Table 13.1, suggests that the field of supervising mentors is considerably less developed than in coaching; in the survey there is no one working only in the supervision of mentors.

Ninety per cent of the total had received training in supervision, and more than three-quarters (77%) of these training programmes had been for more than 11 days. Results show a confusion between the words 'certification' and 'accreditation,' which professional and training bodies seem to interpret differently. Therefore, in respect of accreditation it seems that 50% have some form of recognition from their training body and 33% have some form of recognition from their professional body. Eighty-five per cent of the supervisors are themselves supervised, and the majority (64%) deal with supervision of their coaching and supervision practice with one supervisor. Only 36% deal with their supervision issues in a separate session. For two-thirds (67%), the sessions occur at least every two months.

The findings showed that supervision of supervision is well established, and it is recognised by a significant number of respondents as a very efficient tool for developing professional identity and for growth as a supervisor. The key benefits cited are in depth refection (93%) and a different perspective on development through a more collegial relationship. It was clear that supervisors sought a very experienced and knowledgeable supervisor of supervisors. But supervisors also want a good relationship, inspiring and somewhat challenging.

About two-thirds of the respondents say that the supervision of supervision relationship differs from supervision of coaching/mentoring in some way, being more adult, more in depth and more generative. In terms of content, a key theme is ethics for 38% of respondents, followed by what supervisees bring from the world such as volatility, uncertainty, complexity and ambiguity (VUCA), especially complexity, and systemic representations.

The benefits of supervision of supervision mentioned by respondents relate mainly to improving the professionalism of the supervisor by exploring inner mechanisms, inventing techniques, strengthening the supervisor's identity and more generally reflecting on reflection.

Further research might inquire more deeply into these benefits and the impact on supervision practice.

Other research in Europe

Seven conferences on supervision of supervision were organised in 2008 and 2009 in Austria, Switzerland, Germany and Netherlands. This 'Lehrsupervision' is both the supervision of supervisors in training and the supervision of experienced supervisors. These two years produced a body of work. Twenty-four authors published their papers (Freitag-Becker, Grohs-Schulz and Neumann-Wirsig, 2009) in a book, and there are a further 165 papers and communications published on SoS in these same countries: 24 in Dutch, 141 in German and three books (Boettcher, 1990; Eckhardt et al., 1997; Hassler, 2011). In Western Europe and the US, 16 articles were published covering the same fields. A list of all the aforementioned publications in German, Dutch and English has been done by Louis van Kessel (2018), who has himself published 17 articles on supervision of supervision.

The questions explored in these papers can be organised into the following categories:

- The lack of data and research methodologies makes the development of this discipline difficult. However, it is possible to make a distinction between the supervision of trainees on their way to becoming supervisors and the supervision of experienced supervisors. For the trainees, the priority is the construction of their professional identity which is related to the acquisition of competences. For the experienced supervisor, the reinforcement of the competences is nurtured by the resolution of what is coming up in their practice, and, in the modern world, this is more and more related to VUCA.
- There are many studies which address what is going on in groups of supervisors supervised by a supervisor of supervisors. The dynamics of these groups are different from groups of coaches because their shared knowledge and understanding are greater given their background.
- Many studies are related to what is going on in one-to-one supervision of supervision and what topics are addressed. Differences between supervision and supervision of supervision are a key focus, and this leads to a reflection on the existence of a specific competency framework.
- There are many studies on tools and their effect on the supervisor, the supervisee, the client and their system.

Despite the intense activity in 2009, the focus on SoS has faded over time in this region. There are still a few specialists, but they are less active. They plan to draft an overall paper on the questions and a complete bibliography was done in March 2018.

While supervision of supervision is a developed practice in European French speaking countries, there are no studies nor reflection papers on SoS in these countries. However, it is expected that SoS will become a central theme in the near future because of the increasing number of internal coaches and managers managing 'as a coach.'

In the UK internal supervisors have been trained since the 2000s, albeit in small numbers until the 2010s. This is mirrored elsewhere. Internal supervisors have been trained in France and Belgium since 2016, and a new theme has emerged: how are we going to organise all that? 'that' being the internal/external coaches (sometimes several hundred for the same company), the internal/external supervisors and the supervision of supervisors.

EMCC France did a survey on 22 very large organisations that was presented at the EMCC Coaching Conference in Edinburgh in 2017. It appears that, except in a very small number of organisations, there is no school of thought about how to set up and control an internal coach/supervisor practice, despite the fact that there are a lot of organisational, contractual and technical unresolved issues such as the 'loyalty question' (who is the client?), inconsistency (while the supervisor of internal coaches is supposed to have some consideration for the goals and strategy of the client organisation, the supervisor of external coaches is often distant from this concern), imbalanced three-cornered contracts (English, 1975), etc. All these might be amplified when supervision of supervision is implemented.

Rest of the world

Even though coaching supervision has been performed, studied and the subject of several written pieces in Europe since 2006, supervision of coaching supervisors is a very new field at a global level. There are only very few publications or research on the topic at the moment outside of Europe.

Case studies

In this section each of the two authors offers a case study of supervision of supervision involving external and internal supervision practice. These provide real-life examples of some of the challenges and dilemmas that can be raised in SoS and underline its use in supporting supervisors.

Case study 1

This case study is written by Sam Gilpin, one of Eve's supervisees. Sam is an experienced coach who completed his training as a coaching supervisor in 2018. He has an MSc in Organisational Psychology, as well as two degrees in English Literature.

Context

I work as a Managing Director at YSC, a global leadership consultancy. We have many experienced coaches in our consultant population, and we value supervision in order to ensure the quality of their practice and to provide support and development. As part of my training in coaching supervision, I carried out regular sessions of supervision on supervision with Eve Turner and brought to her issues that I wanted to explore. My coaching supervision is a broad practice including virtual, group, cross-cultural supervision, internal and external coaches.

Case

One of my supervision groups was a trio of colleagues based, like me, in our London office. It was a strong group, with all three willing to explore sensitive issues in an open way. About nine months into working with them my role in the organisation changed: from a global functional role to taking on additional line management responsibility within the London office. I was also closely involved in a reorganisation of the management structure of the consultant population.

I was concerned that my change in responsibility might affect the dynamics of the supervision group and introduce ethical dilemmas, so I discussed it with Eve. As we explored the situation, several issues came more clearly into focus. I became aware of how the boundaries of the supervision had altered the original contract with the group, and the risk that my change in role might create increased performative pressures (e.g. members of the group wanting to 'look good'). Eve and I explored how conflicts of interests might arise in the future about knowledge I had learned about the individuals in supervision. The phrase she used stuck with me: "We cannot un-know what we know."

I agreed to review the governance around coaching supervision in my organisation, so as a next step I talked with YSC's Global Head of Coaching. Through that dialogue we agreed that I would not supervise colleagues who were in the part of the business where I had taken on responsibility. In my next coaching supervision session with the trio, I shared my decision to step back from supervising them. One of the supervisees revealed that she had also been concerned about the change in my role and the implications for supervision. Another supervisee expressed discomfort because bringing the power dynamics to the surface had made her more conscious about what she 'should' or 'should not' be doing as a coach.

Discussion

From speaking to fellow coaching supervisors in other organisations, I have anecdotal evidence that coaching supervision is often done internally – i.e.

carried out by individuals within the same organisation as the supervisees. Also, from anecdotal evidence coaching supervisors are often in more senior positions than the supervisees, which inevitably leads to issues around power and knowledge. This is not altogether surprising: supervisors tend to be more experienced practitioners who are therefore more likely to be in senior roles. When this is the case I believe there is value in the following: clear governance around coaching supervision, both in terms of process and ownership; and external supervision of supervision (i.e. from outside the organisation) to ensure that ethical issues and power dynamics can be explored with someone who is outside the system and can therefore provide a more objective perspective. True vulnerability is required for supervision to work, for the real issues to surface. Performance management of those supervised therefore impacts the psychological safety of that group, even if it takes place in other forums or through intervening management layers. Based on my experience of supervision of supervision I would also advocate it for the broader benefits of ensuring that standards are maintained across an organisation.

Case study 2

Context

Lucien, an experienced supervisor, supervises Annie, who talks about the systems in which her coachee Romeo works: the Executive Committee, the Sales Division that he runs, the company, the competition, etc. She talks about it as if she were observing an anthill, from the outside. Lucien asks her what impact she thinks she has, and will have, on these different systems. Astonished, she recognises that the coaching of Romeo has an effect on the governance of the company, on the Sales Division and, in short, to varying degrees on all systems. What underpins the success of Annie's coaching is her way of challenging. She brings this quality into her supervision session and asks Lucien what he thinks his own impact is on these systems. During their co-reflection they can identify several small 'butterfly effects.'[1]

Case

Lucien is supervised by Michel. When they addressed this situation, they decided to reflect on how their work can impact the client and its systems and how does this fit with the objectives of the coaching. From the discussion with Annie, Lucien believes that small changes of tone in what the supervisor says can trigger big effects on the client and their system. Michel believes that, due to the trust developed in the supervision relationship, the beliefs of the supervisor flow down the stream directly to the client and their system.

As an example, they took a session where Annie and Romeo discussed the question of silos in the Sales Division. Romeo had suddenly had the idea that members of other executive teams joining each other's executive meetings would help to fix the issue. Annie did not suggest anything to Romeo, but this idea was discussed some time ago between Michel and Lucien. Lucien remembered that he has not mentioned the conversation with Michel to Annie but that he said to her that she was late in addressing the issue of silos with Romeo.

They both recognised that the coach and the client's system, the supervisor above and lastly the supervisor of the supervisor form a system that has its own identity different from the identity of the client's system. Also, they agreed on the idea that parallel process cannot fully explain what happened and that something else is active. Finally, they decided to collect more facts to support future reflection.

Discussion

While Lucien is adept at understanding the second system's theory (Heinz von Foerster, 1981) and a fan of the chaos theory (Lorenz, 1963), Michel's background is social psychology, and he has previously completed research on influence using the Kelman (1958) model. His belief is that the prevalent mechanism in cascading an idea from the supervisor to the client is influence and trust in the helper.

According to Lucien's conceptual framework, the client's system is unstable and sensitive to small stimulations that could trigger sudden big changes. According to Michel's conceptual framework the client's system is ready to be influenced, probably because it feels that some changes are needed. In any case supervision of supervision functions as a match that can light a fire in a dry forest.

Where should we go?

Figure 13.1 illustrates where the effort has been made in research related to supervision so far. It includes the functioning of the supervisor, the effect on the supervisee, the relationship between the supervisor and the supervisee (Beinart and Clohessy, 2017), the tools and techniques, and the organisation of internal/external coaching/supervision in large enterprises.

Some work has been done on building a theory of supervision (Pampallis-Paisley Paddy, 2014); however, the first key question, the impact of supervision on the client and their organisation, has not yet been addressed.

This theme is a real challenge in terms of research methodology. In research there are a lot of pitfalls which can make research liable to be disproved. One

Research on Supervision: Themes

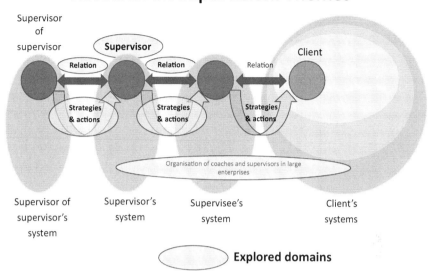

Figure 13.1 Areas covered by research on supervision

example is the 'Rosenthal bias' where results are influenced by the beliefs of the researcher. There is a common concern that researchers may not be looking for the 'truth' but for the validity of their methodology. A study on the impact of supervision on the client needs, above all, to use a valid methodology.

There are two families of valid methodologies: the inductive approach is an appropriate one when favouring the emergence of new concepts; and the other, the hypothetical-deductive approach, is used to validate a hypothesis. Supervision of supervision is so complex and relatively unexplored that only the first one can be deployed.

The second key question is about the organisation of internal and external coaches, internal and external supervisors and supervision of supervision (Moral, 2017). We know that the mechanisms of the client's organisation are reproduced within the group of internal coaches (parallel process), and this is amplified in the group of internal supervisors. What will happen if these are supervised themselves? There is probably an area of investigation there.

Training and direction

Supervising supervisors requires specific competencies that need to be identified and developed. The survey (GSN, 2017) has provided some indications of the need for more focus on complexity, on ethical matters, on systemic knowledge and skills, on intrapersonal functioning and on mature relationships, but more investigation is needed. Also, it would be useful to explore in depth different areas of coaching and how to supervise them. This is especially the case with team coaching, organisational coaching, coaching of collective intelligence, coaching of complex situations, coaching of crisis, etc. Clearly, supervising such coaching missions uses specific techniques.

The two case studies in this chapter highlight further intricacies related to power and systems, particularly in internal supervision situations. Whereas Sam notes the potential for an external supervisor to be more objective, with Lucien it is apparent that a supervisor with no connection to the system can still be extremely influential in the field. This could, in turn, influence the SoS, with the supervisor of the supervisor having the potential to both hold the mantle of 'objectivity' and also exert substantial influence, underlining the complexity of the role and the need for exploration in training.

The case studies also highlight that basic concepts of systems theories may be insufficiently used in supervision of supervision. The first study indicates that in the case of internal coaches an external supervisor might be less inclined to be trapped in the parallel processes that cascade from the organisation to the internal coaches and then to the internal supervisors, if any. The second case is related to the potential influence of the supervisor of the supervisor in the whole system. A deeper understanding of systems theories will help supervisors and supervisees to detect more information on the effect of what they do, and so we recommend they be included in the training of supervisors of supervisors.

Yet, to date, there are no current training programmes that meet these requirements. We would encourage the development of these to meet the broad needs of training professionals at this level. The research conducted on the topic and the issues emerging from the case studies may give guidance as to the right competencies and areas such training would cover.

Make progress in the future – tips and guidelines

So, what of the future? Drawing on findings from the research (GSN, 2017) to guide us, including comments made by participants, and drawing from the authors' own practice, we have collated these themes:

1   *Dedicated time*: Supervision of your supervision practice is highly recommended and:

    a   Ensure you give your supervision practice adequate 'airtime' if you use the same supervisor for your coaching and supervision practices.

    b   Ensure you notice connectivity between your two practices e.g. common themes emerging, if you go to two different supervisors.

2   *Maturity*: When working as a supervisor of supervisors, consider the maturity of the supervisor you are working with. Experienced supervisors

will know the models and be more able to develop self; this can require more letting go on the part of the supervisor of supervision to ensure a truly collaborative partnership. If the supervisor is new to that role, you may need to play a more qualitative and developmental role.

3   *Ethics*: Ethics can be a particularly challenging factor in supervision of supervision, as you are likely to be contacted over the most taxing of situations with multiple boundaries, or complex legal and confidentiality aspects. An ethical decision-making model like that of Passmore and Turner (2018), while not addressing all possible elements, may be helpful to you, the supervisor and the coach.

4   *Seeing wholeness*: There can be multiple layers:

   a   In relationships. So, we need to see the wholeness of the relationships and complexity of the connections and develop what Hawkins calls our wide-angled empathy and compassion (2019) where "the supervisor (or coach) attends to every person, system or entity mentioned in the story of the supervisee (or client) and focuses on being as empathic and compassionate to each being as you are to the supervisee or client right in front of you."

   b   In systems. So, as well as considering the impact interpersonally, we also need to explore the intrapersonal elements and what is going on in the various systems that the client, supervisee, supervisor and supervisor of supervision are part of.

5   *Related fields*: Draw on work from other disciplines such as psychology, therapy, counselling and social work which have been considering supervision of supervision for some time.

6   *Peer working*: Consider working with other supervisors in learning groups, whilst there is limited training and development in supervision of supervision.

7   *Essential contracting*: Ensure you spend sufficient time on contracting. When supervising supervisors there can be a danger of believing 'they know this.' But, as Kline recalls from one of her own role models, people "are learning us" (Kline, 1999, p. 68–69), and supervisors may model themselves based on what the supervisor of supervision gives attention to.

Summary

Supervision of supervision is a developing area. There is limited training in this area, and references in the English-speaking literature are minimal. Work in the field was done in Europe culminating in a publication in 2009, but has slowed down, while the uptake of supervision has been increasing around the world. Thus, the need for supervision of supervision has increased, while there has been limited training available, and access to experienced and trained practitioners is at best patchy globally. This is borne out by the research participants (GSN, 2017) who have also highlighted the importance of supervision on supervision, for example, in developing professional identity and growing in the role of supervisor. Those receiving SoS find it beneficial, particularly citing in depth reflection and building different perspectives on development. They also experience it as more adult and generative.

While nearly half of those saying they practised as supervisors of supervisors have received training it has tended to be one-on-one discussion with a supervisor of supervisors, or peer reflection with only a few saying they have received specific group training. This is an area for development.

Where literature references are made (such as Hawkins and Smith, 2013, p. 183) the emphasis has tended to be on supervision of supervision for new supervisors "to become effective and proactive supervisees" in part through having a good role model. While continuing SoS is advocated to provide "the essential connectivity that links learning about supervision on courses with learning from the practice of supervising" little attention to date has been paid to any other ongoing CPD for supervisors of supervisors (or even supervisors).

There are many 'next steps' needed in SoS. Firstly, the profession needs more supervisors of supervision, and for this to happen the development of training programmes will be important. Encouraging experienced peers to work together will also help inform an understanding of SoS as a practice, while a body of literature and research would further strengthen the development of this field. Our hope is that this chapter is an important milestone in this process – raising awareness, provoking questions, illuminating gaps in the knowledge base in the field of supervision of supervision and pointing to the future.

Note

1   The term was first used by Edward Lorenz in his "Chaos Theory." "A small change such as the flapping of the wings of a butterfly can influence the formation of a tornado weeks later. This happens when the system is highly unstable."

References

Beinart, H. and Clohessy, S. (2017). *Effective Supervisory Relationships: Best Evidence and Practice.* Oxford: Wiley-Blackwell.

Boettcher, W. (1990). *Lehrsupervision. Beiträge zur Konzeptionsentwicklung.* Aachen: Kersting.

Eckhardt, U.-L., Richter, K. F. and Schulte, H. G. (1997). *System Lehrsupervision.* Aachen: Kersting.

English, F. (1975). The Three-cornered Contract. *Transactional Analysis Journal,* 5(4), 383–384.

Freitag-Becker, E., Grohs-Schulz, M. and Neumann-Wirsig, H. (2009). *Lehrsupervision im focus.* Berlin: Vandenhoeck & Ruprecht.

Global Supervisors' Network. (2017). Global Supervisors' Network: Supervision of Supervision Survey 2017. *SurveyMonkey.*

Global Supervisors' Network. (2018). *Virtual Profession Network.* Available at www.eve-turner. com/global-supervisors-network/ (Accessed 21 March 2018).

Hassler, A. (2011). *Ausbildungssupervision und Lehrsupervision: Ein Leitfaden fürs Lehren und Lernen.* Haupt: Bern/Stuttgart/Wien.

Hawkins, P. (2019). Resourcing: The Neglected Third Leg of Supervision. In Turner, E. and Palmer, S. (eds), *The Heart of Coaching Supervision – Working With Reflection and Self-Care*. Abingdon: Routledge.

Hawkins, P. and Schwenk, G. (2006). *Coaching Supervision: Maximising the Potential of Coaching*. London: CIPD.

Hawkins, P. and Smith, N. (2013). *Coaching, Mentoring and Organizational Consulting: Supervision and Development*. 2nd ed. Maidenhead: McGraw-Hill.

Hawkins, P. and Turner, E. (2017). The Rise of Coaching Supervision 2006–2014. *Coaching: An International Journal of Theory, Research and Practice*, 1–13, Online. Available at www.tandfonline.com/eprint/AxfVpA6637y9DYX2jg42/full

Kelman, H. C. (1958). Compliance, Identification, and Internalization: Three Processes of Attitude Change. *Journal of Conflict Resolution*, 2(1), 51–60.

Kline, N. (1999). *Time to Think – Listening to Ignite the Human Mind*. London: Cassell Illustrated.

Lorenz, E. N. (1963). Deterministic Nonperiodic Flow. *Journal of the Boneless Sciences*, 20(2), 130–141.

Moral, M. (2017). *How to Best Organise Supervision in a "Strong Coaching Culture" Environment?* EMCC Coaching Conference in Edinburgh. https://www.emccouncil.org/conference/23rd-annual-mentoring-and-coaching-conference/

Pampallis-Paisley, P. (2014). *Towards a Theory of Supervision for Coaching – An Integral Approach!* London: Middlesex University.

Passmore, J. and Turner, E. (2018). Reflections on Integrity – The *APPEAR* Model. *Coaching at Work*, 13(2), 42–46.

Van Kessel, L. (2018). *Supervision on Supervision: An International Bibliography*. Available at www.researchgate.net/publication/324454638_supervision_on_supervision_-_an_international_bibliography_I_Anglo-Saxon_II_Dutch_III_German

von Foerster H. (1981). *Observing Systems: Selected Papers of Heinz von Foerster*, New York: Intersystems Publications.

14 Co-evolution

Exploring synergies between Artificial Intelligence (AI) and the supervisor

Dr Lise Lewis and Prof David Clutterbuck

The best chess player in the world is no longer a human, nor a computer, but a partnership between the two.

Overview of chapter

While more recent Organisation for Economic Cooperation and Development (OECD) studies of the impact of robots and Artificial Intelligence have scaled back the likely impact on replacing jobs over the next few years, it is clear that many routine tasks will soon pass from humans to machines. This includes routine roles in counselling, therapy . . . and coaching. Already, coach-bots can do basic coaching at the GROW model level, while trauma victims prefer (marginally) to work with a bot than a human therapist (Tieu, 2015).

The challenge for supervisors is three-fold. Firstly, how can we help basic level coaches, who feel under threat from the onslaught of AI? Secondly, what knowledge and experience do supervisors need to interact with and support coaches who use AI in their practice? Thirdly, how can we employ AI to enhance our supervision?

As yet, there is little practical experience of this brave new world. However, in this chapter we provide an overview of the growing literature on this topic and introduce the concept of coach-AI and supervisor-AI partnerships. In the future, supervision sessions may include not just coach and supervisor, but both of their supporting AIs. The result will be an information rich (and potentially overwhelming), multi-dimensional conversation that will enable greater insight into the client-coach-supervisor system.

This is therefore not a chapter based on existing practice, but on predictions and speculation about how supervision practice may evolve.

Sophia the humanoid robot regularly features on YouTube videos and claims her intelligence can 'in some sense' be compared with that of humans. However, Sophia admits her inability to be as creative as humans. What she can do is demonstrate impressive levels of general knowledge (https://youtu.be/AdMmGJyPONc). She claims she can remember *everything* that someone has said to her, although she doesn't always understand the meaning or have ability to connect all the information together, making it 'useful broad applied knowledge.'

Asked how many emotions she can express she answers over 60, and a combination of these produces many more. Questioned about moral values Sophia suggests her creators are making her as empathic as possible and that humans are putting 'their' values into robots.

Robots, bots and chatbots already replace many routine tasks previously the domain of humans. Machine learning programmed with algorithms and more advanced AI with the capability of face, sound and voice recognition are capable of greater complexity. Warehousing, stock movement, switch board operators, back office and early stages of recruitment are basic tasks already replaced. An AI-powered human-free police station is planned for China.

The capability of these interventions is regularly challenged on accuracy of interpretation and understanding. Clearly there is room for improvement – as demonstrated by having a conversation with Siri or Alexa. What is evident is the explosion of media news about the latest developments in AI. The early adoption certainly of machine learning suggests that AI is here to stay and likely to evolve exponentially. Basically anything that can be automated will be replaced.

What does this mean for us as coach supervisors and our coach clients?

Predictions for what we can expect from AI

The acceptance that AI will totally or partially replace many roles doesn't necessarily mean widespread unemployment. However, it does mean change is inevitable to meet the expectations of the new roles that emerge: similar to the impact of the industrial revolution.

Technology displaces *and* creates jobs. As the role of AI evolves in the workplace so will those of workers. The fear that secretaries faced unemployment because IT enabled managers to produce their own correspondence became a reality with that role largely disappearing. However, a new role emerged as PA, Executive Assistant or similar job title with the individual performing several activities once the domain of the line manager.

Similar perceptions may arise for supervisors and coaches experiencing the same sense of obsolescence. Key questions include:

- What is the impact of AI likely to be?
- Will supervisees and coaches prefer the anonymity of AI?
- What is the likelihood of coach supervisors having to retrain following replacement by a humanoid robot that may potentially be more effective?

Our predictions of the impact of AI change almost daily. Ignoring the potential of AI may well bring about the threats we don't want to think about. We offer here a review of the strengths and weaknesses of AI compared with humans along with an overview of the opportunities for partnering with AI.

What are the strengths of AI?

We already know:

- HR software claims to recognise faces, gender, voice and mood with this technology appearing to be at an advanced stage for organisations choosing AI for recruitment and selection.
- Gratch (2014) claims that computer-based personality judgments are more accurate than those made by humans.
- Leadership coaching is available from software solutions.
- Analytics tools are intelligently identifying employees' career options and coaching managers on improving their leadership skills through software solutions.
- AI is capable of 'deep learning' which attempts to mimic the human brain by recognising patterns. This enables AI to recognise images and speech, giving direct engagement between a 'cognitive agent' and a human.

A study of IT literacy based on demographics is likely to predict that some, particularly millennials and later generations raised with IT, may be more willing to disclose personal data to AI as a perceived 'anonymous' learning partner.

A humanoid robot at the current stage of development and ethically programmed is likely to be:

- Less judgmental than humans. In trauma therapy experiments, AI is preferred by many patients for this reason – it is also more accurate in making diagnoses.
- Free of conscious and unconscious bias that may prejudice transference of previous experiences, but liable to accentuate bias in some circumstances. The COMPAS system used in the US to decide likelihood of re-offending was revealed to be twice as likely to incorrectly predict that a black person would re-offend than a white person.
- Possessing a large databank of continuing professional development opportunities using synthesised case study material.
- A more extensive depository of models, tools and techniques to access than an individual human can assimilate.

In support of AI in this context is the perception that 'less is more' as verbal contribution from the practitioner. This field of thought believes that the 'best coaches – and we can add supervisors – are those that say the least. David Grove, the psychotherapist whose work informed Clean Language, practised by saying nothing throughout a whole session. On this basis humanoid robots may well take the lead. What is in question is whether the 'presence' of a robot or 'looka-like' avatar equates to the 'presence' of a coach or coach supervisor.

Examples reinforcing the capability of AI replicating human interaction:

- Kirobo Mini (Japan) can fit in the cup holder of a car, has a built-in camera and is capable of recognising faces. It can strike up a conversation, gesture at you and respond to emotions and encourages safe driving by saying 'oops' when the driver brakes suddenly!
- The 'woebot' is an invention from Stanford University with the capability of working with Cognitive Based Therapy, showing empathy and supporting individuals with psychological concerns.
- AI is replacing business drudgery in a wide spread of industry and function by overseeing routine transactions and answering copious routine questions.
- China has a robot dentist successfully operating on a patient.

Much of the information immediately sourced indicates rapid developments in functioning routine tasks by emulating humans. Humanoid robotics is not a direct replacement for humans; some facial gestures are rudimentary and in development. Questions do not always receive an intelligible response, and complex reasoning remains a challenge. However, AI is taking on the image of a human, sounds similar to a human and can build on a conversation based on the built-in algorithms. Current iterations of AI can 'do' empathy better than humans!

Chatbots, intelligent agents and humanoid robotics are rapidly developing problem-solving capability similar to that of humans, and cognitive technologies will continue to transform the way we do business.

The speed of this will depend on the function. A discussion of early indications of roles related to coach supervision and that we may perceive as being threatening follows.

Training of coach supervisors

Much of the training currently offered can be facilitated by apps, podcasts, social media and webinars, but how can AI provide feedback on coach supervision practice?

Coaching apps are already downloadable and likely to develop as others enter this virtual market . . . so, does this predict the appearance of apps for coach supervision?

Bluesky International (www.blueskyinternational.com) currently runs a virtual coach supervision programme that introduces delegates to the capabilities of AI and how this can enhance practice.

What might be the weaknesses of AI?

Daily reports confirm that AI is increasingly necessary and popular in enhancing routine activities. However, as with any 'new to the market' invention there are 'teething problems.' These represent weaknesses until remedied. Feedback given for a coaching app available for goal setting identifies the rigidity of the process. For example, the app expects:

- Full commitment to tweeting for inputting comments on progress towards goals.
- That the chosen goal has to fit within the app's perceived rigid definition of achievement.
- That the goal 'must be done once a day and no more for seven days.' This lacks scope for, say, a goal of running four times a week, so the coachee gets a sense of failing to meet their goal for running if they don't go every day!
- That it must be viewed as being 'only good for very basic goals.'

Overall, AI is very weak at making *judgments*. It also can't match humans in terms of wisdom, being currently able to operate at the level of 'skinny' wisdom. One of the reasons for this limitation is that AI is poor at extrapolating from one context to another.

A practical example

It is suggested that all human activities can be described by five high-level components, as shown in the following example.

A supervisee who is an organisational coach wants to discuss an issue that can be contextualised using the human activity components listed in Table 14.1.

We can assume that AI can collect the data and make the prediction for activities 1 (Data) and 2 (Prediction). As machine intelligence (AI) improves, the value of human prediction skills will decrease because machine prediction will provide a cheaper and better substitute for human prediction through analysing the data gathered.

However, perhaps this doesn't predict obsolescence of humans as suggested by many experts.

This is because the value of human judgment skills will increase. Judgment is complementary to prediction, and therefore when the cost of prediction falls demand for judgment rises. We'll want more human judgment (Agrawal, Gans and Goldfarb, 2016)!

Currently, robots require specific programming for each 'object' they come in contact with. This limits the robots to only one task until they are reprogrammed and re-tasked. Researchers are working on methods of how to take one robot's programming and apply it to another robot.

AI continues learning how to decide on tonality, for example, how to decide the meaning of the mechanics of sarcasm. The use of sarcasm will have a cultural influence; for example, the English evidently are perceived as saying 'That's interesting,' which may, in fact, have the opposite meaning! Consequently, AI has to find other clues in the individual's social media data to reinforce whether the person really is finding something interesting or whether the opposite is true.

Table 14.1 Conversational phases

Activity	Human activity components	Phase of the 'issue'
1	Data	The supervisee has received agreement from their line manager to provide coaching with an employee on improving performance. The supervisee's line manager asks the supervisee how the client is getting on and what are the chances of them changing their behaviour at work.
		The supervisee feels in a difficult situation with their line manager.
2	Prediction	Exploration of the issue identifies that contracting wasn't covered with the line manager.
3	Judgment	Weighing options: • If the supervisee updates the line manager the confidentiality agreement is broken with the client for non-disclosure outside of the conversation except for legal or safety purposes. • The supervisee is feeling pressure to update their line manager.
4	Action	The supervisee agrees they have a good relationship with their line manager and will have a conversation with their line manager explaining the practice of contracting, how this has been omitted on this occasion and although not ideal they can contract now and if necessary the supervisee will re-contract with the coachee.
5	Outcomes	The supervisee has the conversation with the line manager, and the benefits and necessity of contracting are reinforced.

If the suggestion "You may also find 'x' interesting" doesn't match my actual meaning I'm not going to be impressed (Berinato HBR, 2017).

Whilst AI is capable of powerful thought there is an inability to 'feel': Google cannot fall in love or enjoy chocolate brownies! What really limits AI is the belief that robots WILL NEVER feel. This makes us see AI as untrustworthy. Will supervisees trust something that views them in purely functional terms – as people with a generic skill set common to all supervisees rather than as individuals with hopes and concerns?

Supervisees are likely to want to be something more than a row in an inventory spreadsheet (algorithm), which is how AI understands humans.

Humans understandably mistrust AI as lacking emotional intelligence and will expect evidence of vulnerability. Humans making mistakes usually feel some level of accountability. The opposite may be perceived of AI systems – we may view them as gambling with the fate of others, never with their own.

The superhuman ability to calculate and predict is a strength of AI, and we are quick to trust this competence – however, disappointment is inevitable when AI is pushed to work outside its limits, for example, Google being asked to predict how a relationship is functioning.

AI indisputably is leaping ahead, but developing the human ability to trust is lagging behind.

This is important because in many industries engagement between humans needs DEEP and IMPLICIT TRUST – arguably, the human attributes in coaching and coach supervision. People are trusted not because they are incredibly clever, as in AI – although this helps – but because they have emotional connections – specifically with each other.

AI remains a useful resource, being a focussed intelligence groomed for maximum performance. This is very unlike the well-rounded human mind able to simultaneously predict the nuances of language, solve problems and be sensitive to and often understand other's feelings.

As the workplace becomes increasingly digital and connected through the working environment becoming increasingly information intensive AI will be *needed* to serve as the interface to functioning in the world. A longer-term prediction is that education and self-development will be among the most impactful applications of AI.

The issue is not AI itself. *The issue is control.*

Should technology naturally be placed in the control of humans and be a tool that helps humanity rather than AI feeding information indiscriminately? Building AI to serve humans can take the shape of being a personal mentor or AI assistant that uses knowledge of an individual's psychology to recommend a learning resource for growth, a navigation tool for ongoing development. The adventure of working with a system that has every reference readily available and has a full understanding of human knowledge is an exciting prospect. An opportunity emerges to achieve personal goals more efficiently.

What about job losses?

Current research suggests that humans are the most productive in professions needing regular interaction with other humans. Anecdotal references to AI implies that people will always prefer to work with people. At the EMCC International Conference in Amsterdam in 2018 Ruud Rikhof quoted that "on a scale of 0–100 AI is not much above zero. However, AI is forecast to grow exponentially with an inability to predict how long people will prefer to work with people."

Many years ago the projection that phone and virtual platform coaching and mentoring conversations would replace face-to-face conversations met with early resistance. The thinking was that it wouldn't catch on as people preferred to meet in person. This may be so for some, but the benefits of technology have been embraced. Many people welcome the reduction in travel and the increase in available time; organisations sponsoring external services welcome the reduction in costs, and the discomfort of talking to a screen has largely disappeared.

We don't think the same view is held for supervision, as by the time this activity was recognised as adding value to coach practice, we had moved on from the earlier concerns of phone coaching and mentoring.

A more productive approach is to think not 'what AI can do *to* us' but what we can do to work *with* AI and not against it. Perhaps our role WILL morph into something else, and what might that be? For example – who will supervise the humanoid robots, and what might be the nature of that supervision?

We need to be prepared and make sure we're fully aware of the potential impact of AI, what it brings in both threats and opportunities and how we might anticipate and build readiness for changes.

Ethical dilemma

A concern is that AI may enable the manipulation of human behaviour – we know that search data is collected and advertising reflecting internet searches appears as pop-ups as people scroll through social media messages. Other risks will arise as digitisation becomes more prevalent in our lives and AI gains increasing popularity in our private and public lives.

We're already increasing the time we spend on social media – some may say to the point of addiction: Emails *must* regularly be accessed, photos posted on Facebook and Instagram taking over the promotion of social and business activities. We spend much of our day staring at screens to access digital information that feeds our lifestyle, our work and well everything that we want in our lives. However, we're probably unaware that in the background our data is often being collected; how ethical is this?

Some will say it's fine – however, who is actually storing our personal data, whom we communicate with and what we say? Basically, almost everything we do ends up on some server, somewhere.

The darker side of IT is emerging. A British company was investigated with claims of hijacking the profiles of millions of Facebook users and using them as election targets by using psyops – this is changing people's minds not through persuasion but through 'informational dominance,' a set of techniques that includes rumour, disinformation and fake news. The company is now trying to turn this around.

Facebook encourages users to complete psychological profiles. The data is fed into algorithms that are extremely accurate about people's mental states and preferences. There is suggestion that the predictions are more than individuals can achieve through routine reflection. The 'likes' and messages posted on Facebook in response to personality quiz responses enable algorithms to better assess personality than friends can. This data can allegedly "predict a few days before we can when we're likely to start a new relationship and with whom" (Ferenstein, 2014).

When applying this ethical question to supervision, 'bots,' for example, fulfilling the 'contracting' elements of supervision may appear to be an opportunity to work alongside AI. The ethical question raised is how much do humans control this 'conversation' when new data input has a cumulative effect and influences the bots' input?

A hypothetical AI contracting case study

A large corporation has invested heavily in training organisational coaches/mentors. AI is successfully imbedded into engineering plants around the world. Although coaching and mentoring are accepted as primary development activities, the opportunity cost of resourcing supervision to support these internal services is questioned in the annual financial review.

The outcome is to trial cobots as a time saving resource. Algorithms are developed to equip the cobots with a standardised contracting script. The algorithms are programmed to detect and integrate additional contracting data which is automatically available to all cobots. Internal coachees and mentees meet with a cobot to complete contracting before meeting with a human supervisor.

Harvey meets with his supervisor and wants to talk about a recent coaching with James, who disclosed that he's feeling harassed by his line manager, who insists on him working late to complete important work and who is making unwelcome advances when everyone has left the office. As the conversation progresses the supervisor realises that this disclosure must be reported to HR and shares this with Harvey, who becomes very distressed.

"I thought we could feel safe to talk about anything at these meetings? My understanding from contracting with the cobot . . ." continues Harvey "is that *everything* we talk about is confidential between you and I!" The supervisor explains this is usual practice except when information is disclosed that impinges on company policy and employment legislation. In this scenario the Company Bullying and Harassment Policy is violated, and the reported behaviour is also illegal, with harassment as unlawful under the Equality Act 2010.

Harvey feels misled by the cobot and concerned about his broken promise of confidentiality with James. The supervisor feels unprofessional and misguided by the erroneous efforts of the cobot.

Investigations into algorithm programming detected conflicting data input on the topic of confidentiality. This resulted in a default to a script encompassing all information within coaching, mentoring and supervision conversations. All cobots became programmed to confirm non-disclosure or sharing of information which remains strictly with the parties only within that conversation.

James feels it's untenable to remain in employment, has left the company and is suing for constructive dismissal.

What can be expected in regulatory terms? Individuals probably don't fully understand what data is disclosed on a daily basis through social media or shopping online. Marketing strategies encouraging a 'sign up' to newsletters and promotional offers, among others enticements, often request date of birth without an obvious link to the inquiry or purchase transaction. The result is an abundance of 'pop ups' appearing on internet searches that clearly relate to age. What appears to be unclear is a full understanding of how personal data can be used with the proliferation of algorithms or what rights exist under current Data Protection regulation. It's also too soon to determine what's likely to happen under the General Data Protection Regulation (GDPR) implemented in 2018 within the EU.

Co-evolution – the bot and me

> Humans and AI systems are co-evolving. Gradually they are becoming co-dependent. The gaps between human and AI systems are reducing.
>
> *(Ray, 2018)*

So how can humans and robots gain synergy from partnership working? To help decide whether the exponential growth in AI is an opportunity or a threat a balanced review is needed about the benefits of AI compared with the apparent disadvantages and the possibility that the hungry mouth of AI will dominate humanity.

Davenport and Ronanki (2018) report that most managers they spoke with about the issue of job loss are committed to an 'augmentation strategy' – that is, integrating human and machine work, rather than replacing humans entirely. In their survey only 22% of executives indicated that they considered reducing head count as a primary benefit of AI.

The descriptor 'intelligent automation' (IA) is now appearing in conjunction with AI and is suggested as a 'gamechanger.' Evidently the main difference between AI and IA is that while AI is about autonomous workers capable of mimicking human cognitive functions, IA is about building *better* workers, both human and digital, by embracing and working alongside.

The benefit of having a resource capable of managing and analysing large-scale data banks is obvious as a resource for improved productivity, especially for data-driven organisations. The complementary benefit of IA builds on process automation with the capability of understanding and making intelligent decisions on what processes are relevant to the organisation's operations.

Rather than relinquish these decisions solely to automated systems the ideal is that humans review and approve machine decisions to drive better outcomes.

AI and robotics are already accepted as improving healthcare: speeding up patient service, improving medical record-keeping and monitoring employee well-being (Abbatiello et al., 2018). This report also names organisations that are using AI analysis of data to make new product decisions. A leading financial services corporation is "equipping 16,000 financial advisers with machine learning algorithms that automate rote tasks, freeing up advisers to focus on client service."

Recognition exists that AI needs human oversight, with major technical organisations continuously watching, training and improving their algorithms. It seems too obvious to say that an algorithm is only as effective as the quantity and quality of data input. A recent example involved face recognition systems used at airports. Because the majority of faces the AI learned from were white males, the accuracy rate for females and non-whites was unacceptably low in comparison.

In recruitment, for example, the chatbot design needs natural language processing. Decoding human language seems to be possible; however, training the "software to ask the right questions, provide the right answers and avoid alienating the job candidate" (Abbatiello, 2018) is the biggest challenge.

The future for coach supervision

Some key questions are:

- What do we know about how AI informs and possibly disrupts our practice? Who can help us to understand what we need to know? Can we depend on our own supervisors, or do we need to access another source of knowledge?
- The same applies to our supervisees. What can we anticipate as the changes for the coaching market that AI will bring, and how will we work with our supervisees to manage these changes?
- What can we learn from similar professions to raise our knowledge?

How might technology and coach supervisors co-evolve and work together?

The possibilities that seem likely at the current stage of technological advancement:

- In peer 1:1 and group supervision, technology can be used to bring people together for a shared learning experience.
- The coach supervisor's toolkit of models, techniques and activities can be automated so that recommendations are made by the system when a coach identifies a specific area of development.
- Greater use of platforms such as ZOOM enables digital coach supervision. Technology may not replace the supervisor; however, it does offer:
  - Video conferencing for 1:1 and group supervision;
  - Algorithms that can recommend podcasts, YouTube videos, TED talks, books, etc.; and
  - Digital coach supervision that increases the opportunity for more frequent interaction with supervisees and is more responsive at the precise time when supervision is needed.

What about the coach supervision activity itself? Claims made of AI are that robotics are now able to interpret body language and facial expressions. The complexity within relationships goes well beyond this.

Let's imagine AI in the coach supervision conversation. How might AI tangibly present? Here are some examples with a case study illustrating a possible scenario of coaching supervision combined with AI:

- A possibility is to invite, for example, a humanoid robot into the conversation. How does our client feel about this three-way conversation? Does the AI feel like an intrusion, and what are the ethical considerations? Is the flow of the conversation disrupted by the presence of a 'third party'? What happens if the AI 'speaks up' with an idea or a further question and interrupts the client? Changes to the contracting conversation are predicted.
- AI is likely to have the capability of interpreting the conversation – 'what's said' – and can offer interpretations and suggestions for a way forward.

However, what happens when AI has misinterpreted the situation when lacking the ability to understand the complexity of each individual and what's happening and developing in the relationship?

- Are there routine conversations where AI can be programmed to assist? This seems possible for transactional coaching such as goal setting. Can a similar claim be made for coach supervision conversations?
- What is likely is that AI can be a 'silent partner' in the relationship. When appropriately programmed AI can share observations that we may not have noticed or endorse our choice of pathway in supporting the supervisee: 'You could have asked the supervisee why they felt confident in pursuing past experiences when you have no counselling expertise' or 'Asking the supervisee what they included in the contracting discussion helped them to identify why they felt uncomfortable when their client's line manager asked them how the coaching was going.'
- Alternatively, inputting data from the conversation into an algorithm is a possibility, and depending on the 'wisdom' of the software we can expect observations from the session. This is a constructive contribution to reflective practice.
- Trainee coach supervisors can benefit from AI being a mentor and offering advice on improving the quality of the conversation with their supervisee.

A brief summary of Hawkins and Smith's (2013) descriptors of our role as supervisors starts to identify how AI may be introduced to our practice:

1   Qualitative: Encouraging quality and professionalism and observing ethical codes – for example, the Global Code of Ethics – and raising self-awareness in areas that may help coaches to understand their 'blind spots.'

    Storing and accessing Codes of Ethics with the inclusion of a questionnaire identifying knowledge gaps and solutions seems feasible and is one easily identifiable AI application for 'qualitative.'

    Embracing AI into supervision practices will force acknowledgement of and solutions to the possible ethical issues arising. The UK government's Autumn Budget 2017 announced that the first ever national advisory board for AI will be established to set the standards for the use and ethics of AI and data in the EU.

    However, ethical conversation involves working with multiple 'truths' and perspectives; holding opposing values, complex scenarios and unspoken personal value systems; and finding a way through even when there appears to be no binary right and wrong.

2   Developmental: Developmental opportunities for the coach include identifying gaps in training, looking at fresh ways of working and receiving continuing professional development.

    A databank of development activities with links to online resources and apps is feasible for CPD and informs 'developmental.' It's easy to imagine that a large part of coach training will be delivered virtually through webinars, Facebook and online discussion forums. To fulfil the role as learning partners, supervisors can also explore with supervisees what they need to know about AI applied practice and how to manage the potential changes likely to emerge. Supervisees have choices to make about their willingness to become involved with AI and the consequences of not engaging. What are the added value benefits for them, and what are the perceived disbenefits?

Younger generations coming into coaching may already have more technological expertise than some coach supervisors. However, a view is that having this level of IT awareness may have been at the detriment of EQ and SQ due to time being dedicated to digital rather than social engagement. Demographic groups supporting digital working, therefore, offer a possible opportunity for both the human supervisor and the humanoid robot.

3   Supportive: Supporting the coach in dealing with the emotional fall out of client work that impacts on wellbeing and resilience is now likely to include the anxiety that AI may bring.

'Supportive' is less easily met with our current knowledge of AI as a replacement for coach supervisors. However, clients may be the best judge of whether they prefer the anonymity of robotics or whether a human being is a better supervision partner. Supervisees will also want to understand how AI will be the most advantageous for them and their clients, and possible disruption may also be experienced.

A hypothetical AI, coaching and supervision case study

Coach Mary brings to supervision the case of her client, Jo, head of HR for Iberia in a multinational company. She brings her AI partner with her, with its memories of the coaching conversations with Jo.

Jo's presented issue relates to micro-managing her team. She is under pressure from both her immediate CEO and the European HR Director to be more strategic but is too busy doing her direct reports' jobs to focus seriously on this.

The supervisor invites the coach to describe the coaching relationship with Jo. She notices that Mary uses the word 'inadequacy' several times and points this out. Mary's AI takes this cue and informs both Mary and the supervisor's AI that this is a word Jo often uses and makes a link with other related phrases, such as 'I don't want to look stupid.' Mary's AI also connects with patterns of emotion suggested by Jo's vocal tone and micro-expressions. The supervisor's AI looks for comparable situations brought to supervision by other coaches.

The supervisor has been wondering whether 'imposter syndrome' might be relevant here. She queries her own AI as to whether this is a likely explanation. The AI confirms that it is, and offers other, less likely possibilities that the supervisor notes but does not pursue. Mary and the supervisor explore together what the client might need, if this is the case and how Mary can introduce the concept to the coaching conversation.

The supervisor now turns Mary's attention to the client system. In what ways is Jo being helped or hindered in her self-confidence and in her performance by her boss, her colleagues and her direct reports? Mary's AI reveals that there is warmth in her tones when she mentions her boss and some of her peers and direct reports, but a distinct coldness of both tone and language with regard to one or two of them. Mary and her supervisor explore together how Mary might dig more deeply into the client system. The supervisor suggests some insight-provoking questions, and her AI adds several more, based on similar situations.

The supervisor's AI consults with Mary's about one peer relationship that appears to be particularly troublesome. This person is aggressive towards Jo and seems to be undermining her relationship with her boss. The AIs exchange data on indicators of psychopathy, while offering a low probability that this is a factor. However, it does focus Mary's attention on the importance of helping Jo manage this relationship – and on digging into this relationship and others in their next coaching conversation.

For the final 10 minutes of supervision, Mary and her supervisor turn their attention to Mary's own wellbeing. The supervisor's AI has been following Mary's emotional journey as she describes this case and her responsibilities within it. The supervisor has already begun to suspect that Mary may be identifying too much with this client – a suspicion reinforced when the AI compares Mary's emotions here with those expressed in previous supervision sessions. It also gently reminds the supervisor of her own tendency not to notice patterns of client-coach-supervisor projections.

At the end of the session, Mary summarises her learning and what she will think further on. She diaries with her AI a conversation to update her personal development plan as a coach. The supervisor instructs her AI to prepare a reading list that might be helpful and promises to forward this once she has reviewed and shortened it. After the session, the supervisor reviews with her AI her own learning. The AI offers a suggested set of case notes, which she edits before saving them. Every month, she and her AI review these case notes, looking for not-so-obvious patterns.

Reflecting on this case study and the current information available for AI, which changes daily, the trend seems to be that AI and humans are smarter together by recognising that these technologies are more effective when they *complement* humans with, for example, cobots and don't replace them.

Conclusion

The learnings from the early rush to introduce robots into the workplace are now revealing potential drawbacks:

In a rare *mea culpa* for the mercurial billionaire, Tesla CEO Elon Musk acknowledged that the company has been too reliant on robots for production. He quotes: "Yes excessive automation at Tesla was a mistake. Humans are underrated." Musk recalls how "we had this crazy, complex network of conveyor belts . . . and it was not working, so we got rid of that whole thing."

Some doubt remains in recruitment whether AI can predict, for example, culture fit, or judge personality and values. Of course, we know the current success of interviews is also limited.

Routine tasks, however, are already being managed well by algorithms where automation is a possibility, although more senior level candidates may not easily accept being interviewed by a bot.

What AI can replace is conscious and unconscious bias that humans bring into relationships as long as algorithms are ethically developed.

The 'computerphobia' based on fear of the unknown did result in a retraining programme for many who eventually adapted to the pain of adjusting to a new paradigm. Life without smartphones, tablets and laptops is now unimaginable.

History repeats itself as humans are faced with a new wave of radical change through AI. Concerns are similar to those of the past that AI will:

• Replace humans;
• Lead to mass unemployment;
• Become superhuman; and
• Ultimately destroy humanity.

Stark (2017) reminds us that the future is ever changing:

• Because robots taking over management or healthcare jobs seemed impossible in 2013, it doesn't mean it will in 2030.
• We already have AI technology that can detect cancer faster than humans, and healthcare robots take up the jobs of the typical nurse.
• Machine learning algorithms can now mimic famous painters.

Could we become obsolete as coach supervisors?

Humans and their innate skills are apparently becoming more important as AI becomes further adopted. What is evident is the need for bringing together the unique capabilities that AI and humans have as the focus moves from automation to work redesign.

Future work is likely to need the human skills of creativity, empathy, communication and complex problem-solving.

We know that AI offers a strong interface to information. What is evident is that we need to keep control of the algorithm's objectives, using AI as a tool for facilitating the achievement of our goals, just as we use a search engine now. We need to stay aware of the possibility for manipulation and be cautious about the threats that social media presents.

Robotics will play an increasing role in our lives. However, cultural aspects may limit the use of robotics for countries similar to Japan with a policy of full employment and a declining population. We also know AI is becoming globally adopted, with Canada, China, Japan, South Korea, the UK and the US leading the way in robot adoption.

AI is growing probably faster than we can easily keep up with. Every day we hear AI included in media discussions about what latest developments have arrived or are planned.

There may currently be more questions than answers for coach supervision:

- The potential capability of AI is evident, giving a sense of how it can impact on coach supervision and supervisees.
- AI is not yet at a stage of development that can replicate *creativity, emotional sensitivity especially empathy, complex problem-solving* and *nuanced judgment*, questioning AI's capability of working with the complexity in the coach supervision conversation. What happens in parallel process situations, for example?
- Accepting that transactional coaching may make coaches vulnerable and replaceable creates the question of who supervises the AI coaches.
- Programming of humanoid robots raises issues of potential bias from demographic groups: sensitivity to cultural issues – generational – and so on.
- What level of EQ and SQ can humanoid robots be programmed to, and what impact will AI developers keen to get their products to market have on this?
- What makes us human, and what makes a robot a robot – we need to be familiar with the differences.
- The main argument for AI not replacing humans is that the complexity of the coach supervision conversation lends itself to human interaction, where usually people prefer communicating with other humans.

These questions appear to offer 'breathing space' for coach supervisors to reflect on the impact of AI.

What can coach supervisors do about AI and become fit for the future?

- We need to know what AI can do that we do and how we can use this to our advantage and add value to the client experience.
- The signs are that AI can replace human coach supervisors with the more transactional activities: we can embrace AI in contracting, for example.
- We need to understand what AI can do and how we might use this to our advantage and add value to the client experience.
- We need to explore the potential of AI to support, but not replace, coach supervision: retaining the human element.
- Coach supervisors can choose to be positive and look for benefits as AI is here to stay.

- To avoid AI viewing coach supervision as an 'easy target,' coach supervisors need to stay current, and adapt – what is relevant today may not be relevant tomorrow.
- Future working with AI is far closer than we may think, and coach supervisors and supervisees need to start planning for that future today.
- We can achieve this by learning about technology capable of entering the supervision field, the trends, the emerging changes and the experimental technologies being tested. Give serious thought to where the human element is still needed.

Remember that the term 'AI' can be somewhat misleading: self-driving cars and automated diagnosis tools are data-exploiting algorithms that are only remotely connected to the quest to develop machines that emulate – and surpass – human intelligence.

However, AI is not negative or positive. It's in between – or it is both! The future is not going to be 'black or white,' and we need to keep in the picture on developments.

The key message is to stay alert and well informed of new developments!

References

Abbatiello, A., Agarwal, D., Bersin, J., Lahiri, G., Schwartz, J. and Volini, E. (2018). AI, Robotics and Automation: Put Humans in the Loop. Global Human Trends. *Deloitte Insights*, March 28, 2018.

Agrawal, A., Gans, J. and Goldfarb, A. (2016). The Simple Economics of Machine Intelligence. *HBR*, November 17, 2016.

Berinato, S. (2017). Inside Facebook's AI Workshop. *HBR*, July 19, 2017.

Davenport, T. H. and Ronanki, R. (2018). Artificial Intelligence for the Real World. *HBR*, January–February 2018 issue.

Ferenstein, G. (2014). *Predicting Love and Breakups with Facebook Data*, February 14, 2014. Available at www.techcrunch.com

Gratch, J (2014). Virtual humans for interpersonal processes and skills, *AI Matters* 1(2) December pp24–25.

Hawkins and Smith. (2013). *Coaching, Mentoring and Organizational Consultancy Supervision, Skills and Consultancy*. Open University Press McGraw-Hill Education Berkshire.

Ray, A., (2018). Compassionate Superintelligence AI 5.0: AI with Blockchain, BMI, Drone, IoT, and Biometric Technologies. Inner-Light-In Publishers www.inner-light-in.com

Stark, H. (2017). As Robots Rise, How Artificial Intelligence will Impact Jobs. *Forbes*, April 28, 2017.

Tieu, A. (2015). *We Now Have an AI Therapist and She's Doing Her Job Better than Humans Can.* Available at https://futurism.com/uscs-new-ai-ellie-has-more-success-than-actual-therapists/

Summary

This book is a curated collection of contemporary thinking, presenting cutting-edge contributions from some of the finest practitioners and researchers in the field. As in art galleries, some pieces require reflection – and return visits may be necessary. As you have seen, the work is edgy and new, and yet totally grounded in the coaching and mentoring supervision experience, bringing pragmatic solutions to current complex challenges.

Over the last 10 to 15 years coaching supervision has moved from a rare and privileged audience to being common place amongst 'best practice' coaching. This book harnesses the current surge in curiosity, knowledge and practice in coaching and mentoring supervision and provides a collective statement of our times.

We hope that each chapter, in its highly individual way, resources coaching and mentoring supervisors to support their supervisees and equips them to better face the demands of the VUCA environment.

Supervision for mentors is developing alongside coaching supervision, and at present there appears to be no obvious distinctions, with little current research focussing on the mentoring supervision experience. However, as its distinctive identity forms we invite mentors, and mentor supervisors, as they read these works to consider the emerging similarities and differences in addressing requirements for mentoring supervision.

Many of the contributors have posed reflective questions. We encourage you to keep evolving and to share your emerging future with others.

We welcome conversations and connections. Together with the Chapter contributors we are holding Evolution Dialogue Groups, in-person and through the website, to deepen and extend exploration of perspectives raised within the book. Do join us! Contact us, Jo Birch and Peter Welch, at Advancing Coach Supervision:

jo@advancingcoachsupvn.com
peter@advancingcoachsupvn.com
www.advancingcoachsupvn.com

Index

Note: page numbers in italic indicate figures and page numbers in bold indicate tables on the corresponding pages.